THE
COUNTERTERRORIST
MANUAL

In Memory of My Father-in-Law
Dr. Jules Snitzer (1927–2009)

THE
COUNTERTERRORIST
MANUAL

A PRACTICAL GUIDE TO ELITE INTERNATIONAL UNITS

LEROY THOMPSON

Frontline Books, London

The Counterterrorist Manual: A Practical Guide to Elite International Units

This edition published in 2009 by Frontline Books,
an imprint of Pen & Sword Books Limited,
47 Church Street, Barnsley, S. Yorkshire, S70 2AS

www.frontline-books.com

ISBN: 978-1-84832-514-2

A CIP data record for this title is available from the British Library.

All photographs courtesy of the author's collection.

For more information on our books, please visit
www.frontline-books.com, email info@frontline-books.com
or write to us at the above address.

Design by The Urban Ant Ltd., London

Printed in the UK by the MPG Books Group

Contents

List of Illustrations

Introduction

More than twenty years ago I wrote one of the first books examining the development of special elite military and police units tasked with hostage rescue. My decision to revisit this topic came about in March 2006, when I was working on a TV documentary on the Munich Olympic Massacre for the National Geographic *Seconds from Disaster* series. In talking with Munich police officers and Olympic officials who had been involved, I was reminded of the frustration they had felt at their inability to deal with such an incident.

I considered that today virtually every country in the world—even one as small as Andorra—has a unit trained in antiterrorist/hostage rescue tactics. However, as antiterrorist units have grown ever more sophisticated in their training and tactics, so too terrorists have learned, and have refined their own science of death to foil the rescue attempts. Hostage incidents such as the one at Beslan School in Russia may well be harbingers of scenarios where the main objective is not some political concession but the killing of as many hostages as possible. As a result, even the world's finest antiterrorist warriors may find themselves challenged to constantly improve their tactics, their equipment, and, in the face of incidents involving hostages, their cooperation with other units.

The terrorist attacks in Mumbai between November 26 and 29, 2008, highlight many of the points covered here. In addition to explosions at some locations, six buildings were attacked, which resulted in the deaths of 164 civilians and members of the Indian security forces as well as 9 terrorists. Over 300 were injured. The attacks targeted buildings likely to contain Western visitors such as the Oberoi

Trident and Taj Mahal Palace Hotels and the Leopold Cafe as well as Nariman House, an Orthodox Jewish facility. Thirty of those killed by the terrorists were foreign nationals.

The Indian security apparatus should have been aware of Mumbai as a prime terrorist target for Islamic terrorists. In March 1993, 13 coordinated bombs were detonated in the city, resulting in the deaths of 257 and the injuring of 700. Over the next 15 years, hundreds more were killed in bombings in Mumbai and its vicinity. As India's technology and finance center as well as a center of the massive Indian film industry, Mumbai made an appealing terrorist target as well. There are also reliable reports that U.S. intelligence had warned India of the likelihood of the attacks and named locations. India had tightened security for a period but when no attacks came after the warnings had removed security personnel.

The fact that only ten terrorists managed to kill so many people and wreak such havoc makes an interesting point about civilian vulnerability that has been discussed extensively by some U.S. antiterrorist professionals. The likelihood of such an attack succeeding in Mumbai, London, Mexico City, New York, or Chicago is dramatically higher than the likelihood of success in Dallas or Miami. Most states in the USA have what are termed "shall issue" laws with regard to concealed weapons licenses. Basically, anyone who is not barred by a criminal record or mental problems and who passes a background check and a course in safe firearms usage can be issued a concealed weapons license. As a result, ten terrorists entering any large gathering place in Florida or Texas would be likely to encounter multiple armed civilians who would fight back. Captured terrorists' documents indicate that terrorist groups targeting the USA are well aware of which states have a substantial portion of armed citizens. The USA also legally recognizes that any retired or active law enforcement officer may carry his weapon anywhere in the country. My point is that terrorists like soft targets. Those ten terrorists were free to torture and kill civilians with little fear of being stopped until the Indian security apparatus finally went into action.

The Mumbai terrorists arrived by sea from Karachi, Pakistan, using speedboats that had been carried aboard trawlers. Once ashore, they attacked the Colaba Police Station near their landing site. By attacking this command and control center, the police response was slowed. Police were viewed as primary targets and reportedly 14 officers were killed early in the attack, including the commander of the Mumbai antiterror squad and two of his top aides. The terrorists then split into two-man teams, though by the time the two hotels and the Jewish Center were attacked, three terrorists seemed to be assigned to each one, and, guided by GPS and equipped with satellite phones, headed for their assigned targets. Intelligence intercepts indicate that throughout the siege, terrorists at the hotels and Jewish Center were in contact with handlers who gave them updates from the news and ordered them to kill hostages. Indications are that one of the handlers was a former high-ranking officer in Pakistan's intelligence agency, the ISI (Inter-Service Intelligence). Some of the terrorists took taxis to their objectives while others seized a police vehicle. Taxis were blown up near the airport and docks to spread police response and make it difficult to identify the primary targets. Apparently, the terrorists were well trained in two-man room clearing drills with one covering while the other advanced. They also showed good fire discipline with one reloading while the other sustained fire. As a result, despite only two terrorists being assigned to most targets, the takeovers were carried out quickly.

The attacks had been in the planning stages for months, hence the intelligence gathered by the US and passed to India. Indications are that the terrorists had either carried out recces themselves or had recces carried out by sympathetic Mumbai residents as the terrorists had excellent knowledge of their targets. Other sites reportedly recced included Mumbai's financial center and the U.S. Consulate. Like the Chechen terrorists at Beslan, the Mumbai terrorists had taken cocaine and LSD to allow them to stay awake for days and keep their energy levels high. Reportedly, the terrorists had also used Google Earth to gain an overall picture of the targets and their vicinity. During the attacks, they had Blackberries and wireless laptops to follow the news and access the Internet. By attacking multiple sites—ten including those where bombs were detonated—throughout Mumbai, the terrorists split responders and made it difficult to focus personnel for one rescue operation. These diversions may also have been intended to help all or some of the terrorists to escape after carrying out their attacks as indications are that they did not intend the attacks as a suicide mission.

The Chatrapati Shivaji Railroad Terminus was attacked first by two terrorists who entered the passenger area and opened fire with AK-47 rifles and threw grenades. Those appearing to be Westerners were targeted. At least ten people were killed. The terrorists also threw grenades into the CCTV control room. The two terrorists killed several police officers then headed to the Metro Cinema, another target, but they came under fire by responding police units and one was killed and the other captured. He was the only terrorist to survive the incident.

At the Taj Mahal Palace Hotel, the terrorists reportedly took more than 200 hostages. Numerous blasts were heard from the hotel as terrorists threw grenades and detonated other explosive devices. The hotel was set afire by some of the blasts, and terrorists ignited curtains in various rooms to make it difficult to pinpoint their locations and to create a smoke haze around the building.

The Taj was a well-known Mumbai landmark symbolic of India's colonial past. Many prominent persons were staying there, including members of the European Parliament, but they managed to barricade themselves in their rooms or escape. The fact that the Taj has 565 rooms helped some guests to hide or barricade themselves, but it would also make clearing the hotel extremely difficult for the entry teams, especially since some rooms were reportedly booby trapped. Some intelligence reports indicate that other terrorists may have checked into the hotels a few days in advance and either pre-positioned weapons and explosives or waited to join the attackers.

At the Taj and Oberoi Trident there appears to have been a failure on the part of NSG (National Security Guard) snipers. I have seen a lot of footage shot by news photographers of terrorists visible in windows. With only two to three terrorists operating in each hotel, a sniper with a "green light" could have lowered the odds substantially with one shot. It appears that the initial plan at the Taj hotel was to inflict as many casualties as possible then blow up the hotel and escape, which is why the terrorists had a horde of explosives. The presence of MARCOS (Indian naval special forces) operators may have prevented their escape.

NSG operators cleared the Taj from the roof down, which is tactically sound as it gives terrorists the possibility of attempting to exit the building and surrendering to perimeter security personnel or attempting to escape. The location of air conditioning and other equipment on the roof of the building, as well as access to crawl spaces and various stairways, also make an entry from the roof appealing. NSG operators had master keys to the rooms, but the large number of rooms and the fear of booby traps, plus the presence of hostages hiding in rooms, slowed the clearing operation. Terrorists had also set fires throughout the hotel to slow the clearing operations.

Some reports indicate that Nariman House was the prime target of the attacks. Three terrorists seized Nariman House, which may indicate that more importance was placed on success there. As with the two hotels, the terrorists used gunfire and grenades as they entered Nariman House to seize the initiative and terrify hostages. They eventually killed six Jewish hostages although Israeli sources think one or more of the dead hostages may have been killed by NSG operators during the assault. One NSG operator was killed during the assault and all three terrorists died after holding out for 48 hours.

The initial NSG assault plan was to land operators on the roof to clear downward while other operators assaulted from the ground floor upward. Note that such an assault with teams moving toward each other requires excellent communication to prevent a "blue on blue" incident. Perimeter and operational security were terrible. When the NSG finally went in, operators were deposited onto the roof of Nariman House from helicopters. The assault alternated between periods of intense action as the sound of constant gunfire and exploding grenades were heard, then silences for up to a half hour. Whether the grenades were stun grenades from the NSG, fragmentation grenades from the terrorists, or a combination thereof is not clear. During the assault, snipers were firing into the fourth floor, where the terrorists and hostages were thought to be barricaded, but they do not appear to have had identified targets. There was later a large explosion on the fourth floor. Reportedly, Israel had offered assistance in dealing with the terrorists at Nariman House but was turned down.

The "First Responders," Mumbai's ATS (antiterrorist Squad) was armed with bolt action Lee Enfield rifles and .32 or .38 caliber revolvers; they were definitely outgunned by the terrorists and were not really trained to clear buildings containing shooters and hostages. Despite the fact that India's antiterrorist unit, the National Security Guards, have a strength of 7,500, none was deployed in Mumbai. Elements had to respond from Delhi, which is over 700 miles away. Actually, the first highly trained personnel to respond was a small detachment of MARCOS (Indian naval special forces) from the nearby naval base. I have been told by an Indian special ops source, that the small number of MARCOS operators—reportedly 12–15—defeated the terrorists at two locations and saved numerous hostages by themselves while fighting for 15–20 hours before the NSG arrived.

It should first be noted that the attacks on multiple locations around the city would create a hard scenario for any antiterrorist unit to carry out a quick response. The killing of the antiterrorist commander early in the incident certainly added to the confusion. Should an incident involving terrorists killing hostages and detonating explosives occur at a number of locations in London, the first response would most likely come from members of CO19 who provide armed reaction units for the Metropolitan Police.The SAS CRW (Counter Revolutionary Warfare) Wing—"The Team"—is the squadron assigned antiterrorist duties at any given time. A troop from the Team is generally assigned to the greater London area and would arrive quickly, followed by the remainder of the alert CRW Team. Should only two or three terrorists be involved at each venue as at Mumbai, once the entire CRW Wing was on station backed up by CO19, buildings would likely be cleared quickly.

In Los Angeles, response would likely be quicker because all police are armed. In many metro areas police are now trained to deal with "active shooter" situations and have patrol cars that carry carbines. In LA, as I write this, only sergeants' cars would have carbines, but each patrol car would have a shotgun. Once four officers are on the scene, they are trained to form a diamond or other entry formation and begin to clear the building. With only two or three terrorists to a venue, these active shooter neutralization teams could begin to deal with the problem and at least contain the terrorists. Both the LAPD (Los Angeles Police Department) and the LA County Sheriff's Department have SWAT teams trained to the level of many countries' antiterrorist teams. The FBI SWAT Team from the LA office would probably respond as well. Depending on the number of shooters and venues, it is quite likely these responders would have neutralized the threat before the California Highway Patrol SWAT team or the FBI HRT could arrive on scene.

The Indian security forces were dealing with a difficult incident, but there were many obvious mistakes. First, despite intelligence warning of attacks in Mumbai, there was little hardening of the potential targets. Secondly, Mumbai did not have a real SWAT capability. Their antiterrorist police were armed with obsolete weapons and had no training in dealing with "active shooters."

Given the large number of personnel assigned to the National Security Guards, it doesn't make sense that they should all be located at Delhi. India has now stationed elements of the NSG in major Indian cities including Mumbai to speed response time. Also, operators should not have had to waste time having hotel employees draw diagrams. At the very least, the local fire brigade should have had blueprints or police should have been told to get architectural drawings from the proper agency. Even more to the point, with 3,500 members, the NSG should have sent teams of a few operators to every major hotel, government building, airport, and landmark in the country to prepare video tapes and diagrams of the venue.

Prior to their arrival in Mumbai, India's Home Minister went on TV to announce the number of NSG being sent and the time they had left New Delhi. As a result, the terrorists had a good idea of what they would be facing. Operational and perimeter security was atrocious at Nariman House, where reporters and politicos mingled with snipers and other NSG operators on the building next to the Jewish Center. Reportedly, NSG snipers were letting the gawkers look through their scopes. The deaths in Mumbai illustrate that the units covered here must be vigilant and prepare for larger hostage incidents than in the past.

Although other books have addressed antiterrorist forces, most have either focused on the memoirs of a member of one unit or have been catalogs of the units themselves, with a few pages devoted to their history, weapons, and equipment. I felt that, in the light of the omnipresent and evolving threat, a book focusing on how antiterrorist units have evolved, how they are selected and trained, and how they prepare for diverse missions would be useful. I wanted to discuss the pros and cons of choosing an antiterrorist unit from the military or from the police, or—in some cases—having units drawn from both. I also wanted to touch upon the need for politicians with the courage to give the order for an antiterrorist unit to "go in." A leadership that understands that in some hostage incidents saving 90 percent, 75 percent—even 50 per cent—of the hostages will be preferable to seeing them all die through inaction. That's the "mission" I have set for myself with this book. I hope that when you finish reading it you will feel that I have accomplished it.

Leroy Thompson
St. Louis, Missouri, 2009

Chapter I

Antiterrorism: Background and Evolution

The hijacking of airliners and attacks on El Al flights during 1968 and 1969 certainly brought the threat of terrorism to the attention of world governments. Many governments, however, viewed the threat of Middle Eastern terrorism as a primarily Israeli problem and either ignored the threat or made concessions to Palestinian groups in the hope that they would look elsewhere for targets. The September 1970 hijackings of multiple airliners from multiple countries, their landings in Jordan, and their destruction on the ground should have warned the world that the threat had become endemic and was not going to disappear. As might be expected, however, Israel, the primary target of terrorism, was the first country to see the need for units trained and ready to take action against terrorists. The May 8, 1972 hijacking of a Sabena airliner and its landing in Tel Aviv set the stage for a successful Israeli rescue of the passengers. Using many techniques that would later become standard with antiterrorist units—including practice on a similar airliner, the use of disguise to get the rescue team close to the aircraft, and the use of deception (more than 300 Israeli soldiers posing as freed Palestinian militants on fake Red Cross buses)—the Israeli team successfully killed or captured the terrorists and freed all the hostages. (An interesting side note to this rescue is that two future Israeli prime ministers—Ehud Barak and Benjamin Netanyahu—took part in the assault. Netanyahu was wounded during the operation.) Israel had demonstrated that it was not necessary to make concessions to terrorists and that effective action could be taken if trained personnel and national resolve were present.

Top The scene of the 1972 Munich hostage crisis—#31 Connollystrasse—as it looked in March 2006; note the balconies on which the terrorists observe police activity. Note also the glass-covered stairway.

Above The view of the back of #31 Connollystrasse. The hostages were held in the second floor room to the right rear.

It was not until the September 1972 Munich Olympic Massacre stunned the world, however, that many countries realized that they were impotent when faced with a terrorist act. The German response to the taking of Israeli athletes was a virtual textbook study of how not to deal with a terrorist incident. Long before the Olympics, the Germans had ignored the potential threat and had not trained the Munich police to deal with a hostage incident. A police psychologist had warned of the likelihood of an incident that would play out much as the actual event transpired. Security at the Olympic Village was so lax that the terrorists were able to gain entry to the dormitory that would house Israeli athletes and reconnoiter it before the Olympics began.

Once the hostages had been taken, negotiations were carried out incompetently and offers of assistance from the Israelis, who were considered to be the most experienced antiterrorist force in the world at the time, were ignored. The attempted rescue by the German police at the Olympic Village was inept and was compromised by being broadcast live on television, a broadcast viewed by the hostage takers! The German police ignored the possibility of a rescue when the terrorists were transporting the hostages by bus to two waiting helicopters, an option many antiterrorism experts now think offered the highest likelihood of success. At Fürstenfeldbruk Airport, located 15 miles out of Munich, the Germans did not deploy enough trained snipers. They had not rehearsed the operation with the helicopter crews landing the hostages to offer the snipers optimum shooting angles. The "snipers" lacked intelligence and didn't even have radios. All the elements were there for a disaster and those elements came together to cause the death of all of the hostages.

In the aftermath, many Western democracies vowed not to exhibit the same inability to cope with a major terrorist incident. To implement that vow, however, specialized and highly trained units would be required. Stung by world criticism and by the disaster that had befallen the Olympics it had hoped would truly erase the stigma of Nazism, Germany was one of the first countries to take action. Ulrich Wegener, who had actually been present during the Munich hostage incident as an aide to the West German Interior Minister, would be charged with forming an antiterrorist unit within the German Federal Border

Guards (Bundesgrenzschutz, BGS). This unit, designated GSG-9, became active in 1973. Among other units that became active in 1973 were France's GIGN and Austria's GEK Cobra.

The suspicion toward elite units within the German Army that harked back to the World War II SS made the Border Guards a compromise choice for an antiterrorist unit since the BGS was a paramilitary formation with some law enforcement powers. As countries around the world formed their own antiterrorist units, they faced a similar dilemma. Military units already had elite formations with many of the qualifications that were desirable in an antiterrorist commando. As a result, a pool of well-qualified manpower was there to be tapped. They also possessed ready access to aircraft, helicopters, and

Above During the early days of their existence, members of GSG9 practice free climbing the side of a building prior to an assault. (BGS)

boats/ships to transport troops. Additionally, they had access to the types of training facilities that could be modified for antiterrorist training. On the negative side, many countries either had laws that prevented the armed forces from operating within the country or a historical dislike of the military carrying out raids. Generally, too, military personnel are trained to solve problems with overwhelming firepower rather than in the surgical manner required of the antiterrorist unit.

If a national antiterrorist unit were to be formed within the police, then, substantial time and expense would be required to train it to the standard of military special operations troops. A clear chain of command and jurisdiction for its employment would also have to be established. Some countries with formations having police powers while also functioning in a quasi-military role chose these formations as a compromise. In many countries, more than one antiterrorist unit was formed—a military one with responsibilities outside of the country and a police one with responsibilities within the country. Still a third unit might eventually be deemed necessary to handle MAT (Maritime Antiterrorism) operations. Military units with antiterrorist responsibilities would include the British, Australian, and New Zealand Special Air Service, the U.S. Delta Force, and the ROK 707th Special Mission Battalion. Police units with military or quasi-military status would include the French GIGN, Spanish GEO, Belgian ESI, Italian GIS, German GSG-9, and Dutch BBE (which employed a mix of Dutch Marines and police). Units such as the U.S. FBI HRT or Italian NOCS were drawn from non-militarized national law enforcement agencies. Specialized maritime antiterrorist units included the British SBS, U.S. SEAL Team Six, and Italian COMSUBIN.

There is a less obvious advantage to forming a national antiterrorist unit within a law enforcement agency. A national antiterrorist unit has to be trained to a very high standard. As a result, it is very hard to keep the edge necessary to perform at the level required over years and years when the unit is not employed operationally. A police unit can keep its personnel sharp by using them on high-risk warrant service, apprehension of dangerous felons, prison sieges, criminal hostage situations, and other types of entries. Many antiterrorist units have come to the conclusion that SWAT (Special Weapons and Tactics) teams in big U.S.

cities make more raids and entries in a single month than most major antiterrorist units have in years. Just as the medics for special ops and antiterrorist units find the best place to train is big city emergency rooms, many also realize that the best place to train operators is on big city SWAT teams. This has resulted in personnel from some military antiterrorist units being assigned as "observers" with big city SWAT teams.

While many Western democracies were forming antiterrorist units in response to the Munich Massacre, Israel took a more Old Testament approach as it launched its Wrath of God teams around the world to track down those involved in the Munich Massacre and assassinate them.

Throughout the 1970s, additional countries formed specialized antiterrorist forces while terrorist groups continued to take hostages, offering governments the incentive to spend the money to form such units. Israel, of course, had formed Unit 101 in 1953 with an antiterrorist mission. This unit would evolve into other units with various designations including General Staff Deep Reconnaissance Unit, Unit 262, and Sayaret Matkal. Incidents targeting Israel continued and Israel used its antiterrorist forces not just for hostage rescue missions but for retaliatory operations against the Palestinians. Other Middle Eastern states learned they were not exempt from terrorism, however. In March 1973, the Saudi Embassy in Khartoum was seized by Black September terrorists. The House of Saud would be the target again in September 1973, when a Black September splinter group seized the Saudi Embassy in Paris.

In fact, throughout 1973, governments that may have been hesitant about forming antiterrorist units should have seen the ever-increasing terrorist violence as a call to action. Major terrorist incidents occurred almost weekly during the year, with the later half of 1973 being especially bloody. Although Israel remained a prime target, Western airlines flying into and out of Israel were often targeted as well. On August 5, 1973, at Athens Airport there was a machinegun attack against passengers on a TWA flight that had just landed from Israel. A month later, on September 5, members of Black September attempted to shoot down an El Al flight in Rome using SAM-7s. In a particularly vicious attack, on 17 December, a Palestinian terrorist group set fire to a Pan Am plane in Rome, killing 32, then hijacked a Lufthansa flight to Kuwait.

Top A GIGN Operator practices firing the compact HK MP5K. (Gendarmerie Nationale)

Above Members of GIGN engaging targets from their holsters using the Manurhin .357 Magnum revolver. (Gendarmerie Nationale)

Not all attacks were by Middle Eastern terrorists. In the same year the IRA carried out a fire and letter bomb campaign in England, and on September 20, 1973, the Spanish Prime Minister was assassinated in Madrid by ETA terrorists.

Within Northern Ireland in 1972 alone there were 10,000 shooting incidents. In an attempt to take proactive action against the IRA, the MRF (Mobile Reconnaissance Force) had been formed in 1971 to operate in undercover four-man teams. The MRF made good use of turned IRA members for intelligence. In 1974 this unit was replaced by the highly effective 14 Intelligence Company, which specialized in surveillance of IRA suspects in cooperation with the RUC Special Branch. In 1976, the SAS (Special Air Service) deployed to Northern Ireland, where they set ambushes for terrorists visiting weapons caches or preparing to carry out terrorist acts. The SAS also snatched some of the IRA leadership, reportedly even from within the Irish Republic.

The years 1974 and 1975 might be termed the years of the Jackal as Carlos made his presence felt in various acts of terrorism. Carlos was especially active in France, culminating in June 1975, when he killed two French security agents and wounded another in a shootout during a raid on his Paris apartment. Undaunted, however, Carlos led an attack in December 1975, against the symbol of Arab wealth and power, the OPEC headquarters in Vienna. During 1975, the Baader-Meinhof gang was very active as well, especially in carrying out kidnappings in Germany.

The most interesting event in the evolution of antiterrorist units during this period was the 1974 formation in the Soviet Union of KGB Alpha, designed as a special operations unit capable of SAS-type missions for the Committee for State Security. Antiterrorist operations fell within Alpha's responsibilities.

Israel's reputation for successful antiterrorist operations was somewhat tarnished in May 1974, when the PDFLP seized a school at Ma'alot in Israel, and 22 were killed and 60 injured during the assault by Sayaret Matkal. The various mistakes made at Ma'alot contributed to the establishment in late 1974/early 1975 of the Ya'ma'm antiterrorist unit within the Israeli Border Police.

The Royal Canadian Mounted Police formed an ERT (Emergency Response Team) in 1975 in preparation for the Montreal Olympics of 1976. (The Montreal Olympics would be the first summer Olympics held since the massacre at the 1972 Munich

Olympics; hence the need to have a trained unit available was given high priority.)

The year 1976 would be the year in which some of the newly formed antiterrorist units would prove their value. In February, terrorists seized a school bus transporting the children of French military personnel in Djibouti. GIGN carried out a well-planned rescue using drugged food to cause the children to fall asleep and hence lie down on the seats, thus clearing the way for GIGN snipers to eliminate all but one of the terrorists. An assault team followed up to complete the rescue.

Jordan had formed an antiterrorist unit, the 101st Special Forces Battalion, in the mid-1970s. This unit saw action in March 1976, when the PFLP attacked the Intercontinental Hotel in Jordan. The unit responded and engaged the terrorists in a gunfight, which resulted in three of the terrorists being killed along with two members of the antiterrorist unit.

The hijacking of an Air France flight carrying a large number of Israelis to Uganda by PFLP and Baader-Meinhof terrorists set the stage for the most ambitious antiterrorist operation yet in July 1976. The Israelis launched a rescue that required them to land at a hostile airport and eliminate Ugandan Army personnel as well as the terrorists to effect the rescue. Among the more intriguing aspects of the rescue was the use of a fake Idi Amin to distract the Ugandan guards while the assault force got close enough to act.

In 1977 the Baader-Meinhof gang continued to carry out assassinations and kidnappings in Germany and elsewhere in conjunction with other terrorist groups. In March 1977, the Royal Dutch Marines earned their place among the antiterrorist elite by carrying out a well-coordinated assault against a hijacked train and a school, both taken by South Moluccan terrorists. The train incident had dragged on long enough for psychologists to be able to work up profiles of hostages and terrorists, which aided the Marines in planning their assault. As part of BBE, the Dutch Marines had assumed the responsibility for antiterrorist ops in Holland in 1974 and had brought a prison siege to a successful conclusion in that year.

October 1977 saw GSG-9, the German antiterrorist unit formed in the aftermath of the Munich Olympic Massacre, deployed to Somalia where they performed a successful "tubular assault" on a hijacked Lufthansa airliner. This assault marked the first employment of two antiterrorist weapons that would become almost iconic among world antiterrorist units—the stun grenade and the HK MP5 SMG. The stun grenades, which had been developed by the SAS, were brought to the incident by two members of the SAS who cooperated with GSG-9 in their deployment.

Throughout 1977 and 1978, the PFLP carried out numerous assassinations of Middle Eastern officials—in Europe and elsewhere—whom they felt were unsympathetic to the Palestinian cause. The Red Brigades became one of the world's most recognized terrorist groups in 1978 when they carried out the kidnapping and later murder of Aldo Moro. Prior to the Moro kidnapping, Italy had formed the GIS antiterrorist unit as part of the Carabinieri, but in the wake of the Moro murder, another unit—NOCS—was formed as part of the Polizia di Stato in 1978. In response to Basque terrorist acts and the general threat of terrorism throughout Europe, Spain had formed a unit—GEO—in 1977 as well.

Above An Italian COMSUBIN operator during the early days of that unit's responsibility for Maritime antiterrorism. (Marina Militare)

In 1977 the USA finally authorized the U.S. Army Special Forces to form an interim antiterrorist force designated "Blue Light" until Delta Force was activated in November 1977. (Note that the term "Delta Force" is still commonly used for this unit and will appear frequently in this text, but the current designation of the unit is actually the Combat Applications Group.)

Egypt's first antiterrorist unit, Saiqa, had been established in reaction to terrorist actions against Egyptian diplomats and political leaders. It saw action in March 1978, when it assaulted a hijacked Cypriot airliner. The precipitous assault led to a fire fight with Cypriot National Guardsmen and the death of at least 15 hostages.

The FLNC carried out 379 bomb attacks on Corsica during 1978, then in 1979 took their attacks to mainland France.

As the decade of the 1970s ended, world terrorist groups remained on the offensive despite the fact that there had been some highly successful antiterrorist operations. The IRA carried out a number of high-profile assassinations in 1979, including that of Earl Mountbatten in August. Showing once again that terrorism could strike at the heart of Islam as well as the West, the Great Mosque at Mecca was seized in November 1979, and was not retaken until a bloody assault by the Saudi National Guard and other troops advised by members of France's GIGN.

November 1979 also saw the seizure of the U.S. Embassy in Tehran by members of the Islamic Revolutionary Guards. The impotence of U.S. President Jimmy Carter in the face of this act would lead to his defeat in the 1980 presidential election. Delta Force trained for a rescue mission that was delayed until the last moment due to dithering within the U.S. leadership and finally launched in April 1980. Helicopter problems caused the mission to be aborted with loss of life when a C-130 and a helicopter collided. Delta's reputation suffered as a result of the botched rescue.

Other countries that formed antiterrorist units during the 1970s included Finland; although originally the unit was composed only of trained marksmen—it wasn't until 1978 that the "Bear Unit" was operational with an assault capability as well. In Asia, Hong Kong started the process of forming its SDU (Special Duties Unit) in the late 1970s, but it wasn't until the SAS and SBS (Special

Above During the late 1970s or early 1980s, an operator from Italy's COMSUBIN practices close quarters combat techniques with the Beretta M12 SMG. (Marina Militare)

Boat Service) had assisted in organizing and training the unit that it truly became operational in the 1980s.

In contrast to the 1980 Delta Force mission in Iran, the May 1980 assault by the SAS "Pagoda Troop" on the Iranian Embassy at Prince's Gate in London to free hostages taken by alleged anti-Khomeni forces, but who were quite likely Iraqi intelligence agents, was a great success. The SAS showed the ability to carry out a precise assault, improvise in the midst of the plan when difficulties arose, successfully eliminate all but one of the terrorists during the assault, and save all but one of the hostages. This operation was also an example of how good hostage negotiators can work with an assault team up to the point of entry.

During 1981, noteworthy events in the hidden war between antiterrorist units and terrorists included the shooting of the Pope in May 1981 and the assassination of Anwar Sadat in October 1981. In December 1981, U.S. General James Dozier was kidnapped by members of the Red Brigades. The Italian antiterrorist unit NOCS carried out a successful rescue in January 1982, using distraction and speed to rescue Dozier and arrest the terrorists without bloodshed. During the early 1980s, too, ETA had intensified their attacks within Spain.

The Dozier rescue had been aided by the U.S. ISA (Intelligence Support Activity), a unit staffed by ex-Special Forces personnel and intelligence specialists. Using sophisticated communications intercept technology, the ISA had supplied NOCS with information about Dozier's location. The ISA had been formed after the abortive Iranian rescue mission, as had TF160, a special operations aviation unit.

Pakistan's SSG (Special Service Group) had been given the antiterrorist mission in the early 1970s. The unit's first major operation occurred on September 30, 1981, when Sikh terrorists hijacked an Air India flight to Lahore. In a highly successful operation, the SSG infiltrated the aircraft dressed as airline employees, overpowered the terrorists, and freed the hostages. An interesting side note on the SSG is that veterans of the unit have often been hired by some of the Middle Eastern oil-producing countries as contract members of their antiterrorist units.

Also in 1981, on March 29, the Indonesian KOPASSANDA stormed a hijacked Indonesian plane in Thailand, killing the terrorists and releasing the hostages, though the pilot was killed. KOPASSANDA, though trained for special operations, had not received specialist antiterrorist training. As a result, the Indonesians formed Detachment 81 as a specialized antiterrorist unit.

Among the noteworthy terrorist incidents in the 1980s was the hijacking by the PLF of the cruise ship *Achille Lauro* in October 1985. Seal Team Six (now DevGru), which was established in 1980 by the USA for maritime antiterrorist operations, as well as the Italian COMSUBIN, were in position to launch an assault, but the Egyptians allowed the terrorists to dock in Egypt and gave them safe passage out of the country. Only after the terrorists had been released did the USA learn that an American citizen had been murdered aboard the ship. The USA launched carrier-borne fighter aircraft to force down the Egyptian airliner carrying the terrorists, but a craven Italian government released them. The 1980s were an especially busy time for the Abu Nidal Organization. During the early 1980s the group assassinated many prominent PLO or Fatah members. The organization also undertook many terrorist operations for Libyan leader Muammar Qadhafi, including bombings and attacks on dissident Libyans in London. Members of Abu Nidal Organisation hijacked an Egyptian airliner to Malta in November 1985, which led to another disastrous rescue attempt by the Egyptians. This assault was carried out by Unit 777 and engendered the query among many antiterrorist professionals: Would you rather be hijacked by terrorists or rescued by the Egyptians?

On December 27, 1985, the Abu Nidal Organization acting for the Libyans carried out simultaneous attacks at airports in Rome and Vienna. In September 1986, an Abu Nidal team hijacked a Pan Am plane to Pakistan where the plane was stormed by Musa Company, the antiterrorist force within Pakistan's SSG, and the terrorists arrested.

Amidst the continued acts of terrorism around the world, the USA formed the FBI HRT (Hostage Rescue Team) in 1983 to deal with terrorist incidents within the USA since Delta and Seal Team Six were precluded by law from domestic law enforcement roles.

Other terrorist groups continued to operate throughout the 1980s. ASALA (The Secret Army for the Liberation of Armenia),which had been formed in 1975, carried out attacks around the world on Turkish diplomats. Various Latin

American terrorist groups remained active during the 1980s as well, including, among others, M-19, FARC, MRTA, and Shining Path.

In India the assault, in June 1984, on the center of the Sikh faith, the Golden Temple in Amritsar, which had been taken over by separatists, led to the death of a reported 493 separatists and civilians and injury to 592. (It is possible casualties were at least 50 percent higher.) Indian assault forces were led by members of the SFF (Special Frontier Force), India's antiterrorist unit at the time. Listed casualties for the SFF and other units involved were 83 killed in action and 249 injured. Five months later, on October 31,1984, Indian Prime Minister Indira Gandhi was assassinated by two of her Sikh bodyguards in revenge for the assault on the Golden Temple. In another incident in response to the Golden Temple raid, the June 1985 bombing of an Air India plane resulted in 329 deaths. India's antiterrorist mission was assigned to a new unit, the National Security Guard, which had to assault the Golden Temple again in April 1986, then still again in May 1988, the latter with large casualties among the separatists.

In response to two attacks on RUC stations by the IRA in which they used a

Above One of the original members of the FBI HRT in the assault gear that was in use at the time. (Pilgrim)

JCB digger with explosives in the bucket to breach the reinforced fences around the installations, the SAS acted on intelligence and set an ambush at the RUC station in Loughgall in May 1987. The ambush was highly successful, resulting in the deaths of eight IRA members, the greatest loss of life by the IRA in one incident since the 1920s. In addition to reinforcing the IRA's healthy respect for the SAS, this incident also caused paranoia within the IRA as they searched for the suspected informant who had tipped security forces to the impending IRA attack at Loughgall. This SAS operation was an excellent example of a preemptive antiterrorist strike by well-trained operators.

In December 1988, Pan Am flight 103 was blown up over Lockerbie, Scotland, an act that was eventually attributed to Libyan intelligence operatives. Hezbollah had been formed in 1983 and immediately began carrying out attacks on Western interests in Lebanon. In April 1983, an attack on the U.S. Embassy in Beirut resulted in 63 deaths, but this horrific attack was just a prelude to the bombing of the U.S. Marine barracks in Beirut in October 1983, which resulted in 241 deaths. Almost simultaneously, the French barracks in Beirut was attacked resulting in 58 deaths. Then, in November, 1983, an Israeli government building in Sidon was attacked with 67 killed.

Among the antiterrorist units formed during the 1980s was Portugal's GOE, which ran its first selection course in 1982, then went operational in 1983.

Despite the setback at Loughgall, the IRA remained active into the 1990s. In 1990–91, there were new bomb attacks against British targets both in England and on the continent against British military targets. In an audacious attack in February 1991, mortar rounds were launched against 10 Downing Street. One result was that the SAS was assigned to augment security for the Prime Minister and the Queen when the threat level was considered especially high. Later in that same month, bomb attacks were carried out against the busy Victoria and Paddington railway stations. In an attempt to strike at a prime commercial target, bombs were planted in Oxford Street during the December 1992 Christmas shopping season. Bombings continued in Northern Ireland and mainland UK throughout the remainder of the 1990s.

France came under attack during the 1990s from three terrorist groups, though French antiterrorist forces did have a couple of notable successes. In

August 1994, DST, acting on a tip from the CIA, captured Carlos in Khartoum. Later in the year, a French airliner was hijacked from Algiers Airport in December 1994 by Algerian extremists. It eventually landed at Marseilles Airport where a rescue was launched by GIGN. Four terrorists were killed in the successful rescue mission, though nine members of GIGN were wounded during the assault, pointing up the difficulty of combat in the close quarters of an aircraft cabin.

During 1995, Algerian Islamic terrorists affiliated with GIA planted bombs at Metro and railway stations. Late in 1995, the Corsican separatist movement, FNLC, began carrying out bombings on Corsica. In 1996, bombings also took place on the French mainland. On the island of Corsica, 1997–2000 saw an intense bombing campaign by FLNC supporters as well as some shootings of French officials. Early in 1998, French security forces made many arrests, but in a revenge attack in February 1998, the senior French administrator on Corsica was assassinated.

The bombing offensive by Algerian terrorists continued in 1996. Some ETA terrorists who were plotting acts against France either within Metropolitan France or abroad were arrested in the UK and Belgium, but ETA remained a threat.

Another threat to French interests arose when ETA terrorists who had hitherto primarily targeted the Spanish government began a bombing campaign in France in conjunction with the ARB (Breton Revolutionary Army). As a result, French forces carried out raids in the Basque regions of France and extradited many ETA terrorists who were wanted in Spain. Many members of ARB were rounded up as well.

There was some good news in the battle against Corsican extremists as the population of Corsica became so disillusioned with the violence that they refused to support the FLNC, making it much more difficult for the terrorists to operate as the traditional code of silence was now sometimes broken to tip authorities to FLNC operations.

Although ETA had been relatively quiet in Spain, in the 1990s the Basque group began a new series of bombings and assassinations, the former especially directed against tourist resorts. There were also at least two attempts to assassinate King Juan Carlos. Raids against ETA in France had also netted intelligence about plans to assassinate French officials.

Islamic terrorists targeted Muslim countries as well as France and other Western nations. GIA targeted foreigners living in Algeria as well as carrying out bombings in Algiers. Egypt had been a target ever since its peace agreement with Israel. President Anwar Sadat had been assassinated in October 1981, and other terrorist acts had been committed on Egyptian soil over the next decade. The Egyptian military and police often responded in a Draconian manner.

By the early 1990s many Egyptian militants had returned from Afghanistan, where they had fought on the side of the Mujahideen and had become even more radicalized. Beginning in 1992, the terrorists targeted Egypt's tourist industry with a series of bloody attacks at historical sites against foreign tourists, culminating in the November 1997 Luxor massacre. Egyptian Army officers and officials were targeted as well. During this decade, too, multiple assassination attempts were made on Egyptian President Mubarak. Egyptian targets abroad were not exempt either. For example, the Egyptian Embassy in Islamabad was blown up in November 1995. Earlier in 1995 there had been an attempt on the life of President Mubarak by terrorists affiliated with al-Qaida. Mubarak was not the only Middle Eastern leader in al-Qaida's sights, however, as there had also been an attempt to assassinate Crown Prince Abdullah of Jordan in June 1993.

Egyptian Islamic fundamentalist terrorism was exported as well. In 1990, Sheikh Omar Abdul Rahman came to the USA, where he organized cells that would be involved in various plots against U.S. targets.

Israel remained a prime target of terrorism during the 1990s as three groups—Hezbollah, Hamas, and Islamic Jihad—carried out suicide bombings, rocket attacks, and other operations against Israel. In October 1994, Hamas kidnapped an Israeli soldier, then killed him as a rescue was launched after an intense Israeli intelligence operation had located him. On that same day, October 19, a suicide bomber killed 22 and injured 47 in Tel Aviv. In an eye-for-an-eye campaign terrorists would carry out suicide bombings or other atrocities against the Israelis and Israel would target and kill leaders of Islamic Jihad, Hamas, or Hezbollah.

Certainly a landmark event in the current War Against Terror was the founding of al-Qaida in 1989 by Osama bin Laden and hundreds of veterans of the Afghan war against the Soviet Union. By late 1991, bin Laden and many followers were based in Sudan. The first attack against U.S. interests generally credited to al-Qaida was the December 1992 bombing of a hotel in Aden used by U.S. personnel.

In February 1993 a truck bomb was exploded at the World Trade Center in New York City with extensive damage, loss of life, and injuries. In June 1993, through information from an informant, the FBI arrested terrorists planning to blow up targets around New York City. The most prominent among those arrested was Abdul Rahman Yasin.

By 1994, al-Qaida affiliate Abu Sayyaf was active in the Philippines with many of the fighters drawn from followers of Osama bin Laden who had been with him in Afghanistan. Ramzi Youssef, who was wanted by the FBI for his involvement in the 1993 World Trade Center bombing, was in the Philippines developing bombs to be used on airliners throughout the Far East. However, a fire in his residence in January 1995 caused him to flee leaving behind a computer that became an intelligence treasure trove. The next month, U.S. agents and ISI agents captured Youssef in Islamabad.

Osama bin Laden considered the Saudi regime a primary target as well. In November 1995 and June 1996, al-Qaida-linked bombings at facilities housing U.S. personnel in Saudi Arabia allowed him to strike at both the USA and the House of Saud. In the latter attack at the Khobar Tower, 19 U.S. airmen were killed and 385 injured. Al-Qaida attacked U.S. interests again in August 1998, when a truck bomb at the U.S. Embassy in Nairobi, Kenya, killed more than 200 and injured more than 4,000, mostly Kenyans. Almost simultaneously, a bomb was exploded at the U.S. Embassy in Dar-es-Salaam, Tanzania, killing 11 and injuring 85.

During the 1990s, Iran attempted to export its own brand of Islamic terrorism around the world by financing terror in return for groups attacking targets designated by Iran. The large Shi'ite population in the triangle where the borders of Argentina, Brazil, and Paraguay meet was an aid to operations by Iranian-backed terrorists in Latin America. The large Jewish population in Argentina made it an especially appealing target. In March 1992, the Israeli Embassy in Buenos Aires was bombed, killing 29 and injuring many more. Hezbollah claimed responsibility. In July 1994, there was a more devastating bomb attack against a building housing Jewish organizations in Buenos Aires, resulting in 86 killed and over 200 injured. The day after this attack, a bomb on a commuter airliner in Panama killed many visiting Israeli businessmen.

Other countries in Latin America suffered terrorist attacks during the 1990s, especially Colombia and Peru. In Colombia, FARC was particularly active against the government and foreign businesses. Kidnapping had always been a source of revenue for guerillas in Colombia and during the 1990s more than a billion dollars was paid in ransom. In 1996 alone, more than 30 foreigners were kidnapped by FARC or ELN. The Colombian oil industry was also targeted by terrorists in a move to undermine the Colombian government economically. In Peru, both the Shining Path and the Tupac Amaru remained active during the 1990s.

The most notorious hostage incident of the 1990s in Latin America began on December 17, 1996 when 14 members of the Tupac Amaru Revolutionary Movement took more than 500 hostages at the Japanese Ambassador's residence in Lima, Peru. The incident would drag on for more than four months, with all but 72 of the hostages being released during the negotiation phase. Eventually, 140 operators drawn from Peruvian police and military special operations units assaulted the residence. The rescue operation, which employed a tunnel that had been dug during the prolonged incident, took 22 minutes before the residence was completely cleared. During the assault, all terrorists were killed with the loss of one hostage and two operators; nine operators were injured. Despite the months that passed as the rescue was planned and for which preparations were made, Peruvian security forces kept good operational security, which allowed them to successfully carry out the rescue. Prolonged negotiations also lulled the terrorists into a sense of complacency, which was shattered when operators carried out an explosive entry directly under the residence!

The Kurdish separatist movement PKK committed escalating acts of terrorism against the Turks during the 1990s, particularly targeting the tourist industry.

India faced terrorist threats from Kashmiri separatists and also from the Tamil Tigers of the LTTE, who wanted to undermine Indian support for the Sri Lankan government. In May 1991, a female suicide bomber killed Indian Prime Minister Rajiv Gandhi. Often, encounters between the Tamil Tigers and the Sri Lankan security forces became full- scale battles with heavy casualties on both sides. Sri Lankan special ops troops suffered very heavy casualties fighting the LTTE. In fact, so many government troops were killed fighting against the Tamil Tigers that in 1998 nearly 20,000 troops deserted. By 1995, government troops and bases were under heavy threat of attack, as was the Sri Lankan tourist industry. In January 1996, a truck bomb in Colombo killed 91 and injured around 1,400. In March 1998, another vehicle bomb in Colombo killed 32 and injured more than 250.

Terrorism from the Muslim world hit Singapore in March 1991, when Pakistani terrorists hijacked a Singapore Airlines jet and demanded the release of the imprisoned husband of Benazir Bhutto. When negotiations failed to release the 123 hostages and it appeared likely the terrorists would start executing them, the Special Operations Force of the Singapore Commandos assaulted the aircraft, killing all four terrorists and freeing the hostages.

One of the most feared forms of terrorism struck Japan during the 1990s as a religious sect released nerve gas in June 1994, then in March 1995 placed containers of Sarin on commuter trains killing 10 and injuring up to 5,000.

There were substantial fears that terrorists would strike the USA at the Millennium. What could have, in fact, been a major terrorist attack was thwarted on December 14, 1999 when a U.S. Customs officer noticed a man, subsequently identified as Ahmed Ressam, acting suspiciously and detained him. Within his vehicle they found explosives and timing devices. One of his intended targets was LAX (Los Angeles International Airport).

As the new century dawned in 2000, al-Qaida continued to target the USA as shown by the October attack on the U.S.S. *Cole* in Aden, killing 17 sailors and wounding 40 others. Among other terrorist acts of 2000 that stand out is the bombing of churches on Christmas Eve in Indonesia, killing 17 and injuring more than 150.

Thai operators rescued 700 hostages at a hospital in Ratchaburi, Thailand, in January 2000. Ten terrorists from God's Army, a faction of the ethnic Karen rebel movement, had taken the hostages and held them during a 24-hour siege. The Thai rescue team stormed the hospital and killed all ten hostage-takers with no loss of life to the hostages.

2001 started off as a prime year for terrorist attacks as FARC exploded a car bomb in a Medellín, Colombia, shopping center resulting in 50 or more injuries. In Russia, Chechen terrorists killed 20 and injured 93 in bomb blasts in three Russian cities near the Chechen border. In Colombia, during the month of May, bomb attacks hit the major cities of Cali, Bogotá, and Medellín resulting in 15 deaths and many more injuries. In July, a suicide squad of Tamil Tigers destroyed or damaged 20 aircraft at Sri Lanka's International airport and killed 7 airport workers or soldiers. Suicide bombers continued to be a threat in Israel with an August 2001, attack resulting in 7 deaths and 130 injured.

The most horrendous attack of 2001 occurred on September 11, when hijacked aircraft were flown into the Twin Towers of the World Trade Center and the Pentagon, resulting in 2,997 deaths and launching the USA into a battle against terrorism that goes on as this is written. U.S. and allied antiterrorist forces would cause the fall of the Taliban regime in Afghanistan and would hunt al-Qaida-linked terrorists around the globe as a result of these attacks.

Near the end of 2001, on December 13, an attack by Kashmiri terrorists based in Pakistan on India's Parliament resulted in the death of seven plus the five terrorists and the injuring of another dozen. The attack increased tensions between India and Pakistan and led to increased troop deployments along the border.

The number of major terrorist incidents in 2002 that could be linked to al-Qaida was particularly significant, though other terrorist groups around the world remained active as well. Although only one hostage died: the January kidnapping and brutal murder of journalist Daniel Pearl in Pakistan individualized the threat of Islamic terrorism for many Americans.

Colombia continued to face kidnappings, assassinations, and bombings by FARC. Major bombings took place in January with 5 killed and 40 injured; in April with 12 killed and 70 injured; and in December (in two attacks just four days apart), killing one and injuring more than 50. Elsewhere in Latin America, in March a car bomb near the U.S. Embassy in Lima, Peru, killed 9 and injured at least 30.

The suicide bombing offensive against Israel became even more bloody in 2002 with the March 27 "Passover Massacre" that took the lives of 30 and injured 140. Just four days later, another Hamas suicide bomber in Haifa killed 15 and injured over 40. On June 18, a suicide bomber on a bus in Jerusalem killed 19 and injured at least 74. Later in the year, on November 21, another Hamas suicide bomber detonated a bomb aboard another Jerusalem bus, killing 11 and injuring more than 50. Another major disaster was averted when a diesel truck was detonated in a gas depot at Pe Gillot. The death of hundreds was averted when a sprinkler system put out the fire before the entire depot went up. Jews were the target in April, when an al-Qaida member drove a natural gas truck filled with explosives into a synagogue in Tunisia killing 21 and injuring more than 30.

The Russians suffered a major terrorist attack by Chechens when a bomb explosion at the Victory Day celebrations at Kaspiisk in Dagestan killed 42 or more and injured at least 130. Near the end of the year, on December 27, a truck bomb at the Chechen Parliament in Grozny killed 83.

The most noteworthy incident involving the Chechens, however, occurred on October 23, when Chechen terrorists seized the Nord Ost Theater in Moscow along with hundreds of hostages. The large number of terrorists involved—40 to 50,including female suicide bombers—made planning a rescue very difficult. However, the Russian national hostage rescue unit, FSB Alpha, planned a rescue using Fentanyl gas to knock out the terrorists and the hostages and allow an entry. Given the large number of hostages and terrorists, and the presence of a massive amount of explosives—enough to bring down the entire theater—there were sound arguments for the Russian decision to use gas. However, plans had not been made to give medical assistance to the large number of hostages affected by the gas and 120 hostages died along with 40 terrorists.

Islamic extremists, often fighters for Kashmiri independence, continued to target India. In May 2002, terrorists cut the rails near Jaunpur causing a train crash that killed 12. Another train derailment in September caused by suspected Naxalite terrorists killed 130 people. Still another train derailment caused by Islamic extremists killed 20 near Kurnool, India, in December. In another incident that did not target the Indian rail system, in September, two terrorists from a Jaish-e-Mohammed group attacked the Akshardham Temple complex in Ahmedabad, India, killing 30 and injuring numerous others.

Elsewhere in South Asia, the October 12 bombing in Bali killed 202 people, mostly Western tourists. Many of the tourists were from Australia and may have been targeted because of Australian support for the U.S.-led War on Terror. Five days later, bombings at Zamboanga in the Philippines killed 6 and wounded around 150.

In 2003, Colombia remained under constant threat from FARC guerillas as there were at least a dozen significant bombing attacks including one on February 7 at the El Nogal nightclub in Bogotá that resulted in 36 dead and over 200 injured and another a week later in Neiva that resulted in 18 killed, including the Chief Prosecutor and Chief of Police, plus 37 injured. Although FARC was responsible for most attacks, ELN is believed to have been responsible for a March 5 attack at a covered parking garage in Cucuta that killed 6 and injured 68. Serious attacks began again in the fall with bombings in September, October, and November in Chita, Florencia, and Bogotá, resulting in 26 deaths and over 150 injuries. FARC is believed to have been responsible for these attacks.

Israel faced continued attacks from suicide bombers in 2003 as well. On March 5 a Hamas suicide bomber killed 17 and injured 53 on a Haifa bus. In another bombing aboard a Jerusalem bus, a Hamas suicide bomber killed 23 and wounded more than 130. On October 4, a suicide bomber killed 21 and wounded 51 at a Haifa restaurant.

Russia, meanwhile, fell prey to bomb attacks from Chechen terrorists. On July 5, 15 were killed and 40 injured by a bomb at a rock festival in Moscow. Then, on August 1, an explosion at a Russian hospital in Mozdok, North Ossetia, killed 50 and injured 76. Another bomb blast struck a passenger train in southern Russia on September 3, killing 7 and injuring 90. Early December saw two more high-profile bombings—one on the 5th, when suicide bombers killed at least 46 on a train in southern Russia and a second on the 9th, when a blast in Red Square, Moscow, killed 6 and injured at least 11. There were bomb attacks within Chechnya as well. A truck bomb killed 59 in Znamenskoye on May 12 and a suicide bombing at a religious festival in southeastern Chechnya took 16 lives two days later.

Among other significant attacks in 2003 was one In the Philippines; a March bomb attack on the airport in Davao killed 21. Another bombing on a housing compound for Americans working in Saudi Arabia in May killed 26 and injured 160. Also in May, bombers linked to al-Qaida attacked five targets associated with the West or Jews, resulting in 41 dead and over 100 injured. In August, the Canal Hotel in Baghdad was bombed, killing 22 and injuring over 100. Also in August, two bomb blasts in Mumbai, India, killed 48 and injured 150. In November, two bomb attacks a few days apart struck synagogues, a British Consulate, and the Hong Kong and Shanghai Bank In Istanbul, Turkey, killing 57 and injuring more than 700.

Although there were fewer terrorist incidents around the world in 2004 than in 2003, the number killed was higher as many of the incidents involved very large numbers of casualties. Bus attacks in Israel continued with the January 29 suicide attack on a Jerusalem bus that killed 11 and injured more than 50. Although there were other deaths by terrorism in Israel during the year, tightening of entry from Palestinian areas to Israel cut the number of suicide bombings on buses and in commercial areas but made the checkpoints a new target. Outside Israel, three car bombs in the Sinai Peninsula in October killed 34 and injured 171, many Israeli or other foreign tourists.

Attacks against the Russians by Chechen terrorists were numerous in 2004. In February a bomb on the Moscow Metro killed 41, then, in October, aircraft bombings killed another 90. A week later, on August 31, another Moscow subway station was targeted, resulting in 10 killed and 33 injured.

But the most horrendous attack was at Beslan School, where around 50 Chechen terrorists took between 1,100 and 1,200 hostages on September 1, the opening of school. Having learned from the assault on the Nord Ost Theater, the terrorists planted explosives around the building with "dead man's switches" that would set them off should the terrorist on the pedal switch be killed. The terrorists also took Draconian action, killing a large number of male hostages and throwing them out of the windows. Early on, it became apparent to Russian negotiators that this was not an incident that was likely to be "negotiated out." The intent of the terrorists seemed to be to kill as many hostages as possible. Units from FSB Alpha and Vympel as well as Army Spetsnaz were on the scene and began practicing for an assault, but they faced many problems, not the least of which was the large number of relatives of hostages who were on the scene drunk and armed. Eventually, an accidental explosion of some of the booby traps on the third day of the incident started the terrorists killing hostages, which forced operators from Alpha and Vympel to go in, though the assault was not well coordinated. Snipers found themselves forced to give covering fire to escaping hostages who were being shot by terrorists from the windows. By the time the assault ended, 344 hostages had died. The Alpha and Vympel operators performed courageously, often placing themselves between escaping hostages and terrorist bullets. This incident has been a wake-up call to antiterrorist units around the world that massive hostage incidents such as this with large numbers of terrorists cannot be handled in the surgical manner for which the units train. It has also shown that in such incidents, a substantial number of snipers armed with self-loading tactical rifles may be necessary to engage the maximum number of terrorists.

In February, Abu Sayyaf bombed a ferry in the Philippines, resulting in the deaths of 116; this was only one of many attacks by al-Qaida-affiliated groups during the year. Among others were the coordinated bombings of commuter trains in Madrid, Spain, which killed 191 and injured more than 1,500. In May, 22 died in the attack on an oil compound at Al-Khobar in Saudi Arabia. In August, al-Qaida in Iraq claimed responsibility for bombings outside restaurants in Dubai where 37 died and around 200 were injured. Then, in December, an al-Qaida-linked group attacked the U.S. Consulate in Jeddah, Saudi Arabia, resulting in the death of five local employees.

On March 2, attacks against Shia Muslim processions in Iraq and Pakistan caused the deaths of 224 and the injury of over 650.

The year 2005 saw a rash of bombings and attacks by gunmen in Thailand. One of the largest occurred on February 17 when a car bomb outside a hotel killed 7 and injured 40. Many of the attacks targeted Buddhists. Muslim extremists were linked to many of the bombings. Nearby in Myanmar (formerly Burma), on May 7, multiple bombings in Yangon killed 19 and injured 160.

On February 14, a car bomb in Beirut killed former Lebanese Prime Minister Rafiq Hariri as well as 20 others. April attacks employing bombs and gunmen targeted foreign tourists. On July 23, a much more massive blow to Egyptian tourism was struck when car bombs exploded at tourist sites around Sharm el-Sheikh, killing at least 88 and wounding more than 100.

In June, a suicide bomber attacked a mosque in Kandahar, Afghanistan, killing 20. Jordan was targeted as well for supporting the U.S. War on Terror as explosions at three hotels in Amman, Jordan, on November 9 killed 60 and injured 120.

London was targeted on July 7 as bombs on a bus and in underground stations killed 56 and injured over 700. Two weeks later, attempted bombings on another bus and in three underground stations caused minor damage.

India faced terrorist attacks in July when a bomb on a commuter train killed 13, then again in October when multiple bomb blasts in a market in Delhi killed 61 or more and injured more than 200. Bangladesh also faced terrorist bombs on August 17 as about 100 improvised bombs exploded around the country.

Russia faced fewer attacks within Russia during 2005, but in October, Chechen rebels attacked Russian government buildings in Nalchik, Kabardino-Balkaria. During the fighting 137 died, including 92 of the terrorists.

Although there were fewer bombings in Israel during 2005, the Jewish state was not exempt as a February suicide bomber killed five in Tel Aviv and another in Hadera during October Israel killed 6 and injured 26.

In 2006, a large-scale bombing campaign in Iraq accounted for hundreds of lives and thousands of injures. There were also numerous attacks in Afghanistan. Other terrorist groups, some of which had been relatively quiet for months, struck during 2006 in Northern Ireland, Thailand, and Colombia. On February 1, the South Korean Embassy in Damascus was targeted by extremists linked to al-Qaida resulting in the deaths of 23, 7 of whom were Korean. This attack was most likely because of South Korea's support for the U.S. War on Terror. In April, bombings in Dahab, Egypt, killed 23 and injured 62 others.

Other than in Iraq and Afghanistan, though, the most consistent attacks were against India. In March, bombings in the Holy City of Varanasi killed 28 and injured more than 100. Then, in July, new attacks on commuter trains in Mumbai killed 209 and injured 714. In August, a bomb at a Hindu temple near Imphal killed 5 and injured nearly 50 more. Finally, in November, a bomb exploded on a train in West Bengal killing at least 8 and injuring many more. Most likely in revenge for attacks against Hindus, in September, a bomb blast at a Muslim cemetery in Malegaon killed 37 and injured 125 others.

Sectarian violence among Muslims accounted for a substantial number of terrorist acts during 2006. For example, in April, a suicide bomber in Karachi, Pakistan, killed 57 Sunni worshippers. Elsewhere in Pakistan, an attack by a pro-

Taliban group on a church in Rawalpindi killed 67, including 23 Americans. Pakistani investigators believed that a local Sunni cleric had ordered the attack.

In Sri Lanka, during June, LTTE killed 68 and injured around 60 in an attack on a bus. Later in the year, during September, an LTTE suicide bomber rammed an explosive-filled truck into a bus transporting Sri Lankan sailors, killing at least 92.

In November, the assassination of anti-Syrian politician Perre Amine Gemayel was blamed on Syria, Iran, and Hezbollah, and resulted in large-scale demonstrations and calls around the world for Syria to pull out of Lebanon. In Israel, the suicide bombing offensive had abated somewhat, but on April 17, a Palestinian suicide bomber killed 11 and injured 70. In Somalia, an attempted assassination of President Abdullah Yusuf Ahmed involving a suicide bomber on September 18 claimed the life of the President's brother as well as four bodyguards. During the subsequent gun battle six other assassins were killed.

Europe was not exempt from terrorist attacks during 2006. In addition to bombings of various stores in Belfast by the Real IRA in November, the Germans foiled an attack on the rail system in July and arrested Islamic militants who were allegedly incensed over satirical Danish cartoons of Muhammad. In August, British police disrupted a plot to place bombs on aircraft flying from Heathrow Airport to the USA. In Norway, during September, Muslim extremists opened fire on a synagogue in Oslo. The extremists were captured and it was discovered that they had also planned to attack the U.S. and Israeli embassies in Oslo. Finally, the year ended with a bombing at Madrid Airport on December 30.

Some of the largest terrorist incidents during 2007 took place in Iraq as extremist groups attacked fellow Muslims, either because of their brand of Islam or because they were serving in the police or military of the Iraqi state. American troops and civilian contractors as well as other foreigners were also targeted. Bombing attacks in Iraq often kill in the hundreds.

In nearby Pakistan, the number of terrorist attacks in 2007 seemed to be on the rise. On January 27 in Peshawar, a suicide bombing hit a Shia religious procession killing 14 and injuring 30. Just the day before, a suicide bomber had blown himself up attempting to enter a Marriott hotel in Islamabad. On February 17 in Quetta, a suicide bomber detonated a bomb in a courtroom killing 15 and injuring 24. Some of the attacks were motivated by religious differences, but others were strikes against the government for taking a hard line against Islamic militants. This targeting of government officials was illustrated in bloody fashion on April 28, when Pakistan's Interior Minister Aftab Khan Sherpao (the official in charge of many law enforcement functions) was targeted by a suicide bomber when making a speech. He was slightly injured but 28 were killed and 35 injured in the blast. (Sherpao was targeted again on December 21, when a suicide bombing at a mosque where he was worshipping killed at least 50.) On May 15, a bomb in a restaurant in Peshawar killed around 24 people.

Between July 3 and 11, pro-Taliban/al-Qaida forces occupied the Red Mosque in Islamabad and took hostages. In a battle that concluded after the Pakistanis used a Predator drone to gather intelligence, on July 10, after negotiations broke down, the SSG and Pakistani elite police plus some supporting military units assaulted and retook the mosque. During the prolonged siege, 1,096 people either came out of the mosque or were rescued. Ten members of the SSG were killed and 33 injured during the operation. Many civilians were killed during the siege and numerous civilians and troops were injured. It is difficult to put an exact number to the terrorists killed, as some of those classified as civilian dead may have actually been fighters. Seventy-five bodies were recovered from the mosque at the end of the operation, all or most presumed to have been terrorists. Included in those holding the mosque were foreign al-Qaida fighters including Uzbeks, Egyptians, and Afghans.

During one week in July, more than 150 were killed in Pakistan in incidents resulting from the assault on the Red Mosque by the Pakistani Army. The attacks were organized by Ayman Al-Zawahiri, who had also been involved with those who took the mosque. On September 4 in Rawalpindi, two bomb blasts, one on a bus transporting government employees, killed at least 21 and injured 74. On October 1, a suicide bomber disguised as a woman killed at least 15 and injured 22 in Bannu.

In a preview of the unrest that would accompany the return of former Pakistani Prime Minister Benazir Bhutto, on October 18, twin suicide bombings with suspected Taliban/al-Qaida links struck Bhutto's motorcade, killing 136 and injuring 387. Bhutto was uninjured. But she was not as lucky on December 27 as an assassin shot at her then blew himself up, killing at least 20. Bhutto died in the attack causing widespread belief that elements of Pervez Musharraf's government had been involved in the attack. As an interesting side note for this book since the Pakistani Special Service Group (SSG), which has the antiterrorism mission for Pakistan, will be discussed, some conspiracy theorists in Pakistan believe that Musharraf, a former officer in the SSG, used snipers from the unit to eliminate Bhutto.

Although Pakistan has been active in the War on Terror, the elements within the ISI (Pakistani intelligence) and the Army sympathetic to al-Qaida and the Taliban, combined with the large number of terrorists sheltering in the Tribal Lands along the frontier with Afghanistan, have contributed to instability in Pakistan, an instability that has certainly spilled over in terrorist acts against India as well.

Among the larger attacks in India during the year were another train bombing in February against the Samjhauta Express, which killed 68 and injured 49, and an abortive attack in June against Rajshahi University and other nearby targets. Jadid al-Qaedi claimed credit for the latter attempts. India also had interests in Sri Lanka, where a bus was bombed on January 5 and a resort on January 6; in the two attacks 21 died and 54 were injured. Later in June, Sri Lankan security forces discovered two large truck bombs in Trincomalee and Colombo and managed to defuse them before they exploded. Also in June, a bomb in the city of Yala killed one and injured 28.

Islamic terrorists continued to be active around the Middle East during 2007. An Islamist insurgency began in Somalia in early 2007 with the first car bomb exploding in Mogadishu early in February. In June, a car bomb attack on the Somali Prime Minister's house killed 6 guards and injured 20 others, though the Prime Minister was unscathed. Also in North Africa, on April 11 two suicide car bombers killed 33 and injured 222 in Algiers. Al-Qaida took credit. In December, more bombings in Algiers killed 37 and injured 177.

Saudi Arabia took preemptive action against terrorists in April, arresting 172 suspected al-Qaida terrorists involved in plots to use civilian aircraft for suicide attacks on oil facilities and military installations. Again in December, the Saudis pre-empted terrorist acts by arresting 28 al-Qaida militants.

In Turkey, a May bombing at a market in Izmir killed 1 and injured 14 others. Later that month, a suicide bombing in an Ankara shopping district killed 6 and injured many more. In June, a bomb outside of a store in Istanbul injured 14. In December, Turkish police stopped another bomber in Istanbul outside of a subway station. The Turks also faced attacks from PKK militants in 2007 leading to a threatened Turkish invasion of Kurdish areas of Iraq. In one attempted infiltration of Iraq, U.S. troops detained Turkish special forces personnel.

In the Philippines, there were bombings throughout the year. In June, Nairobi was hit by a blast just outside the Ambassador Hotel which killed one and injured 37 others. French tourists were killed in Mauritania on Christmas Eve by a group linked to al-Qaida.

Although tightened security at border crossings made Israel safer from suicide bombers, there were still incidents throughout the year, including a suicide bombing in January; two Israelis were shot by members of the Al-Aqsa Martyr's Brigades in October; Hamas launched rockets into Israel in May; and two Israeli hikers were killed by members of Fatah in December. In May, Israeli security forces stopped two female suicide bombers attempting to cross from the Gaza Strip. In November, Israeli soldiers shot and killed three suicide bombers attempting to enter Israel by climbing the Gaza fence.

Terrorism continued to threaten the West as well, especially Western Europe and U.S. interests abroad. In June, Canadian police arrested 18 conspirators for planning to blow up the Parliament and behead the Prime Minister as well as attacking other targets. Virtually at the same time, authorities in New York thwarted a plan to blow up the fuel pipeline that feeds John F. Kennedy Airport, an attack that would have likely killed or injured a great many who live nearby. Toward the end of June, Glasgow Airport was targeted by al-Qaida-linked bombers, while two other bombs were set off in London. No one was seriously injured in the attacks and eight were arrested. In September, another group of attacks was foiled in Germany as suspects were arrested before they could carry out attacks against Frankfurt Airport, Ramstein Air Base, and schools attended by American dependants. The group had links to al-Qaida. In October, an attack on the U.S. Embassy in Vienna was thwarted and the suspects were arrested. Later in October, there was a suicide attack on an Amsterdam police station in which two Dutch police officers were stabbed before one of the injured officers shot and killed the terrorist. On December 6, a bomb in Paris killed one and injured one.

Although Russia did not face anything as horrendous as the Beslan School massacre in 2007, there were still some serious terrorist incidents. Among the most noteworthy was the derailing of a Moscow–St. Petersburg train in August that injured 60 and a November bombing of a bus in North Ostia that killed 5 and injured 13.

Attacks by FARC in Colombia were a constant throughout the year. Among the more serious, many of which targeted police officers, was a bombing in March in Buenaventura that killed 16 and injured 16. In April, a bomb targeting police headquarters killed 1 and injured 30. Nine anti-narcotics police officers were killed in May by a FARC roadside bomb. The next day 10 soldiers were killed by another roadside bomb.

One thing that becomes apparent with this overview of terrorist incidents and the development of the response is that over the last decade, terrorists have learned to fear the antiterrorist units who carry out hostage rescue operations. As a result, they avoid these types of incident. A bomb is harder to counter, especially if it is an "Islamic Smart Bomb" (i.e. a suicide bomber). Although antiterrorist units must continue to train for rescue operations, other than their alert section, which remains at home ready to deal with a hostage incident, today many of the most elite antiterrorist units have much of their unit deployed on preemptive operations. Hostage rescue units, close protection teams, and air marshals, however, remain reactive forces. In many cases today, antiterrorist units are used proactively, whether to act upon intelligence and strike against terrorists before they can launch an operation or by taking the fight to the terrorists in safe havens in Afghanistan, the Philippines, Somalia, or elsewhere. Many antiterrorist units now operate on the assumption that if they can eliminate as many terrorists as possible in Afghanistan or elsewhere, they will be less likely to have to react to an incident in their home country planned by these same terrorists in the future.

Chapter II

Recruiting and Selecting the Antiterrorist Operator

Normally an antiterrorist unit recruits from within the parent organization of which it is a part. In many military antiterrorist units, most of those applying to join the unit will come from within the special forces of that unit's country. For example, the U.S. Combat Applications Group will recruit heavily from the U.S. Army Special Forces, but may also evaluate candidates from the airborne forces, Rangers, and other units. In some units, even if the unit is part of the Army, personnel from any branch of the armed services may apply. Canada's JTF2 (Joint Task Force 2), for example. recruits from all branches of Canada's armed forces, as do many other units. The British SAS will also accept candidates from outside the UK armed forces. Citizens of the Commonwealth, Republic of Ireland, the former Rhodesia, New Zealand, and Australia may apply. (Fiji is one of many Commonwealth countries that have produced highly respected SAS troops). In other military antiterrorist units, passing selection for the parent unit allows the soldier to serve on the antiterrorism portion of the unit as a regular rotation. The British and Australian SAS handle the antiterrorist mission in this way.

The level of physical fitness present in those already serving in an airborne or special forces unit gives them somewhat of an edge in terms of selection for an antiterrorist unit, but there are advantages in getting recruits from a wide range of military backgrounds. Candidates who have served in intelligence and have excellent language skills, for example, can be a real advantage, as can trained helicopter or fixed-wing pilots, electronic warfare specialists, or mechanics. Once selected as a member of an antiterrorist unit, an operator will receive very diverse training; nevertheless a candidate who meets all the normal selection criteria while having additional wide-ranging and useful skills is an asset.

For units selecting from national police forces, the pool of candidates will generally be drawn from those with a certain number of years of successful law enforcement experience. Whether personnel are drawn from the military or the police, a certain level of maturity is desirable. As a result, some units will set a minimum age, normally in the mid to late twenties. Many will also set a maximum age for who may apply for the selection course. The British SAS, for example, will only allow males of 32 years or less to apply for selection, though an exception is made for those who are serving in a reserve special forces unit, when the age limit is extended to 34.

As another gauge of maturity, some antiterrorist units will only recruit amongst NCOs or serving officers. This was originally the case with Germany's KSK, for example, though enlisted personnel and even civilians may now apply. They must, however, complete the rigorous Long Range Surveillance course prior to application. In some national police forces with units that perform more hazardous or challenging tasks, these officers will have already proved they have some appealing characteristics. France's GIGN, for example, can draw upon members of the Gendarmerie's EPIGN, a unit that already performs higher-risk missions and is parachute-qualified.

At least some law enforcement agencies may find that the pool of manpower within the normal investigative arms of the agency will not supply enough high-quality candidates. Since a typical FBI agent may work on long-term investigations and make few arrests during a typical year, he may not have the mindset to join the HRT, which may be more likely to attract agents who work street crimes such as bank robberies and apprehend dangerous felons as a matter of course. However, the increased use of the HRT after the 9/11 terrorist attacks has caused the FBI to begin specifically recruiting agents with potential to join this team.

Right GROM operators during an entry–note that the point man is using his HK P8 with his HK MP5SD slung; note also that the P8 is retained by a flexible lanyard. (Grom.mil.pl)

Above A Little Bird helicopter of the U.S. Army 160th Special Operations Aviation Regiment prepares to insert operators onto a rooftop. (SOCOM)

The FBI HRT has instituted what it terms the "Tactical Recruiting Program," which targets those with experience in military or police tactical operations. Candidates are expected to be in excellent physical condition and to score substantially higher than the basic requirements on the Special Agent Physical Fitness Test, plus have three years of tactical experience. Those who meet the requirements will be fast tracked to attend HRT selection; however, they must still complete the FBI Academy and gain two years' investigative experience as special agents before being eligible to apply for the HRT. To apply to be a special agent, a college degree is required, which makes former officers in the SEALs, Special Forces, Rangers, Marine Corps, or Air Force Special Tactics Squadrons particularly appealing. Military academy graduates who have served with a special ops unit are especially desirable.

Initially, Israel's Sayaret Matkal was such a secret organization that recruitment took place from within a small circle, often including family members of those already serving. For example, Benjamin Netanyahu and two of his brothers served in the unit; one was killed during the Entebbe Rescue. This policy of personal selection of recruits by members of the unit ended during the 1980s and recruiting is now from a much broader pool.

The Hong Kong police's SDU has a couple of interesting requirements in its recruiting. Not only must applicants have at least two years of exemplary service, but they must also be nonsmokers and nondrinkers. Whether "nondrinker" means only rarely taking a drink or being completely abstemious is not clear.

Although the selection process will differ among units, most have a process consisting of three or four phases. The first phase is often a physical fitness test since if a candidate cannot display the fitness necessary to perform the tasks of the operator, he need not continue. The FBI's physical fitness test incorporates 50 pushups, 10 pull-ups, 50 sit-ups in one minute, a 110-yard shuttle run, a 1.5-mile run in 11 minutes, and a 200-yard swim. The Delta Force test in the past included a 40-yard inverted crawl in 25 seconds, 37 sit-ups in one minute, 33 pushups in one minute, a run/dodge/jump course in 24 seconds, a 2-mile run in under 16.5 minutes, a 100-yard swim in uniform and boots, and an 18-mile speed march. Canada's JTF2 requires a 2.4-km run in 9 minutes 45 seconds, a minimum of 40 pushups with no rest stops, a minimum of 40 sit-ups in one minute, 5 overhand, straight arm pull-ups, a bench press of a 65-kg weight, and the Canadian Forces Swim Test. Note that many military units require distance runs to be carried out wearing combat boots. Some units, in an attempt to determine if a candidate has phobias that might preclude him performing his duties in the unit, may also include physical tests to determine a fear of heights, confined spaces, or drowning.

Most units will also include a marksmanship test, since a candidate who cannot already shoot well is unlikely to develop the ability to carry out the precision shots required in a hostage rescue scenario. Standard weapons used by the police agency or military forces from which candidates are drawn are generally used, but some units may also include shooting unfamiliar weapons. Generally, handgun, submachinegun, and rifle marksmanship will be evaluated. Qualification will be set substantially higher than the minimum requirements for serving in regular police or military units.

The next phase is often some type of psychological evaluation, though the form will vary from unit to unit. The FBI HRT, for example, has used the Minnesota Multiphasic Personality Inventory, while Canada's JTF2 combines a cognitive ability test with a selection interview. Intelligence is very important for the antiterrorist operator, so along with psychological tests some units may also incorporate intelligence tests. Others may just use the standard test for recruits joining the police or military, but will set a higher minimum score for qualification. Some units also incorporate an interview as part of initial selection, while others save the interview for those who have passed all other aspects of selection. Because the precision use of lethal force may be required of the antiterrorist operator his psychological stability must be given serious consideration. However, it is important not to just assume that psychological evaluation is there to weed out "cowboys" who are too anxious to apply lethal force. Good psychological evaluation will also weed out those who might not be able to bring themselves to use lethal force without hesitation should it be necessary to save innocent lives.

These first three phases will often weed out as many as 50 percent of candidates, but the most rigorous part of the selection process is the final phase, which incorporates rigorous physical endurance, psychological toughness, and mental flexibility in a slog that normally lasts between two and four weeks.

The British SAS selection course is one of the best known in the world and has been copied by many other units so it should offer a good example with which to begin a discussion of such courses. Currently, the selection course is no longer known as the SAS Selection Course, but as the Special Forces Selection Course, since the SAS (Special Air Service), SBS (Special Boat Service), and SSR (Special Reconnaissance Regiment) all undergo the same initial selection process. Prior to undertaking selection, each candidate attends a two-day Special Forces Briefing over a weekend well in advance of one of the two yearly selection courses. Candidates receive a detailed briefing about special forces selection and undergo a map and compass test, swimming test, first aid test, and combat fitness test. Those perceived as having a low likelihood of successfully completing selection are informed, and likely candidates are provided with a training program to get them ready for the rigors of the selection course.

Above Members of the Montenegrin Antiiterrorist Unit SAJ; note the MP5 SMGs and the distinctive mesh face masks. (US DOD)

Recruiting and Selecting the Antiterrorist Operator

The actual selection process takes place at Sennybridge Training Camp in Wales and lasts four weeks. The course, which makes use of the surrounding Brecon Beacons and Elan Valley, stresses navigation and fitness. Weather conditions are known to be harsh and unpredictable here, which adds further to the rigors of the course. Candidates start off with various physical fitness tests, including a 1.5-mile run in under 10:30 as well as various other exercises.

The first week of selection consists primarily of runs up and down the hills in the Brecon Beacons with loaded rucksacks, together with navigation and map reading exercises. Many very physically fit candidates wash out because they cannot handle the navigation part of selection. Runs requiring navigation in small groups through forested areas follow, as do night navigation exercises. During the first and second weeks, the rucksack loads are increased, plus candidates must carry their rifle with them unslung at all times. Fatigue increases and, since food is supplied only intermittently and in relatively small portions, so does hunger.

During the third week, the land navigation problems become more complex, with candidates having to reach checkpoints to be logged in by members of the selection staff. The final week consists of more and more daunting navigation runs, leading up to the final endurance march across 40 miles of the Brecon Beacons, navigating from point to point while carrying 55 lb in the rucksack plus rifle, food, and water. The endurance march must be completed in under 20 hours to pass selection. Although this final march is considered a necessity to pass selection, it does not guarantee selection for continuation training, as a candidate may still be deemed unsuitable for entering a special forces unit. Not only is the pass rate for selection normally below 10 percent, but the weather conditions in the Brecons are so harsh and the candidates are pushed to such extremes that deaths during selection are not unknown.

Right Members of China's Snow Wolf Commando Unit training for their antiterrorist mission at the 2008 Olympics. (Chinese Armed Police)

Here's how some of the other world antiterrorist units run their courses:

New Zealand SAS

The selection course for the New Zealand SAS is similar to that of the British Special Forces, but lasts only two weeks. Selection is open to members of any of the New Zealand armed forces, which requires instructors to determine the ability of those who are not from the Army to handle complicated land navigation problems. A substantial number of those attempting selection are Maoris, who have a long and proud tradition of serving in the New Zealand SAS. Attrition rate in the New Zealand selection course usually runs to about 70 percent.

No leeway is granted in timed runs or navigation courses; being one second over can eliminate a candidate. As with the British Special Forces selection

Above Members of Iceland's Viking Squad practicing with their HK MP5s; note the distinctive Icelandic landscape in the background. (Icelandic National Police)

course, the built-in factors that test self-discipline, self-motivation, physical and mental toughness, initiative, and intellect work well for selecting candidates that will make good Special Forces operators. During the earlier stages of testing, candidates spend three days navigating the New Zealand countryside averaging 3 km per hour. By the end of those three days, fatigue and hunger are already becoming a factor. This training begins to test the ability of candidates to make decisions under stress as they have to decide when to run and when to save themselves so that they do not become so exhausted they cannot finish the course. They must also decide on routes—for example, whether to go over a hill that may be shorter in distance, but is ultimately more tiring.

As each day passes, hunger and fatigue become greater, while the candidate also realizes that things will likely be even more difficult the next day. As they say in U.S. Navy SEAL selection, "The Only Easy Day was Yesterday!" One of the more testing aspects of New Zealand SAS selection takes place at the Kaipara sand dunes, where candidates must carry a 25-kg jerry-can of water up and down the dunes. Six cans are spread among five men, which means that at any given time one candidate must carry two cans. This exercise allows evaluators to see how well candidates share the load and also illustrates teamwork.

Later in selection, candidates must do an escape and evasion exercise within a dense forest while chased by members of the SAS staff. At the point when they begin this exercise, they have been without sleep for 24 hours, yet they must complete the course within the time limit and deliver a message they have been given. The final endurance march covers 60 km through Woodhill Forest and must be completed within the time limit.

FBI HRT

The FBI HRT used the SAS selection course, combined with others, as a basis for their own selection system. One objective was to get agents out of the familiar to see how they would cope with the unexpected. Many prospective HRT members actually found that not having a schedule telling them what would be happening each day was harder than the actual physical tests. Many career soldiers undergoing selection for military antiterrorist units also find the lack of information a difficulty. As with other selection courses, the HRT course is designed to challenge the candidate, to elicit weaknesses and character flaws. For example, during HRT selection, it is common to give a group of candidates half the number of meals needed for the group to see how they share and cope with hunger. One of the toughest challenges in some HRT selection courses has been a run of 22 miles carrying a 45-lb load. To add difficulty and test teamwork, each team of candidates has also been required to carry a bag of medicine balls. HRT candidates have also had to walk 75 ft under water while holding their breath and carrying a 30-lb load in their hands.

KSK (Germany) and GIGN (France)

Among European antiterrorist units, Germany's KSK has one of the tougher selection courses. Lasting three months, it is held in the Black Forest, and requirements include the completion of a 90-hour long distance run and navigation exercise. Candidates must also complete a three-week survival, escape, and evasion course. Only 8–10 percent pass the selection course.

One of Europe's most respected antiterrorist units, GIGN, uses a one-week selection course for personnel who have already served in the Gendarmerie Nationale and met preselection requirements. GIGN selection begins with written tests of intelligence and psychological suitability, as well as an essay about what has motivated the candidate to apply. Written tests are followed by tests of physical strength and stamina, including pull-ups, sit-ups, pushups, and so on. A 9-km run/march carrying 11 kg follows. The final tests for the first day are of marksmanship with the handgun and rifle.

On the next day, candidates must run a very difficult obstacle course. A bungee jump from a bridge is incorporated into the day's activities to test nerve, confidence, and fear of heights. Next is an orienteering race with seven checkpoints that must be completed without a compass or written notes. Before this course is completed, the candidates will also have to pass a test to determine whether they suffer from claustrophobia by passing through various tight obstacles in total darkness. The second day ends with a night navigation exercise through the forest, which allows them a couple of hours' sleep at most.

The third day begins with an observation test, which is carried out in a room filled with tear gas. Candidates must pass through the room without a mask while observing the location of objects about which they will be tested. After a shower (to counter the effects of the gas), candidates must pass additional tests of observation and memorization. The remainder of the day is spent traversing various high ropes, climbing, and covering other raised obstacles.

The fourth day focuses on swimming ability, with tests including diving from a 10-meter board, swimming 100 meters against a stop watch, and covering 50 meters submerged. One of GIGN's traditional challenges follows as candidates must jump into the pool with bound hands and feet to demonstrate their ability to remain afloat under adverse conditions. The rest of the day is spent running obstacle courses, climbing, and in other forms of physical exertion.

The morning of the fifth day is spent in martial arts competition among the candidates, who are matched by weight and previous training. Evaluators are less concerned with who wins than that candidates do not give up and continue fighting. The day finishes with an interview by a panel of GIGN officers and NCOs and a final evaluation of who has passed and who has failed.

Although shorter than some other selection courses, the GIGN selection process still taxes candidates to the utmost and does a good job of evaluating courage, intelligence, and physical fitness. Candidates have already successfully served in the Gendarmerie Nationale, a militarized police force, and will still have to face a long an arduous training regimen before finally joining the unit. GIGN is famous for incorporating some tests into the selection process that offer a "French flair" to the proceedings.

Irish ARW (Army Ranger Wing)

The ARW is tasked with special operations and anti-terrorism for the Irish Republic and hence has a very rigorous selection process based to some extent on the U.S. Army's Ranger course. Unlike many special units, the ARW selection course is open to females. The annual course lasts four weeks. During the first phase, candidates must pass a number of physical tests including land navigation tests, timed assault course runs, water confidence training and testing, and a 10-km combat run. Candidates who do not successfully complete the initial phase are returned to unit, though they may attempt the course the next year. A candidate may attempt the course three times.

The second phase stresses initial training and assessment in various special forces skills, including long-range reconnaissance patrols, small unit tactics—especially ambush/counterambush, surveillance and intelligence gathering—and a 40-km group march, which must be completed within a time limit. Various assessments throughout selection will test the candidate on the following areas: rappeling, jumps from a bridge into water, team river crossings, the ability to work in confined spaces without succumbing to claustrophobia, various physical exercises, a 10-km run, various mountain and hill marches carrying a light to medium pack, a forced cross country march, and a group forced road march of 45 km carrying a medium load. Selection culminates with the group route march. Those who successfully complete course requirements—about 15 percent in a typical year—receive the "Fianoglach" (Ranger) tab.

ARW officers and NCOs then assess the overall performance of each individual against the number of openings in the unit. Those selected for the unit are then sent through another six months of intensive training before being fully fledged members of the Irish ARW.

Canada's JTF2

Canada's JTF2 actually has three separate selection courses depending upon one's function within the unit. The toughest course is the Special Operations Assaulters Selection Process. ("Assaulters" is the term JTF2 uses for its operators.) During the seven-week selection process, candidates are pushed to their limits physically and mentally. While in stressful situations, they are evaluated on weapons safety, their reaction to threats, and decision making. Additionally, over this period, they are tested for their physical fitness; ability to work at heights, in water, and in confined spaces; teamwork; problem solving; and interpersonal skills. Officer candidates must spend an additional three days demonstrating their ability to organize and command a special ops mission. Many units include this additional requirement for officer candidates. Support elements and coxswain elements (who will do boat handling) of JTF2 still have to undergo selection, but it is not as difficult.

Russia's Spetsnaz

Russia's Spetsnaz are known for an especially brutal selection process. In most Spetsnaz units, selection occurs, to some extent, in a Darwinian manner (i.e. natural selection). Many Spetsnaz are actually promising conscripts who are first put through a brutal regimen designed to inculcate obedience and physical toughness. They then undergo what is more akin to the selection courses used in other units to win the red beret that will designate them as fully fledged Spetsnaz. A typical red beret selection course might run along the following lines.

Above A member of Italy's GIS armed with a Benelli shotgun--note the light and optical sight (Carabinieri)

The candidate must cover 10 km in under two hours, during which obstacles including mud, water, sand, dirt, and hills are encountered. He must wear a helmet and ballistic vest and carry his AK74 while covering the distance. The AK74 is loaded with a blank cartridge, which simulates the need to practice weapons safety and to take good care of the weapon. Bullets will be fired in his direction and explosives detonated close to his route. Spetsnaz training incorporates a lot of operations near fire so passing through fire will be part of the selection run as well. To simulate operating in an NBC (Nuclear, Biological, Chemical) environment, he will have to don a gas mask and exert himself by running or carrying another candidate for 2 to 3 km. At points along the way, evaluators will stop the candidate and require him to perform a series of physical exercises. They may also run alongside harassing him by throwing pyrotechnics at his feet.

Immediately upon completion of the 10-km run, the candidate moves on to an obstacle course that simulates operations in urban areas and incorporates trenches and tunnels, the latter designed to be very tight and hard to wriggle through. Upon completion of the obstacle course, he must fire the blank round in his rifle to show that he has not allowed it to become inoperable while performing his various tasks.

Although physically exhausted, the candidate next has to pass a weapons test with standard Russian infantry weapons. The Dragunov sniper rifle will normally not be zeroed and hence the candidate is given two shots to zero the rifle, then must fire two shots successfully on two targets at long range. Normally, he will also have to do a dynamic entry in a hostage scenario and fire two double taps from his pistol on two targets. This phase also frequently incorporates a disassembled radio that the candidate must assemble, then establish contact with his "base."

In the next phase, the candidate must climb a five- story building, then rappel to clear the building from top down. He will encounter shoot/no shoot targets as the clears floors and must engage those which are shoot targets with blank rounds. He will also have a grenade simulator, which he must pitch into a room after kicking out a window. He has 45 seconds to carry out this exercise from the top floor to the ground. He is then put through another series of tough physical exercises to wear him down even more.

Finally, the candidate must fight four others, including Spetsnaz who have already achieved the red beret, for 12 minutes without halting. New fighters rotate in against the candidate so he is always going against fresh opponents. He must avoid getting knocked out and must remain aggressive rather than just defending himself. It is not uncommon for candidates to lose teeth and suffer severe cuts and abrasions during this final phase. Any challengers not deemed aggressive enough will be disciplined.

Although this course is typical of those used in Army Spetsnaz units, it may be assumed that the super elite antiterrorist Spetsnaz units under the FSB (Federal Security Service)—Alpha and Vympel—use a similarly tough selection course, though their candidates are chosen from the ranks of the FSB based on their previous record and often based on proven athletic ability in national or world competition. They then go through a two-month selection process that challenges them to the utmost but is more akin to those of units such as the SAS or FBI HRT, which already have mature highly motivated candidates. Nevertheless, they are expected to be as tough as other Spetsnaz while also being highly self-motivated. Some units incorporate an interview near or at the end of the selection process to evaluate the candidates' poise, intelligence, self-confidence, psychological state after weeks of stress, and various other factors. In many cases, the unit commander and other officers will be present as well as senior enlisted personnel. On at least some selection courses, Delta Force had candidates read Machiavelli's *The Prince*, then discuss it during the interview. Thinking about it, a potential operator's reaction to Machiavelli's classic should offer insights into intelligence, practicality, ethics, and various other aspects of the personality.

A variation on the interview is the interrogation that many units incorporate into selection in order to determine the strength of a candidate's will to resist. Generally, the interrogation occurs as part of the escape and evasion element included in some selection courses. Many of the techniques the press has highlighted with regard to the interrogation of captured terrorists (i.e. water boarding) are routinely practiced on volunteers for special operations and antiterrorist units as part of their selection. For the SAS and SBS, the interrogation phase traditionally includes a session while standing nude with a trained female interrogator from Army Intelligence or MI6 who will make it a point to comment on the smallness or deformity of the candidate's genitals! Interview, interrogation, or both, these are just additional techniques for evaluating the candidate's character and will.

MAT (Maritime Antiterrorism) Selection

Units tasked with MAT undergo an equally grueling selection process though more of it takes place in mud, in boats, and in the water than with land based antiterrorist units. Many national antiterrorist units include a section with the MAT mission who will receive specialized diving and small boat training, while others such as the U.S. Navy's DevGru, the SBS, or the Italian COMSUBIN are naval special warfare units that carry out MAT operations.

The SBS formerly ran their own selection course, which incorporated many waterborne operations, but now goes through the selection process along with the SAS, then moves onto specialized Swimmer-Canoist operations. For many of the MAT units drawn from naval special warfare teams, the initial selection process is considered difficult enough that no additional selection is considered necessary though those assigned the MAT mission will get additional specialized training.

The U.S. Navy SEALs' BUD/S (Basic Underwater Demolition School) serves as an excellent example of the naval selection process. BUD/S is divided into three phases over 25 weeks. The first phase covers eight weeks and emphasizes physical conditioning including running, swimming, obstacle courses, strength and team-building exercises, basic water operations, and lifesaving skills. The second phase, which covers seven weeks, concentrates on diving and other skills of the combat swimmer. Included are dives that require underwater navigation to reach simulated targets. The third phase is the land warfare stage, which lasts 10 weeks and trains the candidate in the basics of special ops out of the water. This phase emphasizes small unit tactics, patrolling, weapons training, and demolitions.

The most rigorous part of the selection process takes place during the third week of the first phase, when candidates have to undergo "Hell Week." This incorporates 120 hours of continuous training with only a few hours' sleep, which candidates must grab when they can. Throughout the five-and-a-half days, candidates are cold and wet almost the entire time and pushed to their physical limits constantly. Hell Week tests a candidate's ability to push on and make decisions despite pain, discomfort, and fatigue. It also demonstrates to future special operators that they can continue to push on to complete a mission despite incredible hardships. It is impossible to make it through without the teamwork that demonstrates the SEAL mantra, "There is no I in SEAL!" BUD/S instructors are also known for reminding candidates, "The Only Easy Day was Yesterday!" Hell Week eliminates a substantial portion of the candidates. Only about 25 percent of candidates normally make it. The swimming section, which covers drown proofing and underwater knot tying, will eliminate a few candidates as well.

Each antiterrorist unit will incorporate a few special touches in their selection process that reflect their culture and their mission, but hopefully this chapter has offered a good overview of the basic nature of antiterrorism selection.

Chapter III

Training the Antiterrorist Operator

The antiterrorist operator will need a wide array of skills to allow him to carry out the diverse missions he may be assigned. Individuals selected for military antiterrorist units who are already serving in elite formations may have many skills that will merely need fine tuning to fit the hostage rescue/antiterrorist mission. Those selected from police units, however, may need to be trained in traditional military skills to allow them to carry out missions that fall outside of normal policing duties. Units such as the British SAS, which rotate operators through the antiterrorist squadron, will have far less difficulty in keeping operators sharp than will the Australian SASR's TAG unit, which is permanently assigned antiterrorist work. Likewise, national police antiterrorist units such as GIGN or GIS that deal with an array of serious criminal operations can keep their skills honed. Nevertheless, at least some antiterrorist training in esoteric skills serves the dual purpose of giving operators "another tool in their tool box" should the need ever arise on an operation while also helping to keep the operator alert and interested and ready for action. Many antiterrorist units have been deployed to Afghanistan or Iraq where their skills can be used in hunting and apprehending real terrorists, but can also be employed to do something other than train, train, train.

This chapter contains an overview of the wide array of skills necessary for antiterrorist operators and some of the special training they receive.

Small Unit Tactics

As with many aspects of antiterrorist training, military special ops units with the antiterrorism mission will have received extensive small unit tactical training as part of their training for an array of special operations. Members of national police units, for the most part, will not have received such training. Small unit tactical training consists of the following:

PATROLLING

This is one of the most basic skills to be learned. Units must understand how to carry out patrols with point and rear security, without bunching up and making themselves an inviting target for an ambush. They must learn to move stealthily through divergent terrain, and how to tape up equipment and pack it so that it does not make noise as they move. Some units will also receive training in tracking and counter-tracking.

SETTING AND COUNTERING AMBUSHES

Operators should be trained in setting ambushes and in methods of countering an ambush by fighting through it. Immediate action drills that train operators to use fire and movement to cover each other as they escape a kill zone or attack directly through the flank of the ambush must be practiced extensively with live fire. The ability to set an ambush may prove invaluable if the mission is to snatch or eliminate a terrorist leader. Many rescues have been launched on terrorists transporting hostages through the jungle by operators lying in wait— in effect, using the techniques of ambush. An ambush set to carry out a rescue is really little different than an ambush set to snatch an enemy. Both require the operators to be aware of no-shoot targets.

MOUT (Military Operations in Urban Terrain)

All antiterrorist units must know how to fight in the warrens that make up many of the cities in developing countries. Should they have to fight their way clear of a terrorist-controled neighborhood after a rescue, their skills at combat in urban areas will be severely tested. In such a situation, it can only be hoped that gun support from helicopters such as TF160's "Little Birds" is close by.

CLEARING AND ENTRIES

Members of antiterrorist units must be especially skilled at clearing buildings, ships, trains, aircraft—anywhere that hostages might be held. As a result, they must practice extensively to carry out entries and room clearing. Groups are normally organized into four- or five-man teams, who are trained to get into position as stealthily as possible, then to dynamically enter the rooms they must clear. The minimum number of operators who enter a room is two, with four being more common. As soon as the room is secure, other operators will move through to the next room to be cleared. Generally, this type of entry is used when hostages are present and/or there is an active shooter so that rescue personnel can get to the hostages as fast as possible.

Operators will also learn to do entries through windows reached via rappeling, through ceilings or walls sometimes breached by an explosive charge, or even through sewers or holes blown in the floor (as during the 1996 rescue at the Japanese Ambassador's residence in Lima, Peru).

Clearing is another tactic that operators must learn. They have to practice clearing hallways with many rooms opening from them, clearing stairways, being aware of possible terrorists located on upper levels when clearing an atrium or other open areas. Trainers can keep operators busy indefinitely when training to deal with the myriad permutations of buildings. Many units work with construction companies that allow them to carry out exercises in buildings that are about to be demolished so that operators can actually break down doors, crash through windows, and otherwise carry out realistic entries. In terms of doors and windows, operators will learn to use specialized entry tools such as the "hooligan bar," cutting torches, "Thor's Hammer," and window rakers (designed to break out a window and quickly rake away glass so operators can enter).

Building clearing tactics must also be practiced using variations that are likely to be required in an operational assault. Operators may, for example, be inserted by helicopters or infiltrated to the target from the sea. The assault may be initiated by a sniper eliminating a terrorist or by an explosion blowing out a wall. As their entry and rescue tactics are honed by hundreds of training exercises, operators will develop the ability to quickly adjust their tactics to fit the situation and when something goes wrong with their plan, as will usually happen, they learn to make adjustments. They also learn to adjust to members of their team, often anticipating what other members will do, based on the endless training they have done.

In some antiterrorist units operators learn to carry out entries accompanied by trained dogs. France's GIGN and RAID, among other units, make great use of dogs that are trained to go in ahead of the rescue team and attack any terrorist holding a weapon. A bounding dog makes a small target and can normally reach a terrorist very quickly. (The dogs, by the way, wear ballistic vests just like their human comrades.)

Parachuting

Military personnel entering a military antiterrorist unit are quite likely to already be parachute-qualified; however, in many cases they will have basic static line parachute qualification. Static line parachuting is designed to insert a large number of airborne troops into an area quickly during a battalion- or brigade-sized drop. It is very unlikely to be used in cases where an antiterrorist unit is inserted clandestinely in small numbers to carry out a rescue or other operation. Many antiterrorist units chosen from national police forces will also receive basic parachute training, often as a confidence builder and as a symbol of being elite. Parachute wings on an operator's chest will also give him more credibility when a police unit has to work with a military special ops unit on an operation or when doing exchange training. The mystique of being parachute-qualified still exists. A GIGN operator once talked a hostage taker, a former French para, into surrendering by appealing to the fact they were both members of the "airborne brotherhood."

There are three main types of specialized parachute insertions and jumps:

HALO (High Altitude, Low Opening)
In some antiterrorist units every member will be HALO-qualified, while in others only a portion of the unit will receive HALO training. HALO jumps allow an

operator to leave an aircraft at high altitude—up to 30,000 ft—and freefall to a much lower altitude—2,000 ft is fairly standard—before opening the chute. This insertion method allows the aircraft to fly above many surface-to-air missile systems and also allows an operator to quickly drop off radar coverage. For example, the SAS and SBS used to practice jumps in Norway in which they would wait to open their chutes until a fjord would block radar from detecting their descent. HALO jumpers are normally on oxygen, have their combat load well distributed for aerodynamics, wear warm clothing for the time they spend at altitude, have an altimeter attached to their wrist or reserve chute, and normally have a back-up system (AAD-Automatic Activation Device) that will automatically open the chute at a certain altitude should they pass out or become disoriented.

Above A member of the Czech URNA antiterrorist unit completes a HALO jump.
(Czech Republic Ministry of the Interior)

HAHO (High Altitude, High Opening)

This variation of the HALO jump can prove invaluable, especially if the unit must carry out a clandestine operation in a country that is hostile or non-supportive. HAHO is designed to allow an operator to jump from up to 25,000–30,000 ft, then open a chute and glide up to 35 miles to his landing zone. This allows the aircraft to fly on the other side of a border yet still insert operators via parachute. HAHO jumps are normally carried out at night with the operator guiding himself in via a GPS system. Skilled HAHO jumpers can form up at high altitude then glide in together with a team leader acting as guide for the group. HAHO jumpers have steerable parachutes and may make course corrections along the way to use the best route to infiltrate to their target.

LALO (Low Altitude, Low Opening)

The LALO drop—yet another technique practiced by some antiterrorist units—is designed to insert a team very quickly close to the ground. In a LALO jump the

Above Members of GSG9 train in engagement of vehicles from a helicopter; it appears the operator at left is using an HK G3 rifle with Trijicon ACOG optical sight. (BGS)

aircraft will swoop in to an altitude of 1,000 ft or perhaps slightly less to insert the operators—in this case via a static line jump—who will only have a few seconds' hang time before hitting the ground. This method can be effective against terrorists who do not have anti-air capability, as it inserts operators right onto a target quickly. Today, in many cases, instead of a LALO jump operators might fast rope from a helicopter instead (see Helicopter Operations, below).

Operators who are assigned a MAT role will also be trained to carry out "wet jumps" directly into the sea. The U.S. DevGru practices HALO insertions into the sea, after which operators inflate rubber boats or don scuba gear to infiltrate their target.

Though the antiterrorist unit needs personnel with a wide array of parachuting skills, in reality, parachute insertion is used only rarely on antiterrorist operations.

Helicopter Operations

The helicopter has become the chariot that takes special operators into battle; hence the antiterrorist warrior must be highly skilled in helicopter operations. Training includes insertion via trooper ladders, rappel, or fast rope as well as direct jumps into the sea or snow. Operators also train in extraction procedures via ladder or various types of extraction rigs, some of which can extract a four-man team at once. (Interestingly, SBS operators apparently first developed fast roping to give them a method of descent as fast as a fireman's pole.) Many helicopters used for special operations will be equipped with benches on the outside so that operators can be quickly inserted from the hovering chopper. Special ops helicopters may also be rigged with harnesses to allow operators to fire their weapons from the helicopter. Many units practice firing upon vehicles from helicopters: GSG-9 has a reputation for being very skilled at engagement from helicopters. Units also train snipers to engage from helicopters, especially for MAT operations. These tactics will be discussed in more detail in the section on sniper training.

Operators also practice parachute insertions from helicopters. MAT operators practice parachuting into the sea, then using inflatable boats to approach their target. In some cases jumps are made, then operators swim to the target. Operators in scuba gear practice jumping a few feet into the sea from hovering helicopters. Specialized helicopter units such as the U.S. 160th SOAR (Special

Operations Aviation Regiment) practice many highly specialized techniques. For example, the 160th has practiced extracting SEALs by hovering just above the water with the helicopter's ramp down into the water. SEAL operators can then run rubber boats directly into the helicopter for rapid extraction after an operation.

Having skilled helicopter pilots to practice with the operators is an absolute necessity since they have to be able to hold the helicopter steady when it is used as a sniping platform or for fast roping. For MAT operations, the pilots must be able to adjust their approach and hover to the motions of the ship. Among the helicopter pilots trained for MAT ops was Britain's Prince Andrew, who worked closely with the SBS.

Combat Swimmer and Small Boat Training

Members of antiterrorist units who receive scuba and boat training normally fall into one of three groups, each trained to a different level of skills. The first group comprises operators who are in one of the naval or marine special operations units that has a MAT mission as well as other naval special warfare tasks. They will be trained to an extremely high level as specialists in all types of naval special ops. Units such as the U.S. Navy SEALs, the Royal Marines SBS, Russian "Delfin," and Italy's COMSUBIN fall into this category. Even within these units, however, there will be some operators who specialize in MAT. For the SEALs it is DevGru; for the SBS M Squadron; and for the "Delfin" those operators from Alpha and Vympel who receive naval Spetsnaz training.

The second group consists of operators within antiterrorist units who are trained in combat swimming and small boats and are assigned to specialized sub-units. For example, SAS Boat Troops or Combat Applications Group (Delta Force) Boat Troop operators could carry out a maritime antiterrorist operation if necessary, but would usually act as support for the SBS or DevGru.

The third group is composed of operators in national antiterrorist units who receive basic combat swimmer and small boat operations as part of their training for the unit. They will have the ability to carry out operations such as assaults on a hijacked ferry or underwater infiltration to a coastal site. At least some members of the unit will probably have received additional training to allow them to carry out more sophisticated maritime operations. GIGN offers a good example of a unit that does not primarily have the MAT mission, but trains operators as combat swimmers. In fact, GIGN has used some techniques especially well suited to their mission to train their swimmers. To get them used to waiting patiently beneath the water until an operation may be launched, operators have had to lie on the bottom of the Seine motionless for extended periods while giant barges pass over their heads just a few feet away. GIGN operators have also spent a great deal of time practicing having their weapons ready and engaging targets located at the rail of a ship or on a bridge as soon as the muzzle of the weapon breaks water.

Operators are trained in basic combat diver skills. These will include the physiology, physics, and theory of diving; specialized physical conditioning for diving, including long swims; use of open and closed-circuit scuba equipment; underwater navigation; diving equipment maintenance; and transport. Navigation over long distances under water, by day or night, using the compass is an integral part of the training. As the combat dives get more sophisticated, swimmers will have to change direction underwater and make turns to reach the objective. They will operate under time limits and must stay in contact with their team. Operators also learn to dive in tropical and Arctic conditions.

Underwater communication via radio or hand signals is another important aspect of training, and personnel are trained to use specialized underwater weapons (see Chapter V). Russian trainees have to carry out a lengthy swim under burning gasoline and with explosions nearby.

As diving skills improve, swimmers will learn to exit and reenter submerged submarines to allow clandestine insertion and extraction. Swimmers will also be trained to use underwater vehicles such as the U.S. SDV (Seal Delivery Vehicle) to allow them to cover longer distances while submerged. Operators will also learn to carry out "wet jumps" via parachute directly into the sea, often with rubber boats, which they will then use to reach their objective. Insertions directly into the sea of operators either in scuba gear or with rubber boats are also in the operator's repertoire.

For silent approach to ships or coastlines, operators learn to use small canoes or rubber boats, while they will also probably have access to larger boats that are very fast and heavily armed for use in hit-and-run operations.

Operators who are part of a naval special warfare unit will be trained in underwater reconnaissance of enemy ships or installations, beach reconnaissance prior to a landing, and underwater demolition. All of these skills have some application to swimmers assigned to an antiterrorist unit as well. For example, their objective may be a ship carrying WMDs (Weapons of Mass Destruction). If it is determined that an assault to take the ship is not feasible, then attaching explosive devices to the hull to sink it may prove the most viable option. If done well, the ship may appear to have sunk accidentally. The USA, Israel, and the Russians, among others, have, reportedly, carried out such operations. The ability to carry out a beach reconnaissance may be useful, too, prior to a rescue operation against a coastal target if a portion of the rescue or support force will be coming in over the beach.

To give an idea of how such skills might be used, a U.S. MEUSOC (Marine Expeditionary Unit Special Operations Capable) will have an element trained in hostage rescue. When deployed, such units will also have a small SEAL element attached to carry out beach reconnaissance. Should the necessity arise to rescue American citizens in an area where the MEUSOC personnel are the closest and only ones likely to be on site in time, the MEUSOC operators and SEALs can work together to put together a rescue over the beach or from helicopters.

Terrorist Psychology and Hostage Negotiation

Members of antiterrorist units study terrorist incidents and terrorist profiles to learn as much as possible about how terrorists operate. By studying the psychology of terrorists, they may be able to predict likely targets or predict actions the terrorists are likely to take once they have taken hostages. Many units will have a psychologist or psychiatrist as an advisor, or perhaps even assigned to the support element of the unit. An important part of psychologically profiling terrorists is determining when it may be necessary to launch an assault. Terrorist actions must be analyzed, as must the possible deteriorating state of the hostages. For example, during the Munich Olympic incident, the fact that the terrorists attempted to disguise their identity seemed to indicate that they did not plan to die and hence might be open to negotiation. But the negotiations were handled poorly and an inept rescue attempt was launched so the incident still ended badly. During the Beslan School incident, all the psychological indicators were that the terrorists intended to kill as many hostages as possible, especially children. As a result, the FSB operators from Alpha and Vympel had to be prepared to take Draconian action against them at the first opportunity.

Psychological profiling of hostages may be important as well. During the DePunt Train incident in Holland (May 1977), psychologists were able to indicate to the Dutch Marine/BBE operators which hostages would be most likely to panic during a rescue operation. When the assault on the train was launched, one of these hostages did indeed leap up into the line of fire. Another psychological prediction based on hostage-profiling was offered when the US Delta Force was preparing to rescue the hostages in Iran in 1979. Psychological advisors emphasized that photos of one hostage should be studied closely as he had a special operations background and was very likely to use the confusion of a rescue to disarm one of the terrorists; hence he might be mistaken for a "Tango."

Some units even send operators into mental hospitals to observe patients with different psychological disorders so that they will be better able to determine how such individuals might react under stress. Operators also watch the interrogations of captured terrorists to gain an insight into their mindset.

The study of hostage incidents will give them indicators of the actions terrorists are likely to take. For example, in lengthy incidents, negotiators and rescue personnel hope that Stockholm Syndrome will start to work and that the terrorists will feel a kinship to the hostages, which will make it more difficult to execute them. In some cases, negotiators try to build this bond by forcing the terrorists to work with the hostages: by sending in food that needs to be prepared, for example. On the other hand, if terrorists separate one or two hostages from the rest and place them in a separate room or put hoods over their heads, this may indicate that they are distancing themselves from the hostages they have chosen to execute when the time comes to prove that they are serious in their demands.

One aspect of Stockholm Syndrome that operators must be particularly aware of is the likelihood of hostages beginning to identify with their captors to the extent of shielding them from rescuers or even picking up weapons to defend the terrorists. This is why most rescue teams will cuff hostages after evacuating them until they can determine that no terrorists are hiding among them, and that none have actively been supporting the terrorists.

Most antiterrorist units have personnel who are trained as hostage negotiators, though they may not carry out the negotiations in all incidents. In some countries, negotiators fall under the national police umbrella and only turn the incident over to the antiterrorist unit if it appears that negotiations will not succeed and that hostages will die. In other units, the negotiators are an integral part of the unit. In either case, operators should have a sound understanding of what hostage negotiators do and how they operate.

The best hostage negotiators provide a source of intelligence based on their conversations with the terrorists. They can also offer educated opinions on the state of mind of the terrorists and the likelihood of their starting to kill hostages. For example, prior to the assault on the Nord Ost Theater in Moscow, negotiators heard some of the women suicide bombers begin chanting prayers, which they felt was an indication that they were about to blow themselves up.

Good hostage negotiators can also prolong an incident to allow time for Stockholm Syndrome to work and to give rescue personnel time to prepare and rehearse for an assault. One technique negotiators use to good effect is wearing the terrorist leader/negotiator down with trivia. For example, if he asks for fruit juice, the negotiator will carry on lengthy discussions about which type he would like and in what type of containers. Not only do these negotiations buy time but they also develop a give and take between terrorist and negotiator. Very skilled negotiators may even be able to lead terrorists to take action that will increase the likelihood of a successful rescue. For example, if the terrorists and hostages are in a barricaded building where an assault will be very difficult, a skilled negotiator might be able to convince the terrorists that taking a bus to a waiting plane at the airport offers their best option. Once the terrorists exit the building with the hostages, they may be eliminated by snipers and an assault team. During the Iranian Embassy siege at Princes Gate, the negotiator even kept the terrorist leader on the phone as the SAS assaulted, thereby locating him so that the SAS could eliminate him while also making it more difficult for him to order his fellow terrorists to begin killing the hostages.

The negotiator should understand how an antiterrorist team works when doing an assault and should train with the team on practice exercises. If the negotiator is not an integral part of the team, then it is normally considered best that he or she not be located with the assault force. Note the terms "he or she." In some instances a female negotiator might be better while in others a male negotiator might be preferable. If the negotiator is not actually an operator, then it is possible that some subtle bond will have developed between him or her and the terrorists that will lead him to give an unintended indicator that an assault is about to go in. As a result, even though the negotiator must be willing to say to the rescue team leader that he feels he will not be able to negotiate the incident out and that it is time for the assault option, he will still not know exactly when the assault is going in. Even when the negotiator is an integral part of the unit, he should be in a separate location while negotiating so there is no chance of the terrorists hearing rescue personnel practicing a rescue or discussing options.

Although antiterrorist units train rigorously to assault with maximum force when necessary, they also realize that if they can properly assess the terrorists' psychological state, the incident might end without loss of life, or if the assault is necessary they may be able to more effectively eliminate the terrorists while saving the hostages. Unfortunately, the current brand of Islamic terrorism seems more intent on killing the maximum number of those perceived as "infidels" than upon negotiating for any set concession, but being aware of this mindset also helps prepare operators to deal with these terrorists.

Surveillance Techniques and Intelligence Gathering

Although the mission of antiterrorist units is to rescue those taken hostage by terrorists, their mission is also to prevent terrorist acts. This may mean that they will carry out surveillance on suspected terrorists before assisting in their arrest. Surveillance may also be designed to identify members of a terrorist cell prior to taking its members into custody. When operating in other countries where hostages may have been taken, operators must also be able to blend in when attempting to determine where hostages are being held.

As a result, members of antiterrorist units are frequently trained in sophisticated surveillance techniques. Among the skills they will develop are those necessary to shadow a suspected terrorist without being detected. Techniques may include the use of multiple vehicles, following a suspect on foot, using multiple operators to box a suspect by moving parallel to his route, choosing clothing that may be changed easily and rapidly to create a simple disguise, and using a multitude of techniques developed by units such as the British 14th Intelligence Company.

Sometimes surveillance will be over an extended period. Specially designed vehicles that look like service vehicles such as those used by phone companies, cable companies, and delivery companies, may be available, but these may also attract the attention of suspected terrorists. As a result, operators also learn to build hides in urban or rural areas in which they are trained to stay for days at a time observing potential targets. The SAS became very skilled at such surveillance in Northern Ireland.

Operators also learn to carry out surreptitious entries to gather intelligence or to place electronic surveillance devices including microphones, video cameras, computer mirroring devices, etc. As part of their training, they may well learn lock picking, how to photograph a room with a digital camera as a record so that anything disturbed is replaced properly, and methods of entering through windows, ventilation shafts, and so on.

As well as planting bugs on phones or computers with land lines, operators will learn how to intercept cell phone calls or text messages and how to hack into computers being used wirelessly. They will also learn to use devices that block electronic signals so that cell phones will not work if they want to isolate a terrorist from his comrades. In addition, operators will learn to track vehicles or persons via GPS or use devices to block GPS tracking should that be necessary. Thermal imagers can be used to track suspects within a building to locate them prior to a raid or a rescue operation, and operators must be trained to interpret the images. Some units will also even have the ability to track suspected terrorists using satellite imagery.

Another skill that is useful to operators carrying out surveillance as well as those planning a rescue is the use of computer drafting programs to quickly

Right Members of the Australian SASR practice their rappeling skills from a helicopter. (Australian MOD)

develop diagrams of a target building and mark locations of important physical features. In fact, all aspects of gathering intelligence at the scene of a hostage or barricade incident are very critical in carrying out a successful assault.

The operators who actually carry out an assault may not be the ones who gather the intelligence, as they will be concerned with developing their options and practicing the assault. Often, antiterrorist units will have an intelligence cell that does the actual gathering of information from witnesses, first responders, relatives of hostages, freed hostages, others from the building involved, electronic surveillance, updates from snipers, building blueprints and myriad other sources of information that will allow them to constantly update the intelligence fed to negotiators and operators. So that they can use the intelligence and aid in gathering, operators will receive some training in gathering intelligence and analyzing the raw data.

Skilled debriefs of freed hostages are especially useful as they help operators assess the mood of the terrorists, their weaponry, presence of explosives, where they may have barricaded doors, and so on, whether they have separated any hostages, where hostages are being held, health problems among hostages or terrorists, and countless other details that may be useful in building the mosaic needed to develop a negotiation and rescue plan.

Members of antiterrorist units will have studied various aspects of building and architecture that will help in gathering pre-assault intelligence. Any team members with training as military engineers or with experience in the building trades will have helped other members of the unit learn about different types of doors, windows, and so on. Details such as whether doors at a target site open inward or outward, are reinforced, have heavy duty locks, or have bars must all be factored into any plan determining whether entry is feasible. The type of roof on a building, for example, may determine whether helicopter insertion is viable or whether access from another building's roof is better. Knowing the thickness of concrete walls on buildings can help plan the strength of charge if an explosive entry through a wall is deemed necessary. Members of antiterrorist teams learn to work with local fire departments, which will often have blueprints of, and information about, buildings within their area.

Members of a unit charged with gathering and analyzing intelligence will try to obtain photos of hostages and terrorists to help brief members of a rescue team as to who are "shoots" and who are "no-shoots." They will also work with psychologists to develop profiles of terrorists and hostages. If listening devices or video cameras have been planted, the intelligence team will attempt to determine the intent of the terrorists from their conversations. Likewise, intelligence analysts will receive information from the negotiator that may help

Above Members of the Republic of Korea's 707th Special Mission Battalion prepare to practice an entry on a tire house. Note that instructors are above to evaluate the entry; note also the large "707" on their ballistic vests so they can immediately identify each other. Their weapons have EOTech sights; note the drop holsters for their pistols. (ROK Special Warfare Command)

determine the terrorists' mindset and plans.

One of the most important skills for the antiterrorist unit intelligence operator is the ability to give very concise briefings illustrated with diagrams or models so that he can keep the rescue team constantly updated and so that they can keep refining their rescue plan. An intelligence operator who has been trained to do entries, even if that is not his primary assignment, has a much better understanding of the type of information the operators need before going in.

The mission of intelligence operators does not end when the entry team goes in. They must be trained to debrief hostages to determine if there are remaining booby traps, terrorists unaccounted for, and numerous other bits of information. They must also be ready to interrogate any surviving terrorists. Operators who have done the entry are also trained to watch for computers, cell phones, documents—anything that may be used to gain intelligence about the terrorist group, future targets, or methods of operation.

Every member of an antiterrorist unit will normally receive some training in surveillance and intelligence gathering. Those who show a special aptitude or have special skills that lend themselves to intelligence gathering may be assigned the intelligence portion of the unit full time.

NBC (Nuclear, Biological, and Chemical) Warfare

Although antiterrorist operators may not have the sophisticated training to actually deal with WMDs (Weapons of Mass Destruction), they quite possibly will end up going in first during an assault on an installation or ship containing WMDs. As a result, they must be trained in the basics of such weapons and to work in support of specialists. For example, after 9/11, combined teams of NEST (Nuclear Emergency Search Teams) and FBI HRT were deployed along the East Coast of the USA to search for and counter any attempt to bring nuclear weapons into the USA. At least some members of U.S. and Russian antiterrorist units drawn from special ops personnel may well have nuclear training, too, related to the backpack "nukes" they were trained to deploy during the Cold War.

In general, however, training in NBC warfare for antiterrorist operators consists of basic familiarity with the types of weapons they might encounter so that they can immediately call for specialists if suspicious items are encountered. Operators must also train wearing NBC suits so that they can move and engage targets while fully kitted up should they have to carry out an assault on a suspected WMD site. This training will include techniques for assaulting a nuclear power plant should there be an incident. Training will include briefings on sensitive areas of the plant where bullets could cause damage though generally nuclear power plants are built so sturdily that small arms fire is very unlikely to reach any critical areas. Operators are also trained that though their mission may be to rescue hostages, the integrity of the nuclear facility takes precedence based on the "good of the many over the good of the few" doctrine.

Operators will frequently be trained to use basic detection devices so they will be aware of radiation leaks or the presence of hazardous chemicals or bio-weapons. Team medics will be trained to administer counter-agents to likely chemical or biological weapons and will normally take the antidotes or medications along during an assault.

Although there may be a tendency to think that such concerns affect only the antiterrorist units of major countries, it should be borne in mind that in April 2007, Slovak operators of UOU intercepted 37.4 lb of radioactive material being smuggled in a vehicle with Hungarian license plates.

Communications and Related Technology

All operators in an antiterrorist unit will learn the basics of communication using different types of radios and computer links, while at least some personnel will receive advanced training that enables them to set up and maintain communication equipment. Most units will have a wide array of radios available to fit different missions.

Since many units respond to incidents within their own country, they will have police radios available to monitor police calls and communicate with officers setting up a cordon around an incident scene. Units will also have a secure net that allows them to communicate with their headquarters throughout an incident or deployment. On an overseas deployment this net is likely to be established via a SatCom (Satellite Communication) link. For operations, each operator will have a radio that allows him to communicate with fellow team members during the operation. It is important that both the command link and the operator link be secure so that reporters or terrorists cannot listen in. Snipers will normally be on the same link as the command element and the entry team, though teams may have a separate channel for talk with the snipers. When multiple snipers are being used against multiple targets, establishing a secure and clear radio link that allows the "Shoot!" command to be given simultaneously is highly critical. In some operations, a ground-to-air radio link with supporting helicopters or flying fire support may need to be established.

Operators will learn to use simple radio codes that designate doors and windows of a target building or entry points on a railroad car, bus, or aircraft. They will also develop a radio code for different terrorists and hostages. The codes will normally be simple and easily remembered. For example, the four sides of a building may each be designated by a color, while terrorists could be "Tango One," "Tango Two," and so on. More complicated codes may be used when sending messages regarding an operation via SatCom.

For use on close protection details, operators will have small ear pieces and throat or wrist microphones. This same equipment can be used when doing clandestine surveillance. Specialized radio systems with microphones in the mouthpiece for underwater use are available for a unit's combat divers.

Operators must also know how to use laptop computers with satellite links to either send photos shot with digital cameras or to receive intelligence such as satellite photos, blueprints, photos of hostages and terrorists, or other important data. Very durable computers—such as the ToughBook, which is used by U.S. personnel—are designed to stand up to the rigors of special ops usage. In conjunction with their computers, operators may employ GPS tracking to locate terrorists via their cell phones or devices planted on their vehicles. They may also obtain intelligence about an incident by gaining access to surveillance cameras in the area and playing the video on the computers. In large metropolitan centers such as London, there are very few areas that will not be covered by closed-circuit television (CCTV). In addition to tracking terrorist cell phones, operators also have the ability to blanket an area around an incident so that terrorists cannot call out or receive calls on their cell phones.

Because communications and information technology change at such a rapid pace, an antiterrorist unit's communications specialists must constantly receive training updates, which they will then pass on to operators.

Target Designation

Although target designation normally falls within the missions of military special operations units, there are circumstances where the ability to guide in precision munitions could be useful for the antiterrorist unit. Currently, some units have a proactive mission against terrorists to prevent them from carrying out atrocities. In such a mission if a terrorist headquarters, bomb factory, bio-weapons lab, or other facility is located, especially in another country, rather that face large loss of life attempting to assault the installation operators might "paint" it for a precision munition.

Antiterrorist units drawn from military special forces will probably have some operators who are already trained in the use of laser target designators. National police antiterrorist teams, on the other hand, will probably only train operators if they have an international mission that could take them to areas with terrorist strongholds or if such areas exist in their own countries.

Operators who will use laser target designators must be trained in selecting the best sites from which to laze a target, be aware of what types of surfaces lend themselves best to being "painted," and know how to communicate with the aircraft that will be launching the munitions. (Note that naval missiles or guns as well as artillery pieces can also launch laser-guided munitions.) Many of the same skills used by snipers or surveillance teams to get into a hide will be required when getting into position to designate a target.

Although man-portable laser designators will vary, most use a pulsing laser that is compatible with munitions to be fired at the designated target. Designators may be used with night vision devices and usually have a magnification of 10x and a field of view of three to five degrees. Minimum range is normally around 300 meters with a maximum range out to 10,000 meters. Operators will be aware from their training with different types of munitions what constitutes "Danger Close" for the specific mission, which, along with available cover and terrorist patrols, will influence how close to the target they set up. In some cases, operators may also designate a target for a Specter gunship that is overhead.

Surgical strikes are the specialty of antiterrorist units. However, the "scalpel" used can vary. It might be a precision sniper shot to a terrorist's head or it might be a precision JDAM (Joint Direct Attack Munition) delivered on a terrorist haven.

Languages

Language facility is useful for antiterrorist operators in many ways. If deployed to another country for training or on a mission, the ability to communicate in the local tongue is invaluable. When listening to wire taps or other electronic surveillance product, language ability is also vital. The ability to read other languages not only allows operators to judge if captured documents are important, but also allows them to read open source material in newspapers, magazines, books, or on the internet that might give them insights into potential enemies. The ability to read foreign languages and understand them may also be invaluable in learning from materials written about other antiterrorist units or documentaries about them.

Many military special ops units have a language requirement for personnel, who must learn at least one foreign language. Some antiterrorist units also require that each operator speak his native tongue plus two others. There are also advantages for units from countries with diverse populations to recruit personnel who speak their ancestral tongue fluently. Operators from wide-ranging backgrounds may also be useful when it is necessary to infiltrate another country in order to gather intelligence or prior to an operation. For example, having operators who are black or Asian might have obvious advantages since "Anglos" would stand out in African or Asian countries. Israel makes excellent use of the fact that Jews have immigrated from so many countries and thus know the language and culture of their former homeland. Israel also has many operators who speak fluent Arabic and specialize in undercover missions into Gaza, the West Bank, and elsewhere.

When sending personnel for language training, it makes sense for an antiterrorist unit to try to get a wide array of language skills among operators. Although it is possible to predict which languages are most likely to be useful, alliances change and today's foreign friend might be tomorrow's foreign enemy. Also, terrorists may choose to take hostages at an embassy or other facility in any country. Just as an example, the SAS traditionally did not emphasize Spanish as a language skill for its operators. Then, in the Falklands War, it found itself very short of Spanish speakers. Within the U.S. Army Special Forces, each Special Forces Group is oriented toward a certain part of the world. The 1st Special Forces Group (Airborne) focuses on Asia and has Chinese, Vietnamese, Japanese, Korean, and other Asian speakers; the 3rd SFG (Abn) focuses on Africa and has Swahili and other African-dialect speakers; the 5th SFG (Abn) focuses on the Middle East and has Arabic, Farsi, and other language speakers, the 7th SFG (Abn) focuses on Latin America and has Spanish and Portuguese speakers, and the 10th SFG (Abn) focuses on Europe and has Russian, French, German, Italian, Hungarian, Polish, and various other European-language speakers.

In many cases, the ethnic makeup of a country will aid in recruiting personnel with certain language skills. In the U.S. armed forces, for example, Spanish speakers are relatively common and, therefore, it is rarely necessary to send operators for training in this language.

A substantial portion of antiterrorist units around the world require English as one of the languages for their operators as it is the most universal language today and will give them the best chance of communicating with other units and in other milieus. In at least some cases, operators will be given a crash course in a few basic phrases should they have to carry out a rescue of hostages most of whom do not speak the native language of the country in which they are held. Just knowing how to say "We're here to rescue you!" or "Stay down!" may be invaluable.

Still another advantage of language training is that when a native speaker of a language is employed to train personnel, the instructor will often incorporate information about the country, people, and customs into the language instruction, which will help operators should they ever have to operate in that country.

Explosives and Booby Traps

Antiterrorist operators drawn from military special ops units will probably have already had basic demolitions training. It is possible that at least a few operators on national police teams will also have had some EOD (Explosives Ordinance Disposal) training. In some countries, especially where one military or police unit handles all special tasks including antiterrorism, the EOD mission may fall under the purview of the antiterrorist unit.

Explosives training that is specially tailored to the antiterrorist mission will stress explosive entry of buildings and possibly trains, buses, or other transport. Explosive entry to a barricaded facility where hostages are being held offers speed and shock to both get the rescuers to hostages as quickly as possible and disorientate the terrorists. In some cases, an explosive entry may be used so that booby traps between the entry point and the point where the hostages are being held will be detonated.

One of the most common types of charge used to gain entry is the cutting charge designed to cut doors. Many antiterrorist teams use a cardboard silhouette target to which they attach detonating card to create a door breaching or cutting device that may be quickly created if needed. In addition to learning how to create breaching charges, operators must learn how to quickly approach a target and how to place them. For breaching steel doors, operators will need to know how to create and place a linear cutting charge. However, the use of a linear cutting charge does cause fragments of metal to enter the room and so is not normally the optimum technique to gain entry directly to a room where hostages are being held.

In situations where a steel door will be breached directly into the area where hostages are held, teams will have been trained to use a water charge (a container containing detonating cord or other explosives and filled with water that is hung against the door). A water charge not only makes fragmentation far less of a danger, but also eliminates the fireball present with a standard linear cutting charge. Teams are trained to back away from doors that are being blown, then to rush through the breached door while terrorists remain stunned by the blast.

Window charges for use against non-armored windows are normally thrust through the window, then detonated, so that the glass is blown outward to protect any hostages inside the room.

Part of training, especially for demolition specialists within a unit, will cover various types of explosives, including C3/C4, PE3/PE4, Semtex, RDX, PETN, etc. By learning the characteristics of different explosives, specialized operators can select those that best fit a mission and properly calculate the amount needed for different types of target.

Operators will receive extensive training in creating charges and using pre-packaged charges. Drills to learn to safely place charges and detonate them as well as how to carry out approaches prior to placing a charge are carried out extensively. Although many teams will send every operator through explosive entry training, there will usually be operators who are especially skilled with explosives who have received more extensive training. These operators will usually have responsibility for setting charges.

Antiterrorist operators also receive extensive training in booby traps and IEDs (Improvised Explosive Devices). They need to be aware of the different types of ignition devices used on booby traps as an aid in avoiding them should they have to carry out a rescue in a building or vehicle which has been booby trapped. This knowledge of IEDs and booby traps will also be valuable if an operator is assigned to do security surveys or aid in dignitary protection operations. If it is necessary to carry out a rescue, then evacuate rescued hostages to a helicopter or boat pickup, operators may also set booby traps to discourage pursuit. Particularly in military antiterrorist units, operators will learn to make improvised explosives themselves. Although this skill is usually considered most valuable when carrying out sabotage missions or working with insurgents, it could conceivably be useful in antiterrorist ops.

Although they are used during tactical entry training, stun grenades and other distraction devices may also be covered as part of explosives training. If commercial stun grenades are not available, unit explosives experts will know how to use grenade simulators or other improvised distraction devices.

Weapons Training

Operators chosen for antiterrorist teams will normally have already displayed a high level of marksmanship to even be considered for entry. However, because of the precision necessary to surgically eliminate a terrorist hiding behind a hostage those skills will be honed even more. No matter what other training he may be undertaking, the special operator constantly practices with his weapons to keep his skills sharp. Members of the U.S. Navy's DevGru are known in the antiterrorist community for the large number of rounds they expend annually—reportedly 2,500 to 3,000 rounds per week—but other units shoot a great deal as well. Operators in France's GIGN, for example, are known to fire 100 to 300 rounds per day. Members of India's NSG (National Security Guards) fire about 2,000 rounds per year during normal practice and qualification. However, during the two months that operators serve on the alert team, they will do range time each day and fire around 14,000 rounds over this period.

As part of their specialized firearms training and as part of continuation training, operators learn, then hone various skills. For example, they learn to engage after rapidly drawing their weapon from its holster. They learn to fire from nonstandard firing positions—on their backs, while moving sideways, or toward or away from a target; to fire from within vehicles, from helicopters, while aboard boats or ships, while rappellng, while skiing, and as soon as they break water after a scuba approach to the target. They will also learn to shoot in situations where only a small portion of a terrorist's body is visible, and particularly to take head shots into the eye/nose triangle (Note: the SAS/SBS teach to take the shot into the mouth) to eliminate a hostage taker before he can harm the hostage.

To add stress and realism, many units incorporate other factors into their firearms training. The SAS and other units will have operators exert themselves physically while wearing full equipment and a gas mask, then make them engage targets with precise shots. India's NSG incorporate a 780-meter course with 26 different obstacles that must be overcome within 18 minutes. After completion of this course, operators must then engage targets and qualify. This exercise is part of selection but experienced operators still run it as well. Some get their time under 10 minutes and still shoot high scores.

The NSG stress rigorous exertion combined with shooting to duplicate the exhaustion a heavily equipped operator may have to overcome by the time he is in position to engage terrorists. NSG operators also practice on a 400-meter shooting course spread over 11 zones and incorporating 29 electronically controlled targets that are exposed for only two to three seconds Operators must move through the course engaging the "shoot" targets in 6 minutes 30 seconds or less. The score is based on a combination of quality of hits on the targets and speed of engagement, as well as speed moving through the course.

The operator will learn to deal with problems that arise during engagement and deal with them quickly so that he can keep fighting. He will learn malfunction drills so that if his weapon goes down he can quickly correct the problem and get it back into action. He will also learn transition drills so that he can instantly switch from his primary weapon to a secondary one should there be no time to clear the malfunction. So that they can keep fighting if injured, operators learn to operate a weapon with their "support hand" (i.e. left hand for a right-handed shooter). Some units will teach operators to fire a "double tap" (two quick shots as close to each other as possible) while other units now teach to shoot until the terrorist goes down. The operator will learn multiple engagement techniques to fit the tactical situation. For example, if he faces multiple terrorists, he might have to quickly fire one shot on each one, then scan to see if any of them need another hit.

Tactical training will be discussed in another section, but to allow operators to receive the best training possible, most units will have real or mock aircraft fuselages, train cars, buses, or other typical targets on which they may practice. Many will also have a "killing house" that is constructed to allow 360-degree live-fire shooting during entry training. The one used by the U.S. Navy DevGru is typical of the best of these killing houses. Built at a cost of $25 million, it incorporates walls that use a rubberized ballistic material to absorb bullets for 360-degree firing. Targets include movers, pop-ups, turners, and realistic humanoid dummies that will only go down if hit with a killing shot. Video cameras allow instructors to critique training operations upon completion. The SAS Killing House at Stirling Lines is very similar, as are those of other units. For some types of assault, operators will practice force-on-force training using weapons altered to fire Simunitions, a sophisticated paint marking cartridge that can be fired from standard weapons.

In addition to the Killing House, India's NSG use a sophisticated Combat Shoot Room. Operators are required to enter the dark room and, using a white light or laser illuminator, engage their target in three seconds. The NSG also use a realistic force-on-force system that has two contiguous rooms, each equipped with video camera and screen. Each operator enters his room and engages the other operator on screen. This exercise builds reaction time and attunes the operator to the movements of a live opponent. (The SAS also use a version of this system.)

Many units also have operators act as "hostages" standing next to targets in the Killing House while other members engage the targets. This exercise forces the shooters to be precise in shot placement when a live "no shoot" is nearby and also helps those acting as hostages to develop coolness under fire.

Since operations will often take place at night and/or in an environment where gas has been inserted, operators will practice in the Killing House wearing their gas masks and NVGs (Night Vision Goggles). They will become skilled at using the illuminators mounted on their weapons, which may include flashlights, visible lasers, and infrared lasers.

The primary weapons used by most antiterrorist units are the handgun, SMG

Above Members of the Colombian Special Forces practice building clearing drills in a tire house that allows them to shoot in multiple directions. The tires are filled with packed earth and will stop bullets; however, steel-belted radial tires must not be used! (US DOD)

(submachinegun), and carbine, and operators will constantly practice with these weapons (see Chapter V for the use of specific weapons). Operators will also learn to use specialized versions of these weapons such as suppressed pistols and SMGs. Suppressed weapons will not only be used in stealth situations to silently eliminate an enemy but also in situations such as ship assaults when the sound in a steel passageway would be multiplied and also where the suppression of muzzle flash is important in case compartments are flooded with fuel or other fumes. The flame suppression is also valuable if raiding a terrorist bomb factory, a drug lab, or a source of suspected WMDs. Suppressed weapons are important, too, should a team have to infiltrate through the sewers where flammable gases could be ignited by muzzle flash.

Operators will learn to use other weapons as well. The shotgun may be used in the antipersonnel role, but also to blow the hinges or locks on doors. The sniper rifle is another important part of the antiterrorist arsenal. Most units train specialized snipers, but all operators receive some training with the tactical

Above Members of Czech MP SOG train for building entries on a mock doorway. (Amada Ceske Republiky)

rifle. Sniping rifles will be discussed in more detail in the sections on training snipers and weapons (see page 147).

Operators will be skilled in the use of support weapons such as the LMG (Light Machine Gun), which may be necessary to give covering fire when carrying out some rescues. They will also be proficient with the grenade launcher, which will often be mounted directly on their carbine or rifle. Although the grenade launcher may be used to insert CS or other gas, antiterrorist teams will also know how to use gas guns. Units carrying out MAT operations will also have access to specialized underwater weapons.

Generally, antiterrorist units will have an extensive arsenal of world weapons so that operators can become familiar with them. This familiarity training not only allows operators to use virtually any weapon that falls into their hands skillfully, but also allows them to evaluate the strengths and weaknesses of these same weapons in the hands of terrorists. For example, an operator who has practiced with the AK47 or AK74 realizes that if a terrorist has one with the safety on, it will take a moment to shift his hand to the proper position to release it. The operator will also know how to render various weapons inoperable during a struggle with a terrorist. If it is a pistol with a magazine safety, for example, he will know that pressing the magazine release and dumping the magazine will render the pistol inoperable. An additional advantage of having knowledge of a wide variety of weapons is that it allows an operator to render safe any weapons taken from terrorists during operations.

Sniping

Although all operators will receive at least the basics of precision tactical marksmanship, some will be especially trained as snipers who can often end a hostage incident with one well-placed shot. Generally, operators who have already shown outstanding long-range marksmanship will be selected, but those with a background in hunting and stalking will also have an advantage.

Part of sniper training—such as learning the ballistics of different cartridges so that allowances can be made when using them for distance and wind drift—is technical. The sniper trainee will also learn the advantages of different types of

Above An operator from the Czech SOG unit practices handgun engagement drills; note the extended magazine. Because of the position of his carbine, it is quite possible he is carrying out a transition drill from carbine to handgun. (Amada Ceske Republiky)

cartridges, such as expanding, AP (Armor Piercing) and APT (Armor Piercing Tracer), so that he can choose the one best suited for the mission. For example, if he has to takeout a terrorist through hard cover he may choose an AP round. Today, sophisticated minicomputers are available to aid in calculation, but snipers must still know how to figure their elevation or windage should the computer go down. Sniper trainees will also learn to estimate distance based on use of the Mil Dot or other reticle with a range-finding capability. Once again, laser range finders will be used today, but the operator must know how to calculate as well. Snipers will also develop their observation skills since they will often be in a hide for days waiting for a shot and sometimes gathering intelligence.

Improving marksmanship is, of course, critical, as is learning to shoot a variety of weapons that may be in the unit's arsenal. Many units, for example, will have a combination of 7.62 NATO, .300 WInchester Magnum, .338 Lapua, and .50 BMG rifles so that the one best suited to the mission may be chosen. Skilled snipers using a precision .50 rifle can now make hits at a mile or more. Snipers must also learn to maintain the rifles and their optics and learn about the different optics available. In addition to day scopes, some of which will have illuminated reticles for low light usage, the sniper must learn how to use night vision optical sights.

Snipers must be able to infiltrate to their shooting position and build a hide, so a good portion of sniper training is spent on camouflage, stalking, and the ability to remain very still once in a hide. Many of the same skills needed to gather intelligence by manning an observation post are also invaluable for the sniper.

Antiterrorist snipers may have to support their comrades while hovering in a helicopter or lying prone on the deck of a ship. As a result, operators must practice with the special ops helicopter pilots to develop the teamwork needed to shoot from a helicopter. Snipers must also learn how to rig a shooting position aboard a helicopter. The sniper who will operate in the MAT role must learn to adjust for the motion of the ship from which he is shooting and the motion of the target ship. Often, for heliborne or shipborne sniping, the operator will have a special rifle that is self-loading and employs a scope with lower magnification and a wider field of view.

It is important, too, that the sniper practices his skills in conjunction with the rest of his team since he will often initiate an assault by taking out a terrorist leader or sentry. He must also practice feeding intelligence to operators doing the entry since he will usually be on the high ground and have a spotting scope with his observer and the scope on his rifle. After the incident at Beslan School, where so many children died trying to escape, snipers must also train to give rapid covering fire by eliminating any terrorist shooter who shows himself at a window. In large incidents such as Beslan, it is advantageous if snipers have a self-loading rifle with detachable magazines and a substantial number of spare magazines available. On some teams, the observer is armed with a self-loading optically sighted rifle to support the sniper.

The antiterrorist sniper must be prepared to remain hidden for many hours so that he may possibly end the incident with one precise shot, but he must also be ready to constantly update his team on what he sees from his vantage point.

Above A sniper and observer team from Slovenia's Specialna Enota antiterrorist unit. (Slovenian National Police)

Unarmed Combat

First, it should be noted that although this section is titled "unarmed combat" in reality most units include training with knives, clubs, and other weapons as part of their hand-to-hand/unarmed/martial arts training."Without firearms" would probably be a better designation. Although many antiterrorist units put great emphasis on martial arts on the assumption that situations may arise at close quarters—an aircraft takedown, for example—where the use of martial arts may be preferable to firearms, the training is still far different from that offered in most martial arts schools. That doesn't mean that many operators aren't skilled martial artists who have competed at national or international levels. When Italy's NOCS was formed, the initial intake of personnel was chosen from among the top martial artists in the Polizia di Stato sports club.

Antiterrorist units need martial arts training that is mission-specific and is

Above Members of Croatia's ATJ Lucko Antiterrorist Unit practice martial arts. (Croatian Police)

based on the assumption that any time the operator must rely on his martial arts training it will be a life and death situation. The martial arts training should therefore give the operator the confidence to go against any terrorist at close quarters without apprehension. Martial arts training should give the operator not just a physical edge but also a psychological one. The antiterrorist operator will resort to his martial arts skills either because of the extreme close quarters at which he must engage a terrorist, or because he has lost his weapon or it has become inoperable. To prevent loss of the weapon to a terrorist at close quarters, therefore, weapons retention skills should be included in the martial arts training. Firearms training will also cover transitioning to a secondary weapon should the primary one go down.

For the operator, martial arts techniques should be ones that can be learned relatively quickly, retained with a modicum of practice, and employed quickly and devastatingly, even when wearing body armor, gas mask, and gear. Techniques relying on set stances and reactions that must be practiced assiduously are less desirable than those that train the operator to counter an attack from any position with natural movements. Versatile techniques that train the operator to react to typical motions (i.e. an overhead strike, whether with the hands, a knife, or a club) can be used against various types of attack. Usable techniques for striking and blocking with the bare hands, grappling and fighting on the ground, techniques using blades, clubs, and improvised weapons as well as techniques to counter these weapons and firearms are all important.

Incorporating regular martial arts training into the physical training program is the best way to keep the skills sharp. Russian Spetsnaz troops incorporate techniques for using the blade and martial arts strikes and parries into their calisthenics program, which keeps their reactions quick and instinctive.

The U.S. Special Forces Combatives Course incorporates an array of techniques that give the operator a chance against virtually any type of attack. The first component is rigorous physical fitness training to give the operator the endurance and flexibility to overcome an enemy.

Sentry elimination teaches operators techniques for stalking and quickly neutralizing an enemy who stands in the way of completing a mission. An antiterrorist team making a stealth approach prior to a takedown might well have to resort to such techniques using bare hands,a knife, garrote, or club. Filipino martial arts are favored, as they combine bare-handed close combat with knives and clubs to prepare the operator quickly for a wide array of combat situations. Kicking techniques are designed on the assumption that the operator will be wearing boots and will not have had time to practice flying snap kicks or other such moves. During training, kicks that are quick and devastating to the enemy are taught. Kneeing and stomping are considered basic skills, while punches, slaps, and elbow strikes in conjunction with blocks and kicks are once again designed to eliminate the opponent quickly. Grappling techniques include throws, arm bars, chokes, joint manipulations, and other techniques to control and eliminate an opponent. Knife techniques emphasize the constant movement of the blade as well as the use of stabs, snap cuts, slashes, and other knife techniques including blocks against an opponent armed with a knife.

Using various types of pads and protective gear, operators practice their techniques using full contact as much as possible so that they are used to aggressively delivering kicks, throws, blows and other moves against an opponent who is fighting back. The Special Forces Combatives Course is designed to not just give the operator the physical techniques needed to overcome an enemy at close quarters, but also the mental toughness and aggressiveness to fight to win in life and death encounters.

Among martial arts training that has proved especially well-suited to special operators is Israeli Krav Maga. Like other martial arts systems that are useful for antiterrorist operators, Krav Maga is strongly oriented toward practical, combat usage in no quarter situations. Krav Maga gives the practitioner the ability to inflict maximum pain and damage to an opponent, and then to escape quickly. The basic principles of Krav Maga include: Neutralize a threat quickly, Avoid personal injury, Go from the defense to the attack as soon as possible, Employ the body's natural reflexes, Attack any vulnerable point, Use any improvised weapon available. To enhance its practicality, Krav Maga teaches the practitioner to fight against several opponents, while protecting someone else, with a leg or arm injured, against armed opponents, and in other situations where the advantage seems to lie with the enemy. Training scenarios may incorporate flashing lights, loud noises, or other disorienting factors to help the Krav Maga practitioner remain focused. Students also learn strong situational awareness so that they can spot potential attacks before they are launched. In addition to Israeli antiterrorist units, other world units including France's GIGN train in Krav Maga.

Russia's FSB Alpha and Vympel as well as other units with an antiterrorist mission such as SOBR train in Systema, another martial art designed for real world application. Systema was developed from traditional Cossack close-combat styles. As with the other martial arts that have the best application for special operations, Systema does not train based on set fighting stances and movements; instead, high-speed elliptical strikes are used along with kicks and ground fighting techniques. Systema incorporates a lot of training in countering and using weapons. It also stresses fighting in situations that many martial arts do not address—while sitting in a chair or a vehicle, for example. An interesting aspect of Systema is that students are trained to not adopt an aggressive expression nor to use loud yells when fighting on the assumption that the practitioner will move directly into an attack from a neutral physical appearance, thus granting him surprise.

Spetsnaz martial arts training emphasizes combat against multiple opponents on the assumption that teams will operate in small numbers, generally clandestinely and at night. Techniques against multiple opponents stress putting each one out of the fight as rapidly as possible with deadly or incapacitating strikes. Another aspect of this training is disarming opponents and turning their weapons against them and their comrades. This ability to fight multiple opponents is considered so important that an endurance bout against multiple opponents is incorporated into the brutal Spetsnaz selection procedure.

As part of their martial arts training, Russian special ops units put great stress on the use of the blade. One assumption is that the Spetsnaz operator will have more than one blade available, including an AK74 bayonet, a fixed blade combat knife, a survival knife, a folding utility knife, a hideout knife, and one or more throwing knives. Spetsnaz have also used a ballistic knife that fires the blade at the enemy through a strong spring action. As with other good knife-fighting training, Spetsnaz training emphasizes continuous movement so that an enemy cannot anticipate where an attack will take place. Movements should transform quickly and flawlessly into others and lead to advances, feints, withdrawals, turns, lunges, and slashes so that the enemy will leave himself vulnerable to attack. Spetsnaz are also highly trained to use their sharpened entrenching tool as both a striking and throwing weapon.

Russian naval Spetsnaz and some other units with a MAT mission also train specifically in underwater martial arts to be used against enemy combat swimmers. Russian "Delphin" (naval Spetsnaz) not only spar under water but also practice knife combat underwater not just against humans but against sharks and dolphins, the latter because the U.S. uses dolphins to guard ships and installations. Reportedly, Spetsnaz swimmers have killed enemy swimmers with the blade, including some South African swimmers who may have been attempting to sabotage a Russian/Soviet ship delivering weapons to Africa.

The Republic of Korea's 707th Special Mission Battalion, which is that country's antiterrorist unit, draws on a long and rich martial arts tradition in Korea. TaeKwanDo and Hwarang Do are two disciplines that have been taught to Korean special operations personnel. However, a special martial arts system was developed for the most elite Korean special operators. Known as *Tukong Moosul*, this system was developed in the late 1970s by a group of martial arts masters, but, unlike other Eastern martial arts, which have a strong sport orientation, it is designed as a combat system applicable to the battlefield. As with other military-oriented martial arts, it stresses quick elimination of an enemy as a threat using techniques an operator wearing combat gear can perform readily.

This has been a quick overview of martial arts training designed for antiterrorist operators. Many other systems may be taught or practiced by individual operators, especially those who act as instructors within the units who are constantly looking for techniques which fit their special needs. In addition to knives and clubs, operators may also learn to use crossbows, tomahawks, blowguns, or other silent killing weapons. Whatever the system taught, however, the goal remains the same: to eliminate a threat quickly using techniques readily employed by the operator. no matter what the situation.

Driving

Training is designed to give the operator multiple skills. On the most basic level, he learns to drive an automobile at high speed safely whether in pursuit or escape and evasion. However, high-speed driving training also hones the operator's reflexes and develops his nerve and judgment. As part of their driving training, operators will learn how to drive both defensively and offensively. When driving offensively, the operator learns techniques for ramming another vehicle, for forcing a vehicle off of the road, and for driving through roadblocks. Part of the ability to drive through roadblocks or to ram is knowing exactly where to hit different types of vehicles to spin them out of control or out of the way. For example, a vehicle with the engine in the front will normally be rammed in the rear, which is lighter and easier to shove away. Operators will also learn to drive on roads that are wet or otherwise slick and how to counter skids. In some cases, they will use controled skids to turn the vehicle. They will learn to perform J-Turns, Bootlegger Turns, and other specialized driving maneuvers.

Once these skills are mastered, the operator must learn how to apply them to tactical situations. For example, he will learn to incorporate his training into VIP driving. He will learn, when operating a vehicle as part of a VIP escort team, to use the vehicle to block traffic for the VIP car as it turns, and to otherwise position the vehicle to protect the VIP car. He will also learn the various vehicle escort techniques and how to operate vehicles when embussing or debussing a close protection team.

As part of his training, which can apply to VIP Protection or other tactical situations, he will learn vehicle anti-ambush drills, including the pick-up of personnel from a disabled vehicle under fire and immediate action drills when in a disabled vehicle.

Many antiterrorist units have specialized vehicles designed with ladders on the roof or in the bed of a truck. Operators will learn to drive these vehicles directly up to a building an aircraft or other venue to deliver operators during an assault.

Operators may also have to know how to operate a wide array of other vehicles, such as motorcycles, trucks, buses, even tanks. Trucks or buses may be used to infiltrate operators close to the site of an assault, or an operator might be inserted into a hostage situation posing as a bus driver. To prepare for dealing with an aircraft hijacking, operators may learn to drive the people movers and service trucks that are used at airports. The SAS used to even put operators through the simulators for large aircraft so that they could board the plane posing as a pilot and at least know the preflight drills.

Though it can only loosely be called driving, some operators learn to ride horses and operate horse-drawn vehicles in case they are deployed to a country where animal power is still widely used. Or, they may learn to use trail bicycles or street racing bikes, which will let them approach an incident site quietly yet quickly or when posing as a cyclist.

Some units will have their own facilities for driving training, but many will use closed airfields that offer long runways for acceleration. Some have access to more sophisticated facilities—France's GIGN, for example, has done driving training at LeMans. Others use the driving test tracks at car manufacturers.

Many units will send operators through mechanics training on a wide array of vehicles on the assumption that it might give them some useful knowledge in a hostage incident. Many buses, for example, are designed so that mechanics working on them can shut them down or start them in a location other than the driver's compartment. An operator may want to have the knowledge to rig a remote ignition cutoff for a vehicle supplied to a hostage taker. Knowledge of the mechanics of various vehicles is useful when doing explosive ordnance recces of a VIP car or other vehicle.

Operators may also spend some time at a facility where they harden vehicles used for heads of state or other VIPs, learning how they are designed and built so that they have the knowledge to advise on them while also having the knowledge to deal with a situation should a leader be carjacked in his hardened vehicle.

Teams send operators on a wide array of driving courses so that they are prepared for diverse situations, but also to help keep the operators sharp and motivated. High-speed driving classes, for example, give the operators valid skills but also offer an interesting and exciting change from the normal training regimen for the adrenaline junkies who are members of many antiterrorist units.

Close Protection

Many antiterrorist units will be assigned to close protection details as part of their duties. Most countries already have some type of law enforcement agency that has the mission of protecting government officials. Antiterrorist operators are generally brought in to augment these law enforcement assets in special circumstances. For example, should a country face an increased threat of terrorist assassinations, then antiterrorist operators may augment protective teams. Frequently, if a leader visits areas where threat assessment indicates that he or she is facing particular danger, then anti-terorist operators may be included as part of the security forces. The British SAS, for example, has accompanied members of the Royal Family on some overseas visits. Leaders of countries taking part in the War on Terror who choose to visit their troops in the war zone are very likely to be accompanied by antiterrorist personnel. When the antiterrorist unit is drawn from the armed forces of a nation, they may also be assigned to protect senior military leaders in combat areas.

Members of a nation's antiterrorist unit may be called upon to provide specialized skills in conjunction with regular protective details. For example, in some countries, the antiterrorist unit is trained to function much as the U.S. Secret Service CAT (Counter Assault Team) to provide heavier firepower should an attack be launched. Skilled snipers from the antiterrorist unit may also function in the countersniper role when world leaders visit their country. In some cases, members of the antiterrorist unit will be brought in to carry out security surveys of venues that will be used during high-level VIP visits.

A similar mission carried out by members of antiterrorist units is assignment to embassies to assess security measures and to augment the regular security force. Not only does this give the embassy additional highly trained security personnel, but it also means operators will be familiar with a country's overseas embassies should they ever have to carry out a rescue of diplomats held hostage there.

As part of their training of special operations and antiterrorist units of friendly countries, personnel will often provide close protection training. Not only does this training help the client country develop more effective close protection for leaders who are presumably friendly to the country supplying the antiterrorist trainers, but it allows its operators to work more effectively with other units on VIP junkets. Many of the skills needed to perform effectively in the close protection mission will be gained as part of the training of antiterrorist operators. They will already possess excellent close combat skills with firearms and without. They will have received high speed offensive and defensive driving training that will allow them to perform as a VIP driver or train VIP drivers. Their experience with explosives and booby traps will allow them to carry out explosive recces for IEDs. Antiterrorist units receive training in terrorist psychology, which will have a carry over to providing a threat assessment when doing close protection work.

Operators will need to be trained in vehicle and foot escort formations and techniques as well as specific AOP (Assault on Principal) drills that apply in the close protection mission. They will already know how to assess a building for its security, but they will learn to apply these skills specifically to determining whether it offers a secure residence, office, or venue for a principal. Antiterrorist operators will have to learn to adjust to working with a principal and his staff, which should be made somewhat easier due to the fact that they are likely to be only called in when there is a heightened threat. Antiterrorist operators may have to do some adjustment of their rules of engagement when operating in the close protection role, but they normally train for scenarios where terrorists are "shoot" and hostages are "no shoot;" therefore, they should have little trouble operating in the politically charged environment of close protection.

Mountaineering and Skiing

Countries that have mountainous and snowy areas within their boundaries obviously need an antiterrorist unit with the capabilities of operating within them. Just as an example, Austria's EKO Cobra and the Jagdkommando both train extensively for Alpine operations. Countries without mountainous areas may not need such a capability, yet having at least a few members of the unit who have received mountain warfare training could conceivably prove useful if a rescue were necessary in another country. Some countries, on the surface, might not seem to need a high-altitude capability, yet even the Israeli Army needs ski troops since there is a ski resort on Mt. Hermon.

Some units such as the SAS utilize their Mountain Troops for extreme warfare. As a result, when an SAS Squadron is on its antiterrorist rotation, it will have one troop trained for mountain warfare and probably a few members of other troops who have been through mountain and Arctic training. At least some members of the SBS will also have received cold weather training should an assault in Arctic waters or onto beaches in the Far North be necessary. The Royal Marines Mountain and Arctic Warfare training ranks among the most rigorous in the world and prepares graduates to fight in the most extreme conditions.

Mountain training will include free climbing, rope work, rappeling, movement across glaciers, and numerous other mountaineering techniques. Along with learning the techniques operators will have to learn how to survive at altitude and avoid altitude sickness, conserve energy, and protect themselves from frost bite. In fact, survival is an integral part of extreme warfare training. This includes learning to build shelters in Arctic conditions.

Although operators may learn downhill skiing, especially if they are from countries such as Switzerland, Austria, or others where this is a long-held tradition, cross country skiing, which will help an operator move across the snow quickly, will be more useful. Operators may also learn to use dog sleds or snowmobiles.

Operators will learn to survive and move in extreme conditions, but they must also learn to fight in adverse conditions. They will learn to camouflage themselves to blend with the terrain. Another very important skill is learning to shoot using crossed skis as a rest or using other specialized techniques. Operators must learn to keep their weapons operating in extreme conditions as well. Choosing lubricants that won't freeze and avoiding condensation on the parts that can freeze a weapon making it inoperable are just two important skills that need to be learned.

Should a rescue under extreme conditions be necessary, operators may have to be inserted into mountains or snowy areas via helicopter or parachute. In fjords or other areas that are reachable from the sea, operators must also know how to operate small boats in extreme conditions or carry out underwater approaches from a submarine. Because such insertions are dangerous, they require substantial training if operators are to be adequately prepared.

Since operations in extreme conditions require careful planning, teamwork, attention to detail, and physical fitness, mountain and ski training not only gives the operator skills that may prove invaluable on an actual operation, but also help in his overall development as a highly professional antiterrorist warrior.

Urban Ascent and Descent

Although antiterrorist operators learn various climbing techniques during mountaineering training, they must also learn specialized techniques for ascending or descending buildings that will apply to rescue in urban settings. In addition to standard rappel techniques from roofs, they will also learn techniques such as the Australian repel, in which they descend head down. This technique is useful for reaching a point just above a window, then peeking in with the face just barely over the top sill. Operators also learn to shoot from this position.

Shooting during a rappel is an important aspect of operator training. Not only will operators learn to stop during a rappel and brace their feet against the building for a shot with a handgun, but they may also learn to shoot while swinging past a window. France's GIGN practices a technique based upon the large number of windows that open inward in Paris and other large French cities. They position themselves, then swing out and kick open the window with their feet. Once in the room they practice quickly engaging any terrorists they see.

Although operators may reach the roof of a building through helicopter insertion or via another roof top, they may also have to ascend on their own. As a result, they have an array of grappling hooks, some of which may be fired onto a roof or other anchor point. Once the climbing rope is secure, they can then ascend the building. Operators practice free-climbing the faces of buildings and often become extremely skilled. GSG-9 operators are known within the anti-terrorist community for being especially good at this. As a trick, they will often direct visitors to climb the stairs in their headquarters to an upstairs room, while they will beat the visitors by free-climbing the side of the building and entering through a window.

Other ascent and descent techniques are practiced, including the use of ladders—often attached to a truck—ramps, poles, and via the shoulders or a stack or other operators. Learning a variety of techniques of this nature not only gives the operators useful skills that may be applied in a rescue, but also helps keep them extremely fit. Most units will have specialized towers built at their training facility that will allow them to practice techniques including shooting from the rappel. Various types of ascents or descents will also be incorporated into training exercises to keep operators sharp.

Survival, Evasion, Resistance, Escape (SERE)

As with other aspects of operator training for antiterrorism, the extent to which SERE training is incorporated will depend upon whether units may be deployed to carry out a rescue in areas where there is a danger of being captured. Units operating only within their own country might not receive SERE training, but, on the other hand, if they are deployed against insurgents who control portions of the country, they might still need these skills. By the very nature of their behind-the-lines missions, military special forces operators will generally have received extensive survival, escape and evasion, as well as, counterinterrogation, training. Just as an example of the potential need for SERE training when carrying out the antiterrorist mission, the aborted Delta Force rescue mission into Iran still managed to get all operators out of the country; however, a scenario in which some had been left behind could certainly have arisen. In that case, operators would have had to attempt to reach Turkey or a sea coast on their own or have instituted an E&E (Escape and Evasion Plan) on which they had been briefed in advance.

SURVIVAL

Operators are first trained to survive should they find themselves in a hostile environment. Such a situation can arise if their helicopter goes down or they become separated during a fire fight from their comrades. It is not inconceivable that, even after a successful rescue in an enemy/terrorist-controled area, operators might have to evacuate hostages to an alternate extraction point or even to a nearby border.

Survival training covers an array of skills that prepare an operator to survive in the water, the desert, the jungle, mountains, even urban areas controled by an enemy. Trainee operators learn to find water; live off of the land by fishing, trapping animals, and recognizing edible plants; provide shelter for themselves, avoid dangerous plants and animals (unless they plan to eat the latter!); and perform first aid to deal with injuries sustained in the field. They also learn to build fires (or not to if a fire could compromise their position), to build rafts for crossing rivers or streams, and to generally make a hostile environment less hostile.

Experienced operators will usually carry a small E&E kit containing basic survival tools—including a knife, fish line for fishing and making snares, waterproof matches and/or a firestarter, a signal mirror, water purification tablets, and possibly tubing and plastic sheeting to make a solar still. Experienced operators may well tailor the kit to the AO (Area of Operations). For example, in mountain or cold areas, compact solar blankets may be added, while for the desert collapsible bladders to carry additional water may be included.

EVASION

Whether it is necessary for the operator to exfiltrate an area alone or with hostages, he must be trained in techniques of counter-tracking, misleading tracking dogs, setting booby traps along trails to slow pursuers, using streams or other terrain to make himself harder to track, and communication procedures for contacting search and rescue or other units sent to retrieve him. Land navigation, with and without GPS or other aids, will be an important skill, as will camouflage. Training will have taught the operator just how far he can push himself before he must stop and rest. If accompanied by hostages, operators will have to take into consideration their physical condition which may not be good, thus slowing attempted movement. Some operators may lag behind to slow pursuers with ambushes or sniping, particularly when hostages are being exfiltrated.

In some cases operators may have to be extracted via trooper ladder, STABO/SPIES rig, or other devices lowered from a hovering helicopter. Operators must be familiar with a variety of small boats and their engines in case they can steal a boat to exfiltrate via a river, lake, or ocean. They should also know how to start a vehicle without the keys in case they get a chance to steal one to speed their movement.

Perhaps the best known examples of evasion by special operations personnel are the stories of British ex-SAS members Andy McNab and Chris Ryan during the First Gulf War. McNab was captured and some of his fellow soldiers killed, but Ryan made it to the border.

RESISTANCE

This portion of SERE training prepares the operator for the eventuality of being captured. He will learn what the code of conduct is when captured and normally how long he must hold out so that other operators will have a chance to leave the AO or complete the rescue. As part of their counterinterrogation training, operators will be subjected to various physical and psychological techniques that are likely to be used against them. One of the ironies of the angst expressed in some parts of the media over using water boarding during interrogation of captured terrorists is that all members of U.S. special operations forces have been subjected to water boarding as part of their counterinterrogation training.

Members of an antiterrorist unit sent to rescue hostages will be viewed as very high-value captives and hence must be prepared for harsh interrogation. Should they be forced to appear on television as captives, operators are often trained to provide intelligence via subtle eye or finger movements or other techniques.

ESCAPE

The best time to escape is right after capture. As a result, operators must be ready to use their martial arts training or hidden weapons to eliminate any guards and escape before they can be transported to a secure facility. Even in a highly secure lockup, operators may be able to apply some of their skills (i.e. lock picking, wall scaling, and so on) to escape. In the UK, SAS members used to be called upon to test new maximum security prisons and often escaped in a matter of minutes.

Medical Training

Normally, every operator will receive basic first aid and CPR (cardiopulmonary resuscitation) training, which will be updated at set intervals. However, a number of operators will also receive more advanced combat medic training. Those military units that draw from special operations units will have operators who have been through the advanced military medical training, while units drawn from national police units may have to send personnel through combat medic training.

The most advanced combat medical training can take up to a year and include immediate care to stabilize traumatic injuries, triage of injured operators and hostages to determine the care that will be needed upon evacuation, cardiac life support, administration of fluids and drugs, and treatment of common team injuries during training and operations. The special ops medic assigned to antiterrorist duties will also be in charge of preventative care for members of his team. This may include knowing the basic steps necessary to remain healthy in the desert or Arctic, or anywhere in between, and making sure they are followed. The medic will know about infectious deceases common to areas of operations and how to prevent and treat them. He will also know the symptoms of special health issues affecting operators from mountaineering, carrying out HALO/HAHO jumps, or doing combat diving. Medics must be aware of the likely problems that can arise from eating indigenous food and be able to treat stomach disorders. Myriad other duties may fall to the medic with a deployed unit, from making sure fresh, potable water is available to checking that latrines are dug downstream. Since the operators with whom the medic works will be highly motivated and well trained, not to mention quite intelligent, many of these issues will be handled as a matter of routine by experienced personnel.

Good combat medics will also look at uniforms, equipment, and supplies to determine if their design is such that harnesses will chafe, edges will cause cuts, or that there are no other design features that can impact on a unit's health and safety.

Operators train hard so parachuting or diving injuries are to be expected despite precautions. Doing high-speed entries and rappeling can also lead to injuries. One reason that operators now wear elbow and knee pads is the large number of injuries they can sustain to joints by banging against doorways or leaping into and out of vehicles. By immediately dealing with relatively minor injuries, the team medic can keep them from becoming serious and, should bones be broken or major traumas sustained during training, the medic can stabilize them until the operator gets to a medical facility. Since operators work with explosives, cutting torches, stun grenades, and other such devices, the team medic must also be trained to deal with burns and have available in his kit materials needed to treat them.

Speaking of kit, combat medics learn to organize their medical kit very carefully so that they can immediately put their hands on needed equipment. Some antiterrorist teams actually carry out exercises requiring the medic to determine simulated injuries in complete darkness by feel, then locate the necessary medical supplies in his bag and treat the injuries in total darkness. Flashing lights and sounds of gunfire in surrounding areas may be included to simulate an actual rescue operation.

Special ops medical personnel must be very aware of how helicopter medical evacuation works and how to communicate with the medical evacuation crew, and possibly the doctors at the facility to which the patient will be evacuated. The medic has to know what steps are necessary to prepare the operator or other injured party for medical evacuation and also what diagnostic information they need to send with the patient.

The best trained combat medics will have done a rotation at a big inner-city emergency room, where they will see more gun shot and knife wound victims in a couple of months than they would anywhere other than intense combat. In case it is necessary to save their comrades or rescued hostages, some of these highly trained medics will know how to perform basic surgical procedures such as opening an airway or tying off an artery. At least a few antiterrorist units actually have doctors who are trained operators assigned to the unit. Many former U.S. Special Forces medics go to medical school on leaving the armed forces and at least a few return to serve with special operations units.

It is important that combat medics assigned to antiterrorist units should also be trained as operators. The general SOP (Standard Operating Procedure) during a rescue operation is that once the operators "go in" they do not stop to deal with injured comrades or hostages. Their job is to get to the terrorists as rapidly as possible to prevent them from killing or injuring anyone. The combat medics will usually be with a group of operators that follows the initial entry team and takes control of captured terrorists, secures hostages until their identities are verified, and deals with operators who are down or injured hostages. The combat medic must be able to operate as part of these follow-on teams and, should additional terrorists be encountered, engage them with his weapons effectively. He may be there to save lives, but that might still involve taking the life of a terrorist who suddenly leaps from hiding with plans to kill him or his patients.

Antiterrorist medics also have a responsibility to prepare their teammates for the possibility of injury and brief them on what will happen should they go down. GSG-9 used to actually insert a catheter into the arm of each operator taking part in an assault and tape it off to save time in getting him fluids should he take a hit. As part of their training, antiterrorist teams will incorporate scenarios that simulate a member of the unit being shot or otherwise injured so that other team members learn to move in and assume his duties and the medic learns to stabilize and evacuate him.

Exchange Training

Some of the most valuable training antiterrorist operators get is from other teams with which they carry out exchange programs. Many teams will have developed their own approach to a typical problem faced in anti-terrrorist operations and other teams can learn from that approach. Exchange training may be carried out in a variety of ways. Most of the major antiterrorist teams will have one or two members from allied units on long-term assignment—up to a year or more. Likewise, they will have a few operators on assignment to other teams. The U.S., Australia, Great Britain, and Poland have teams that work together so often that they can virtually interchange members for operations. Other exchanges may only cover a couple of weeks when a substantial number of operators from one unit will visit another to carry out training exercises.

Certain units have developed a reputation for special expertise in certain areas. The British SBS, Australian OAT, and DevGru, for example, have practiced oil rig takedowns extensively and hence can offer a great deal of expertise to members of other units. The Israelis have more experience with suicide bombers than anyone else; so other units can learn from them. Austria's EKO Cobra and Jagdkommandos are particularly skilled at Alpine operations so those on exchange can learn from them. Other units have specialized skills. Because there are so many good combat shooting schools in the USA, many teams will send exchange trainees to the Combat Applications Group or DevGru so that they can attend courses at Blackwater (now known as Xe) or other facilities. Operators training in the USA may also get a chance to observe big city U.S. SWAT teams who often do more high-risk warrant entries in a month than many antiterrorist units have carried out in their entire history.

Another reason to visit friendly units is to try out their hardware. Operators learn to use a variety of weapons and equipment and sometimes come back to their units and say, "We have to get...!" For example, the SAS adopted the HK MP5 after seeing it in use by GSG-9, And other units who saw the SAS use stun grenades quickly added them to their arsenal. The U.S. Trijicon ACOG (Advanced Combat Optical Gunsight) became widely used among antiterrorist units when they encountered it with U.S. units. A more low-tech example is the use of elbow and knee pads by operators. Once operators saw other teams using them and realized how many injuries they prevented when doing entries, rappeling, and other things, they became *de rigeur* for teams all over the world. Reportedly, in fact, since only Spetsnaz wear knee and elbow pads, in Chechnya, terrorists have been known to abort ambushes when they see troops wearing them!

Major SWAT competitions around the world are another way that operators can interact with members of other teams and pick up techniques and gossip. They also get a chance to see new equipment on display with vendors who attend. Likewise, there are a few large trade shows of equipment for antiterrorism/special operations that offer a chance to exchange ideas and view equipment. The one in Jordan each year has an especially good reputation. It helps when the king is a former special operator!

Chapter IV

Antiterrorist Unit Organization

Generally, the antiterrorist unit will operate as part of a larger military or police organization. As a result, many higher-level administrative tasks will be carried out by the parent organization. Nevertheless, the unit will need its own administrative elements to make sure that the parent unit is addressing the operators' needs. For example, in many antiterrorist units the secrecy required dictates that operators are shown as assigned to some phantom unit or to a unit other than the antiterrorist unit. In such cases, administrative personnel must make sure that operators still receive pay and benefits, that their dependents are properly cared for, and that they remain on a promotion track.

Antiterrorist units also need creative administrative personnel who can deal with the sometimes odd needs of the unit, which may well include having to provide large sums of cash at short notice. As various units around the world have discovered to their dismay, these administrators must walk the line between responding to the operators' needs and making sure that they remain accountable for the cash. Most people who opt to become antiterrorist operators don't choose that career after taking accountancy degrees! Some of the best administrators for antiterrorist units are drawn from former operators who may have sustained an injury that renders them unable to carry out the most rigorous of operations, but who have a knack for getting things done and a first-hand knowledge of operations. In some units, retired operators with the relevant skills may also be hired to continue to work with the unit.

Few units will have their own aviation assets and hence will have to work closely with their police air wing or military special ops aviation units. Units will need technicians and mechanics to keep the electronic gear and vehicles of the unit running. Operators will need the skills to maintain equipment when deployed and may work with specialists when at their HQ, nevertheless having specialists is still important. Skilled mechanics, whether operators or non-operators, are valued for their ability to help create the specialized equipment.

Above Operators of Croatia's ATJ Lucko offer a good view of their ballistic helmets and face shields. Note the elbow pads built into their coverall. They are armed with the HK G36C. (Croatian Police)

Antiterrorist Unit Organization

Unit armorers are very important as well. Operators shoot a lot and are hard on their weapons; therefore, they need experts who can keep the weapons operating and who can make special alterations when needed. Once again, all operators will be trained in basic weapons maintenance and some will receive additional training, but having one or more full-time armorers, either drawn from the ordnance department of the parent military or police unit or hired as civilian specialists, is very important.

There is a selection and training element need as well, though units that only run selection once or twice a year will normally have personnel who perform this function then return to other duties. Certain personnel will be charged with supervising the training of new unit members, often as mentors. Some training will be performed by other specialist units. Parachute or scuba training, for example, may be carried out by specialist military facilities.

Intelligence personnel for the antiterrorist unit must work with the larger military and police intelligence apparatus of their home country and friendly states but must also be highly skilled at evaluating intelligence related to terrorist groups and incidents. In addition they must be able to quickly assemble intelligence that is specifically related to an incident in progress and organize it to give operators information that may be useful in terms of planning a rescue operation.

In many units, there will be trained psychologists and negotiators who assess the state of mind of terrorists and hostages and attempt to reach a resolution to a hostage incident without the need to resort to deadly force. In selecting the psychologist or hostage negotiator care must be taken to choose an individual who will not develop so much empathy with terrorists that he or she loses their objectivity. The psychologist or negotiator must be able to say at some point: "This incident is not going to end through negotiation. The assault team is going to have to go in or the snipers are going to have to get a green light."

A wide array of support personnel is also required to assure that operators are fed, housed, and receive medical care. Those who carry out these support functions must have been vetted for security as they will be in close proximity to those assigned highly secret operations. Some units have learned that making as many of the administrative and support personnel as possible feel an integral part of the unit is very advantageous. As a result, they may arrange for such personnel to go through parachute training or do a course each year in Close Quarters Combat or survival for non-operators assigned to the unit. Not only does this give support personnel additional skills but it also makes them feel more a part of the unit.

There will be operators who are highly trained as combat medics, but the unit will also need medical support from doctors, dentists, and—if dogs or other animals are part of the unit, as with GIGN, RAID, and some other units—veterinarians. In the USA, a substantial number of special forces medics later go to medical school and become doctors. Should they choose to remain in the military, they would make perfect doctors for an antiterrorist unit.

Operators themselves will be organized into sub units for purposes of command and control and also for assignments. Typically, units may have three teams that rotate among roles. One team is on 24/7 alert, ready to respond to an

Above Members of Italy's GIS antiterrorist unit use a special ramp designed for building or aircraft assaults. (Carabinieri)

Antiterrorist Unit Organization

incident. It will carry out some training while on alert but must be ready to drop what it is doing and proceed to an incident site. A second team may be carrying out more intensive training or another assignment, but will remain available within a certain time frame to reinforce the on-alert team should a major incident take place. The third team might have members who are on leave, away on exchange training, carrying out security surveys at overseas embassies, or performing other duties.

Each of the teams will normally have specialist skills among their members. The SAS, for example, will have a squadron assigned to the antiterrorist role, normally for a six-month rotation. Within the squadron will be a HALO/Air Troop, Boat Troop, Mountain Troop, and Mobility Troop, thus providing specialists in various methods of approaching an incident site if needed. There will also be medical, communications, and demolition experts among the personnel. Operators will normally function as either surveillance/snipers or members of assault teams. The SAS normally assigns a portion of the squadron on antiterrorist duty to locations near London. Somewhere between 8 and 16 personnel will normally be assigned to the London area. Their job will be immediate response to an incident while the remainder of the alert squadron is deploying.

The smallest operating element for most antiterrorist teams will consist of four or five men. In the SAS, it is the four-man patrol. The basic operating element will normally be trained to work together clearing rooms or in other assault skills that require choreographed teamwork.

What I have just given is a general overview of organization in antiterrorist units. To gain a better understanding, though, it may be useful to look at specific units in more detail. In fact, since the SAS has just been used as an example it makes sense to expand on a discussion of its organization first.

The British SAS comes under the command of the Director Special Forces. The regular Army SAS regiment is 22nd SAS. There are also Territorial Army (reserve) units. Primary support elements for the SAS include 18 UKSF Signals Regiment.

Left A five-man entry team from the Austrian military police demonstrate their technique for "stacking." Note the shield man is aiming his Glock pistol around the shield while other team members have Steyr AUG carbines. The rear man is also armed with a pistol with light mounted; he may be the breacher. (Osterreichs Bundesheer)

Many members of this regiment are parachute-trained and some have received additional special operations training. The Special Forces Flights of 7 Squadron at RAF Odiham and 47 Squadron at RAF Lyneham provide air support to the SAS. For MAT operations M Flight of the Fleet Air Arm's 848 Squadron might be called upon.

The 22nd SAS Regiment is divided into four squadrons, each of which is divided into four troops. Members of Air Troop are trained in static line parachuting, HALO, and HAHO. Although a substantial portion of an SAS squadron may be HALO or HAHO qualified, it is members of Air Troop who are expected to keep up with the latest developments in parachutes, oxygen equipment, GPS steering systems, and other innovations. They will also be charged with checking over their own equipment and that of other operators when carrying out a parachute insertion.

Members of Boat Troop are capable of being inserted in various types of boats. including Klepper canoes, Gemini inflatables, Rigid Raiders, and other craft. They are trained in open and closed circuit scuba techniques and in deployment from submarines. They are also trained in wet jumps carried out directly into the water via parachute. Members of SAS Boat Troops train with the Special Boat Service (SBS) extensively and should a MAT mission arise might assist the SBS if additional operators are needed.

Members of Mobility Troop specialize in vehicle operations including Land Rovers, Supacat HMV (High Mobility Vehicle), motorcycles, Light Strike Vehicles, ATVs, and various other vehicles. Many of the vehicles are heavily armed and may be used for raiding or fire support in certain antiterrorist operations. Reportedly, the SAS has practiced using vehicles to quickly reach a hijacked Eurostar train beneath the English Channel. Members of Mobility Troop are trained to carry out maintenance of their equipment in the field and would supervise maintenance of equipment for other troops.

Members of Mountain Troop are trained in mountaineering, skiing, and cold weather survival among other skills. Some have attended the Royal Marines Mountain Leader course or the German Alpine Guide course.

The SAS Operations Research Unit is constantly evaluating and developing equipment for all SAS missions including the antiterrorist mission.

The SP (Special Projects) Team is drawn from the squadron serving its six-month rotation as the alert antiterrorist team. (Note that since the SAS uses this system of rotating squadrons through the antiterrorist role, there will be trained antiterrorist operators deployed with any SAS squadron should the need for a rescue operation arise.) The basic SAS CQB course is six weeks long and involves firing thousands of rounds of ammunition. The SP Team will fire many more thousands of rounds while on alert status to hone their shooting skills even further. The SP Team is still based on the system of four troops though there may some additional augmentation personnel. Personnel are organized into a Red

Above Members of Greece's DYK Maritime Antiterrorist Units in one of their Unconventional Warfare Craft. (Hellenic Navy)

Team and a Blue Team, each with sniper/surveillance personnel, assault teams, and explosives entry and breaching experts. One team will be on alert for immediate deployment throughout their period on antiterrorist standby. At RAF Lyneham, a C-130 is always on standby for immediate deployment of the SP Team. As mentioned earlier, a portion of the SP Team is also detached and based close to London for immediate response to an incident.

Here's how organization works in other antiterrorist units:

GSG-9

While the SAS is illustrative of a military antiterrorist unit, Germany's GSG-9 offers a good example of a unit drawn from the police. In the case of GSG-9, the parent organization is the Bundesgrenzschutz, the German Federal Border Guard. GSG-9 draws upon assets of the federal border guard including air assets, but many functions are integral to the unit. Based at Saint Augustin-Hangelar outside of Bonn, GSG-9 has four primary support groups:

- The Technical Unit deals with the testing and procurement of an array of equipment, other than weapons. This unit also contains GSG-9's EOD experts.
- The Central Services Unit is in charge of the GSG-9 armory and purchases weapons, ammunition, and explosives. Gunsmithing and other weapons maintenance is carried out by this unit as well.
- The Documentation Unit deals with communications (commo) and surveillance equipment. This includes procurement, testing, and maintenance.
- The Training Unit is charged with selecting and training operators for GSG-9.

Operational personnel are assigned to one of three sub units. The first group is assigned to antiterrorist operations on land. Operators who specialize in entries and sniping are assigned. The normal strength is about 100 operators. The Maritime Operations Unit is charged with MAT. It also has about 100 members.

Plate 1 Insignia of FSB Alpha

Plate 2 Insignia of Czech URNA

Plate 3 (a) Insignia of the Chinese Snow Wolf Commando Uni

Plate 3 (b) Insignia of the Chinese Snow Leopard Commando Unit

Plate 4 Insignia of Lithuanian ARAS

Plate 5 (a) Insignia of the Slovenian Specialna Enotari

Plate 5 (b) Insignia of Dutch BBE

Plate 6 (a) Insignia of Spanish GEO

Plate 6 (b) Insignia of the Spanish UEI

Plate 7 Insignia of Austrian EKO Cobra

Plate 8 (a) Insignia of GIGN

Plate 8 (b) Insignia of Italian NOCS

There is also an Air Operations Unit, which specializes in parachuting and helicopter insertions. About 50 operators are assigned to this unit.

Currently, GSG-9 does not have a mission outside of Germany's borders or territorial waters. The Army's KSK (Kommando Spezialkrafte) now has the mission of carrying out hostage rescue outside of Germany. The German Navy's Kampfschwimmers have the MAT mission outside of German territorial waters, while GSG-9 would be assigned missions on the Rhine or other rivers and possibly in port.

GIGN

France's GIGN is another antiterrorist unit within a national police organization. Overall supervision within the unit falls to the command cell, which is supported by an administrative group. For much of its existence, GIGN employed

Above Operators from Italy's GIS take up all around security positions after being inserted by a helicopter. (Carabinieri)

four operational troops of 20 operators each who formed the "teeth" of the unit. This has now changed to three sections each of greater strength. However, plans are in effect to form a fourth operational section, which may be on line by the time this is read. One operational troop is available for immediate deployment at any time within 30 minutes. Additional elements can follow within two hours if the incident is a major one. There is also an operational support element that handles negotiation, breaching, intelligence, communications, sniping, dogs and handlers, and special equipment. Attached support elements deploy with the "door kickers" on operations. The special equipment cell tests and develops special equipment for the unit as well as maintaining it.

Operators may specialize in either HALO/HAHO or combat diving. A substantial portion of the unit are also sniper-qualified. Dog handlers train with the assault elements as GIGN uses dogs extensively during assaults.

NOCS

NOCS, which is now sometimes designated as the Polizia di Stato's AntiTerrorism Special Operations Division, is one of Italy's antiterrorist units. It has an especially sophisticated computer and video support section drawn from the assets of the Polizia di Stato. The unit has three tactical assault teams and one protection team. The protection team works on high threat dignitary protection assignments and provides countersniper and CAT (Counter Assault Team) services as well as trained drivers. On the three assault teams, all operators are HALO-qualified and many are trained in scuba, EOD, or sniping. As is typical, the three teams rotate through a cycle with one on alert at all times. The logistics branch of the Special Operations Division takes care of NOCS's specialized vehicles, weapons, and equipment.

URNA

URNA, the Czech antiterrorist unit, serves under the Ministry of the Interior. It is divided into three sections: operations, special services, and administration. URNA has approximately 100 personnel. The operations section has three 21-

man assault teams. Each team has members who specialize in assaults, sniping, EOD, negotiations, and driving attached. The special services section includes snipers, negotiators, technical specialists, and vehicle specialists. SInce some of these specialties are included with the assault sections, it may be assumed that elements are detached to any deployed assault teams. The administrative section handles logistics, training, and equipment.

URNA is based in a suburb of Prague. The 24/7 on alert team is expected to be ready to respond to an incident in 45 minutes or less. A second team would be able to reinforce the first one within four hours. The third team can normally respond within 24 hours. However, teams have rotated through Iraq providing embassy security for Czech diplomats and carrying out other operations. It is possible, therefore, that only two teams are available for phased incident response.

GEO

Another European police antiterrorist unit is Spain's GEO, which reports to the Adjunct Commander of the Spanish National Police. Support divisions include administrative staff, training, research and development of tactics and equipment, security, vehicles, communications, and weapons. The Assault Division consists of two groups, each of which is divided into two sub groups. Within the sub groups are six teams, each with five operators, a team commander, two snipers, a breacher, and a driver. The Alpha and Bravo teams alternate being the on call team every other week, while the one not on call does training and administrative work.

FBI HRT

The FBI's HRT draws upon all assets of the Federal Bureau of Investigations for support. Operationally, the HRT is organized into three teams, each of which has assault elements and sniper/observer elements. Two of the teams specialize in land operations and one in maritime operations. Normally, the HRT's jurisdiction is only within the USA, its possessions, and its territorial waters. However, since U.S. law grants it jurisdiction over terrorists wanted for acts against the USA anywhere in the world, the HRT does deploy overseas, often along with the Army's Combat Applications Group or the Navy's DevGru. The three HRT teams operate on a 60-day cycle. On the training cycle, the team gains new skills, practices skills it already has, and takes part in exercises designed to prepare it for operations. By moving from the training cycle to the operations cycle, skills will be very sharp. When on the operations cycle, the team is ready for immediate deployment to deal with an incident. The final cycle is the support cycle, during which the team works on various special projects and maintains the HRT's equipment.

The current strength of the HRT is around 90–100 personnel, though in larger incidents the HRT can draw from regional FBI SWAT teams. As with many units, the FBI HRT organizational structured has evolved. The unit originally had two sections: Blue and Gold, each comprising two assault teams and a six-operator sniper team. The assault teams were further divided into four-man assault elements. Each element had a specialty (e.g. aircraft assaults, maritime operations, barricade situations, etc.). This organization evolved with each section having two larger 7-operator assault elements and an 8-operator sniper team. Then, in around 1995, the HRT was restructured to incorporate even more snipers. As a result, each section had two 7-operator assault teams and two 7-operator sniper teams. This makes the HRT one of the most sniper-heavy antiterrorist units in the world.

There are two U.S. military antiterrorist units for operations outside of the USA. Delta Force (now often known as Combat Applications Group) is charged with antiterrorist ops anywhere in the world on land. Some estimates of Delta's strength have run as high as 1,000 personnel, but this includes specialists in intelligence, commo, and other support activities as well as HQ staff. Although Delta often uses assets from the 160th SOAR, it has also had its own helicopters painted to look like civilian choppers. Although these numbers are classified, reportedly somewhere around 250 operators would carry out hostage rescue and other direct action. When Charlie Beckwith founded Delta Force he drew heavily on his time with the SAS so the organization has many similarities with that unit.

The basic unit is the "team" of four or five operators. Teams specialize in HALO/HAHO, SCUBA, or other skills. Four or five teams form a troop. For the antiterrorist mission, troops are normally broken up into sniper troops and assault troops. Although organization can vary to suit the mission, the primary operators are assigned to one of three squadrons—A, B, and C—each of which has three troops: assault, sniper. and recce.

DevGru (formerly SEAL Team 6) falls under the U.S. Navy's NAVSPECWARCOM but is also a component of the Joint Special Operations Command. Estimates of DevGru strength usually run to about 200 operators plus 300 administrative and support personnel as well as a section that specializes in testing new Naval special warfare weapons and equipment. Since SEALs shoot so many rounds of ammo per year, an important part of their support staff are armorers.

DevGru operators are organized into cells that have different specialties such as Evasion and Recovery, Force Protection, sniper, and such like. Evasion and Recovery cells have the mission of recovering U.S. downed flight crews, evacuating U.S. civilians from a coast, hostage rescue, and various other tasks. Force Protection can include VIP protection duties. A group of these diverse cells is organized into a team which is designated by a color. For example, Gold, Red, and Blue Teams are assault teams, with Gold considered the primary team. Gray Team specializes in transport and Black Team in Recon and Surveillance. Green Team is the training team.

Team members, especially assault team members, will rotate through three categories. When they are on SPECTRA (Special Training) status, team members will be off attending specialized schools. This can include anything from HALO and high-speed driving to advanced shooting schools. Afghanistan deployments have added schooling in riding and managing horses and mules to the agenda for many special operators. Those on Standby status are the 24/7 ready team for MAT (Maritime Anti-Terrorism) missions. They remain close to the base ready for instant recall and deployment. The final status is Deployment Status. Teams on deployment status may be on a mission, training foreign naval special warfare personnel, providing protection for high-ranking U.S. officers or officials, providing security at U.S. embassies, or various other duties.

SSG

Pakistan's SSG (Special Services Group) performs an array of special operations missions much like the SAS or the U.S. Combat Applications Group. The SSG has four commando battalions: 1st, 2nd, 3rd, and 4th. Operators from these battalions carry out some antiterrorist functions including providing security for nuclear weapons and at some nuclear facilities. Members of the SSG also carry out clandestine missions for the ISI (Inter-Services Intelligence) Directorate. Reportedly, these include direct action. There are also reports that some members of the SSG are assigned to the Saudi Royal Family to provide security. However, since many "former" members of the SSG serve in the antiterrorist units of various Gulf States, it is possible that any SSG serving the Saudis are not active personnel.

In addition to the four commando battalions, the SSG also includes Zarrar Company, which is the designated antiterrorist unit on-call to deal with terrorist

Above A team from Greece's EKAM practice an exit from a building while giving cover all around; their HK MP5s have EOTech optical sights mounted. (Hellenic Police)

incidents. There is also Musa Company, which is a combat diver unit. Although Musa Company has training applicable to MAT operations, there is also the Naval SSG. With a strength of around 1,000, the Naval SSG is trained to operate in a similar manner to the British SBS or U.S. Navy SEALs. There is also an Air Force unit designated the Special Service Wing, which performs functions similar to USAF Special Tactics Squadrons, though it is also trained to carry out rescues aboard aircraft.

Because Zarrar Company and other antiterrorist elements are part of the larger SSG structure and have close links with ISI they have access to a wide array of air, naval, and intelligence support.

As should be apparent by now, the basic structure of the antiterrorist unit remains relatively constant among units around the world. Each unit must have support personnel who will take care of the day-to-day needs of maintaining a military or police operational group. There must be armorers to maintain the special weapons and mechanics to keep the vehicles in operation. Most of all, there must be highly trained operators capable of dealing with myriad types of terrorist incidents at any time and anywhere within their area of responsibility, whether national or international.

Particularly important is a streamlined chain of command. Large military or police organizations are not normally particularly friendly to small, elite units. The antiterrorist unit should preferably report directly to the director or deputy director of the parent organization. A direct chain of command will allow the antiterrorist unit to be deployed more quickly in an emergency, will insure that needs for special equipment or training are not lost amidst budget infighting, and will prevent the unit from being misused on missions that waste its talents. Antiterrorist units have to wage a constant war, not only against terrorists but also against bureaucracy.

Chapter V

Weapons and Equipment

Although antiterrorist operators will have access to the standard weapons and equipment used by their country's armed forces or police, they will also have specialized kit to fit specific missions. These may include suppressed weapons for scenarios where stealth is a necessity, specialized underwater weapons for dealing with enemy combat swimmers, or extreme long-range sniping rifles that will allow a terrorist to be eliminated at up to a mile. The operator may need HALO or HAHO gear to get to the site of the incident or scuba gear to silently infiltrate under water. Some units allow their operators to choose from a wide array of weapons or equipment those items that suit each operator. Other units issue each operator with a range of weapons and equipment from which he or she will choose those that fit their specific mission.

The weapons chosen by antiterror units will often be the latest, most high-tech available; however, classics such as the HK MP5 or Steyr SSG remain in wide use as well. Sometimes an antiterrorist operator needs a weapon that will function as a scalpel and occasionally he may need one that will function as a hammer—the unit's armory should contain both types. Likewise, he may need equipment to allow him to reach the site where terrorists are barricaded or equipment to breach that site once he arrives. He may have to gather clandestine intelligence about the terrorists and their intent, which will involve a need for the latest electronic gear and imaging equipment. Or he may simply need an effective automatic knife to cut a tangled line.

In conclusion, then, the antiterrorist operator must have a wide range of weapons and other gear available, as well as the training to use them effectively.

SUBMACHINE GUNS

Although there is a trend among antiterrorist units away from the SMG (submachine gun) as the primary weapon it is still widely used. The SMG has the advantage of being compact for use in entries or tubular assaults, and of using a pistol caliber round that has light recoil for fast repeat shots and lower penetration in buildings, aircraft, ship's passageways, and such like. SMGs also lend themselves to the attachment of suppressors, which are tactically advantageous for missions involving clandestine approach and assault.

Overwhelmingly, the most popular SMG for antiterrorist teams has been the HK MP5. Highly accurate and reliable, the MP5 was first used by Germany's GSG-9 followed by the SAS and other units. The basic MP5 models are the MP5A2, which has a fixed stock, and the MP5A3, which has a sliding stock. The former is a bit easier to shoot accurately while the latter is better for parachute or helicopter insertions, waterborne operations, or any other movement where a more compact weapon is desirable. There are other variants, which have a three-shot burst mode. The MP5SD is widely used by antiterrorist teams as well. This suppressed version of the MP5 both offers the advantage of a low noise signature and cuts the flash for use in areas where there might be flammable fumes or materials. The MP5K is in the inventory of many antiterrorist units for use in VIP protection assignments or other situations when compactness is paramount.

Above A member of the Special Air Service in full assault kit including the HK MP5. (22nd Special Air Service Regiment)

Traditionally, after the MP5, the most popular SMG with antiterrorist units was the Uzi, which has a reputation for being very durable and reliable. Combat swimmer units in particular have chosen the Uzi. The Uzi was around before the MP5 so some units already had it in the inventory, a major consideration in the early days of many units. The MP5 fires from a closed bolt, which is generally considered an advantage, while earlier Uzis fired from an open bolt. Later versions of the Uzi were, however, available in closed bolt models. More compact "Mini" and "Micro" versions of the Uzi are also available.

The FN P90 SMG has been adopted by many antiterrorist units over the last decade. The P90 has many advantages. Though only 19.7 inches overall due to its bullpup design, the P90 holds 50 rounds, thus offering a lot of firepower. Its 5.7x28 mm cartridge has received mixed reaction from users. Its AP (Armor Piercing) ammo offers excellent penetration against body armor, one reason it was used during the assault on the Japanese Ambassador's residence in Peru. The stopping power of its light, fast bullet is open to some question. Still, its ability to punch through vests and its compact size have caused a lot of units to adopt the P90.

Above A sniper of the Slovenian Specialna Enota antiterrorist unit prepares to engage a target with the Steyr SSG rifle. (Slovenian National Police)

CARBINES

There has been a trend for antiterrorist units to adopt a rifle caliber carbine. The rifle caliber weapon offers many advantages and if frangible ammunition is available for use in an urban setting, aboard ship, etc., it is an excellent choice. The rifle caliber carbine offers better performance against body armor or terrorists behind cover. It also gives the operator better range.

The U.S. M4 Carbine version of the M16 is widely used by antiterrorist units. The M4 has a 14.5 5-inch barrel and is just under 30 inches with stock collapsed and jut under 33 inches with stock extended. Current versions of this stock have multi-positions to allow the operator to tailor length of the stock for use over body armor and to his own arm length. The M4 may also be configured with Picatinny rails to take an array of optical sights, illuminators, and such like, as well as an M203 grenade launcher

In Russia and many countries that were formerly part of the Soviet Union, the AKSU short version of the AK74 is used by antiterrorist units. The AKSU fires the 5.45x39 mm round used in the AK74, a round that has a reputation for tumbling once it enters a target's body to increase stopping/killing power. Overall length of the AKSU with stock folded is only 19.3 inches and with stock extended 28.7 inches; however, to achieve this compactness, barrel length is only 8 inches. Russia also has various specialized assault rifles and carbines available such as the AS Silent Assault Rifle, which fires a special 9x39 mm round that uses a heavy 250 grain subsonic bullet at relatively close ranges. There is also the A-91 Compact

Above A combat swimmer of Greece's DYK leaves the sea ready to engage with his Glock 17 pistol. (Hellenic Navy)

Top These operators from Ukraine's Berkut still use weapons of the Kalashnikov family, in this case with suppressors. (Ukrainian Ministry of the Interior)

Above A member of the Irish Army Ranger Wing with a Steyr AUG mounting grenade launcher, optical sight, and an IR illuminator. (Irish Defense Forces)

Assault Rifle, which goes back to the 7.62x39 mm round used in the AK47 as opposed to the 5.45x39 mm round, which has been the Russian standard for decades. For Delphin, Russia's underwater Spetsnaz, the APS Underwater Assault Rifle that fires darts is available.

Another carbine used by a substantial number of units is the Steyr AUG. The most widely used "bullpup" design in the world, the AUG in original format has an integral 1.5x optical sight, though versions with a flattop are available to take an array of other optics. The carbine version of the AUG has a 16-inch barrel yet is only 28.1 inches overall. There is an even more compact version with a 13 8-inch barrel that is only 24.6 inches overall. France's FAMAS is another bullpup assault rifle, which is used by French units and a few former French colonies.

The German G36K model or the even shorter G36C is in use with some antiterrorist units, particularly German and Spanish ones. The sighting system comprises an integral 3x sight as well as a 1x red dot sight. Backup iron sights are incorporated as well. The K model of the G36 has a 12.5-inch barrel and is 24.2 inches with stock folded or 33.9 inches with stock deployed. The C model has a 9 9-inch barrel and is 19.7 inches overall with stock folded and 28.4 inches overall with stock deployed.

FN's F2000 is seeing some use with antiterrorist units. It is another bullpup design with either integral optical sight or flat top. Even though it has a 15.75-inch barrel, overall length is only 28.6 inches.

Many other countries including China and Singapore have bullpup designs, which are in use with their antiterrorist operators. The bullpup design lends itself well to use by operators who may have to move through tight spaces during entries or may have to take a shot very near to a hostage or fellow operator in close quarters.

There are antiterrorist units that use the standard infantry assault rifle of their country, but they are few. The ability to handle the carbine or bullpup rifle in confined conditions quickly makes it a far better choice.

Above The HK G36K has achieved substantial acceptance among antiterrorist units; note this one mounts a light. (C&S)

HANDGUNS

The handgun serves multiple purposes for the antiterrorist operator. It is the secondary arm to which he will go should his primary weapon malfunction during an operation. In some tactical situations, the handgun will serve as the primary weapon. For example, in some assaults where conditions are extremely tight (e.g. when. infiltrating through heating or air conditioning vents), the handgun may be the weapon of choice. In some cases, suppressed handguns will be carried to take out lights or terrorist sentries. The operator may also have to get into position by posing as a member of an aircraft maintenance crew or some other less threatening individual. In these cases, the concealed handgun may be the weapon of choice. Many members of antiterrorist units sometimes draw the close protection assignment as well; in which case they will normally carry one or more handguns. Some units, in fact, issue at least two handguns, with one being more concealable for the close protection mission.

For many years the most commonly encountered handgun in use with antiterrorist units was the FN P35 "Hi-Power." Though the P35 is an excellent pistol, it was often chosen because it was the standard military and/or police pistol of a given country. Though units using the P35 will still be encountered, and a few units allow more senior members to retain the P35 even after switching to a newer design, it has been replaced within most units that formerly used it.

Today, the most widely used pistol among antiterrorist teams is probably the SIG P226. Highly reliable, accurate, and with a 15-round magazine capacity in 9x19 mm caliber, the P226 makes an excellent choice. For antiterrorist use, many units will select the P226R—the "R" standing for rail to allow attachment of various types of illuminators. Tritium night sights will often be incorporated as well. There are variations of the basic P226 in action type (i.e. traditional double/single action or DAK constant action). Although most units around the world use the P226 in 9x19 mm, versions are also available in .357 SIG, or .40 S&W. Some units may also choose the P228 or P229, which are slightly more compact than the P226, or the P220, which is available in .45 acp.

Also widely used among antiterrorist units is the Glock pistol. The Glock 17 in in 9x19 mm caliber is overwhelmingly the most popular version of the Glock with operators. Some combat swimmer units—Greece's DYK, for example—add an extended threaded barrel for a suppressor and the sub aqua spring cups to make the

Above One of the few revolvers to have achieved use among antiterrorist units is the Manurhin MR73. The example shown was formerly used by Austria's EKO Cobra.

Glock more effective for firing as the operator breaks water. Other variants of the Glock 17 used by some units include the compact Glock 19 and subcompact Glock 26, the latter two often intended for close protection duties. The select fire Glock 18 is in the inventory of some units. A few units also use larger caliber Glocks such as the Glock 22.40 S&W caliber or the Glock 21.45 acp, the latter used by Austria's Jagdkommando among others.

Versions of the Heckler & Koch USP are used by a substantial number of units, including Australia's SASR. The USP is relatively compact for a full-sized combat pistol at 7.64 inches overall. There is also a compact model that is only 6.81 inches overall. The USP is available in 9x19 mm and .40 S&W as well as .45 acp in a larger version. The USP Tactical model has a threaded extended barrel for use of a suppressor. The HK P7 was used by some units in the past but has generally been replaced by the USP, which is designated the P8 in German and Spanish service versions. A few units also have the HK Mark 23 SOCOM pistol, a large .45 acp pistol sometimes termed an "offensive" pistol since it is designed to use a suppressor and various types of illuminators. At 9.65 inches overall without suppressor and weighing in at 2.42 lb, the Mark 23 is not a good choice for most operators who carry the pistol as a secondary weapon. It does, however, serve relatively well as a primary weapon for combat swimmers or others who may have to silently eliminate the enemy.

Some U.S. antiterrorist operators and a few others around the world still use modernized versions of the Colt 1911 pistol. Normally, current versions such as the Springfield Operator, which incorporates a rail for illuminators, are used—by the FBI HRT, for example. These pistols are in .45 acp and can be extremely accurate and reliable as well as offering a lot of stopping power. Some MEUSOC and MARSOC U.S. Marines who may be charged with hostage rescue use high high-quality versions of the 1911 pistol, the MARSOC version being produced by Kimber Mfg.

Italy's Beretta 92 is used by some units, often because it is the standard military or police arm of their country. At 8.54 inches overall, the 92 is a relatively large pistol but it has a reputation for extreme reliability. U.S. troops deployed to Iraq have had some reliability issues with their M9 versions of the Beretta 92, but these are normally traceable to the government's purchase of cheap magazines rather than the

Above The HK USP/M8 has become one of the more popular handguns among antiterrorist units.

Top Some U.S. antiterrorist units as well as a few allies have adopted 1911 type pistols with rails for lights or lasers; these Kimbers are similar to those adopted by USMC MARSOC personnel.

Above The Beretta 92/M9 is one of the pistols used by antiterrorist units. Note the extended magazines to give more firepower.

pistol itself. Among users of the Beretta 92 is Italy's NOCS antiterrorist unit. Copies of the Beretta 92, such as those by Taurus, are used by some units as well.

Many Russian antiterrorist units still use versions of the Makarov pistol, including the standard PM model and the PMM, a product-improved version of the Makarov, which takes a more powerful version of the 9x18 mm cartridge and has a higher magazine capacity. Some elite units such as Alpha and Vympel also have the 6P35 Grach, which chambers a more powerful 9x19 mm AP round than the NATO standard and has a 17-round magazine capacity.

At least a few units have some FN Five-seveN pistols available for use against suspects wearing body armor. The Five-seveN fires the same 5.7x28 mm round as the P90 SMG and has a magazine capacity of 20 rounds. At 8.2 inches overall, the Five-seveN is a relatively large pistol. Very flat shooting due to the high velocity cartridge, a skilled operator can readily score hits on a man-sized target with it at 100 yards or further.

For combat swimmers assigned to MAT missions, there are two specialized underwater pistols available. HK makes the P11, which fires 7.62 mm darts from a sealed five-barrel unit. Reloads are by replacing the barrel. The P11 is in the inventory of many of the world's naval special warfare units. For Russian Naval Spetsnaz, the SPP-1 Underwater Pistol is available. It fires 4.5mm darts from a four-round magazine.

Some countries use their own indigenous pistols as a matter of national pride, but overwhelmingly antiterrorist units will choose among those that have been discussed above.

SNIPING RIFLES

The sniping rifle and the trained marksmen who use it are a key element in antiterrorist operations. An antiterrorist unit needs enough trained snipers so that at least two can be assigned to each terrorist during an operation. As the French GIGN did in Djibouti, an incident may be quickly ended if the snipers can acquire all or most of the terrorists and eliminate them surgically. At Djibouti, only one terrorist remained after the snipers did their work, and he was neutralized by a follow-up assault. In incidents involving a lone terrorist or a relatively small number of terrorists, the snipers can wait for the green light to act or until they see a terrorist about to kill a hostage. There are other scenarios, however, where a skilled tactical marksman can influence events. At Beslan in Russia, for example, there were a large number of terrorists who began shooting children as they attempted to flee the school amidst explosions and fires. Russian snipers saved many hostages by engaging the terrorists with fire whenever they showed themselves. Snipers can also be used to initiate a dynamic entry during a rescue by eliminating a terrorist sentry who might stop or slow down the entry team just before the entry begins. In maritime antiterrorist operations, snipers on other ships or in helicopters can give covering fire to the boarding team as it moves to seize the target vessel. The uses of the sniper rifle for antiterrorist missions are myriad.

In looking at sniping rifles in use with antiterrorist units today, it is important to understand that rifles in different calibers are chosen for different missions. The .308 (7.62x51mm NATO) chambering, for example, is still widely used for urban sniping and for shots out to 500–600 yards, though skilled snipers can take much longer shots with the .308. The Russian 7.62x54R round ranges to approximately the same distances. Some units now use the .300 Winchester Magnum round to extend the range of the sniping rifle another 200 yards or so. However, many units jump from the .308 sniper rifle to one in .338 Lapua caliber for shots to 1,200–1,500 yards. The .338 Lapua round has proven so effective, in fact, that many units now use it as their long-range sniping rifle. Finally, there are the extreme long-range "anti-material" rifles in .50 Browning MG caliber that can be, and have been, used to take shots out to a mile or more.

One of the most popular and longest serving precision rifles is the Austrian Steyr SSG. The SSG has a cold hammer forged barrel, which has always been a boon to accuracy. The basic SSG model is chambered in .308 caliber and has been available with different barrel lengths. An updated version, the SSG 03, is also available in .300 Winchester Magnum, but most antiterrorist units that use the SSG have retained the classic P1 model in .308.

The Accuracy International line of precision rifles manufactured in the UK has achieved wide acceptance among special ops and antiterrorist units. The Accuracy International PM was the first model adopted in the British Army and is still in very wide service. In the version marketed as the Counter-Terrorist model, a 2.5-10x variable scope is standard. The AW (Arctic Warfare) model in .308 is also widely used these days, as well. (The Arctic Warfare designation, by the way, comes from the fact the rifle is specifically designed to perform well in extreme cold weather.) There is also an AWMP that is fully suppressed.

Above Four of the most widely used rounds by antiterrorist snipers: from left to right, .308 NATO, .300 Winchester Magnum, .338 Lapua Magnum, .50 BMG.

The Accuracy International AWM Magnum series of rifles is widely used at longer ranges. Available in 7 mm Remington Magnum, .300 Winchester Magnum, and .338 Lapua Magnum, these rifles allow a killing shot at much greater ranges. The SAS, among other units, has been especially impressed with the performance of the .338 Lapua AWM.

Among units that want a self-loading tactical rifle, the HK PSG-1 has proven popular. The PSG-1 normally comes standard with a 6x42 scope with illuminated reticle. This rifle will take 5- or 20-round magazines, the latter being useful to cover an assault team or escaping hostages.

French antiterrorist units such as GIGN and RAID have used the French produced FR-F1, FR-F2, FR-G1, and FR-G2. The FR series of rifles have detachable 10-round magazines and are bolt actions. Normal chambering is .308. The standard scope is a relatively low powered 4X .

Finland produces some of the best tactical rifles in the world. The Tikka T3 Tactical is a light precision rifle capable of well under a MOA (minute of angle) accuracy yet is easily transported. The most widely used Finnish tactical rifle, however, is the SAKO TRG42, and earlier TRG-21 or TRG-41 models. The TRG-42 is available in .308, .300 Winchester Magnum, and .338 Lapua. A folding stock version is available, which is a real boon for snipers who may have to carry and climb with the weapon to get into shooting position. Folding stock versions of the Accuracy International rifles are available as well.

There are various U.S. sniping rifles used by American operators and some allied antiterrorist units. The USMC M40A1 sniper rifle, which is based on the

Above The SAKO TRG-42 in .338 Lapua is widely used among antiterrorist units as a long-range sniping rifle. The version shown has the folding stock to make it even easier for special operations/ antiterrorist personnel to transport it on parachute, helicopter, boat, or other insertions. The scope is a Leupold LR/T.

Remington 700, has seen some use. The latest improved version is designated the M40A3. Also based on the Remington 700 is the M24 SWS (Sniper Weapon System) developed as a complete package for the U.S. Army. The disadvantage of the Remington 700 as the basis for an antiterrorist precision rifle is that the magazine is a fixed integral one rather than a detachable one. One of the most widely used tactical rifles from the USA is the Springfield Armory M21. This self-loading, match grade, semi-auto version of the M14 rifle is very accurate, offers fast follow-up shots, and takes either a 10- or 20- round detachable box magazines.

Above Among U.S. antiterrorist forces and some allies, the self-loading Springfield Armory M21 has achieved popularity. In this case it mounts a NightForce scope that has an illuminated reticle for night usage as well as day.

Though not known for its tack-driving accuracy, the 7.62x54R caliber Russian SVD Dragunov remains in wide service in Russia and former republics of the Soviet Union. The detachable 10-round magazine and 4x scope with illuminated reticle make the SVD a good choice for relatively close range usage against a substantial number of terrorists as at Beslan. The Russians have developed various sniping systems that are in use with Alpha, Vympel, and other Spetsnaz units. The SV-98 is a bolt action rifle in 7.62x54R, though 7.61x51 mm NATO versions are available for export; it can take a suppressor. The standard sight is a 7 power, which retains the same reticle as the SVD, allowing easy transitioning of snipers.

One other sniping system which should be mentioned since it is used by various antiterrorist units is the PGM Ultima Ratio rifle in 7.62x51mm NATO, .300 Winchester Magnum, and .338 Lapua. Produced in France and marketed by FNH, PGM rifles have a reputation for superb accuracy rivaling the SAKO and Accuracy International lines.

The term "anti-material rifle" is used for .50 caliber and larger sniper rifles. These rifles may also be used in that role, too, to destroy communications equipment, rocket launching panels, and various other high high-tech gear. In the antiterrorist role, there are situations when a large caliber rifle might be used to stop a vehicle or destroy some type of weapons control device. However, the "anti-material" rifles also see substantial use as long-range antipersonnel weapons as well.

The USA pioneered the use of large-caliber sniping rifles and many units around the world still use the Barrett M82A1 or the more compact M95. Also produced in the USA is the McMillan .50 caliber tactical rifle. Accuracy International offers a .50 version of their tactical rifle in the AW50F with folding stock. Finland produces various Helenius .50 anti-material rifles, which, like all Finnish rifles, are very accurate. Hungarian Gepard .50 rifles also see some use, especially in Eastern Europe. Gepards are available in 12.7x108 mm as well as 12.7x99 mm (.50 Browning MG). The Gepard is also produced in 14.5x114 mm caliber (Russian heavy machinegun caliber). PGM Precision produces the Hecate, which is used by French units and some others and has a reputation for being one of the best of the heavy sniping rifles. Russia offers the self-loading V-94 anti-material rifle, which is chambered in 12.7x108 mm. Its reputation among Russian snipers using it in Chechnya was not good.

Above A U.S. Marine fires a Barrett M82A3 .50 Long Range sniping rifle. (USMC)

TACTICAL SHOTGUNS

In antiterrorist units, the tactical shotgun serves primarily for quickly taking down doors by shooting hinges or locks during a dynamic entry. It can also be a useful weapon during MAT operations since penetration when clearing passageways or cabins will be less of a problem. In some situations, the shotgun may be used to deploy less lethal munitions when clearing sensitive areas of protesters or in other situations where lethal force is not deemed necessary. For antiterrorist units who are used for security when transporting valuable commodities or dangerous prisoners, once again the combat shotgun has a very real mission. The 12-gauge is the standard in use with virtually all units.

Above A GIGN operator wearing gas mask and carrying a SPAS-12 shotgun, which is widely used among antiterrorist units since its dual action allows it to be used for breaching loads, combat loads, or less lethal munitions. (Gendarmerie Nationale)

The most popular tactical shotgun probably remains the venerable Remington 870, which is highly reliable and proven over decades of military and police usage. Other U.S. shotguns that have seen use with antiterrorist units are the Remington 11-87P, a self-loading tactical shotgun, and the Mossberg 590 series. Some Winchester 1200 tactical shotguns remain in use with a few units as well.

Many units use one of the Italian dual action tactical shotguns. The Franchi SPAS-12 is in wide usage as is the Benelli M3. These shotguns have the advantage of use as a self-loader for most applications but offer the capability to be quickly switched to slide action for deployment of less lethal ammunition that might not cycle the bolt if used in self-loading mode. The M1 Benelli and M4 Benelli have been used by some units as well. The latter was adopted by the USMC as the

M1014 and is in use with Marine MARSOC and MEUSOC units as well as a growing number of non-US antiterrorist units.

The Russian Saiga 12 shotgun is a self-loading, magazine-fed weapon that is highly thought of for tactical use outside of Russia as well as within. Some Russian special units use the Saiga as a tactical shotgun. Spetsnaz units also have access to the KS-23, which is of approximately 4 gauge. This powerful shotgun can fire tear gas, rubber bullets, buckshot, or an extremely effective anti-vehicular round. Recoil is reportedly quite fierce.

As with the pistol, a few units use locally produced tactical shotguns, but the ones discussed above remain the standards.

GRENADE LAUNCHERS

Used to deploy gas or smoke grenades primarily in the antiterrorist role, the grenade launcher may also be used to deploy antipersonnel munitions, flares, or other munitions as well.

Today, grenade launchers such as the US M203 40mm grenade launcher, which is mounted on the M4 or M16, are the most widely used since they allow an operator to serve as a "grenadier" while still retaining the full capabilities of his primary weapon. Among other popular rifle- or carbine-mounted launchers are the Russian GP-25/GP-30 for the AK74, the German HK79 for the G3 rifle, and the British ISTEC ISL 274 40 mm launcher for the Steyr AUG. Russia also produces the BS-1 30 mm silenced grenade launcher.

Some units prefer stand alone grenade launchers. The most popular is probably the HK 69A1 single shot 40mm grenade launcher. Russia offers the GM-94 43 mm grenade launcher, which is fed by a tubular magazine above the barrel and holds three or four rounds. The US M79 single-shot grenade launcher still sees services with some units as well.

OPTICAL SIGHTS

Optical sights have been used since the nineteenth century for sniping rifles, but the use of highly durable optical sights for battle rifles is a much more recent

Top A U.S. Special Forces operator armed with a carbine that mounts an Aimpoint optic, M203 grenade launcher, white light illuminator, and infrared illuminator These may be from the SOPMOD kit. (SOCOM)

Above Members of FSB Alpha offer a good view of equipment used by Russia's premier antiterrorist team. The rifle carried by the operator in the foreground appears to be one of the Kalashnikov 100-series of rifles. Note that each operator has his rifle set up to fit his individual tastes. The one in the background has a vertical fore grip with built-in light of the type produced by SureFire and has an ACOG type sight. (FSB)

occurrence. The SUSAT sight used on the British L85A1 and the integral optical sight used on the Steyr AUG helped prove that optical sights could stand up to the rigors of field usage. As a result, today most armies, and virtually all antiterrorist units, use some type of optical sight on their SMGs or carbines.

The choice of optical sights for SMGs or carbines basically divides into one of two options. The first is red dot sights, which are normally 1x, such as the US AimPoint, Trijicon Reflex, or EOTech. These are widely used for CQC (Close Quarters Combat) applications on both carbines and SMGs and hence are very well suited to use for antiterrorist teams carrying out entries. Among other widely used red dots are the Russian PK-AS/B.A.R.S. and Kobra, widely used by FSB Alpha and Vympel as well as other Spetsnaz units and the tiny Doctor sight manufactured in Germany. The latter is especially useful for compact SMGs since it is so small.

The second option comprises sights such as the Trijicon ACOG or the Canadian ELCAN, which offer magnification of 4x plus or minus. These are very versatile optics and allow the operator to use the reticle for CQC but also to rapidly engage a target to hundreds of yards using stadia lines if necessary. The RCO, the U.S. Marine ACOG, employs a red chevron reticle that is very fast at CQC yet is also quite effective at 500 yards or more. Among satisfied users of the ELCAN are the Special Air Service and Royal Dutch Marines. Both the ACOG and ELCAN have established an excellent reputation for standing up to hard usage.

For use on sniping rifles, the standard has changed with many antiterrorist units. For decades, precision rifles employed a fixed power scope. The Steyr SSG, for example, was often supplied with a Hensoldt 10x42 mm scope that was of extremely high quality. Other European sniping rifles were often supplied with fixed power Khales, Swarovski, or Schmidt & Bender fixed power scopes. Often sniping rifles were supplied with a 6x or even a 4x scope. In the USA, Unertl, Leatherwood, and Weaver fixed power scopes were often used for sniping rifles. In Russia and the old Soviet sphere of influence, the 4x24 PSO-1 scope was the standard.

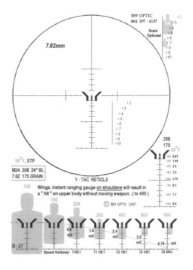

BW Optics Y-TAC Reticle The Y-TAC Reticle, which is designed particularly for use with the M21 sniping rifle, offers a good illustration of a complicated reticle designed for use by sophisticated marksmen. Only the portion within the circle is actually seen by the sniper. The illustrations below and to the side show how the reticle may be used in determining range, compensating for bullet drop and so on.

As higher powered .300 Winchester Magnum, .338 Lapua, and .50 sniping rifles have come into use, variable power scopes that allow them to be used effectively over a range of distances have become more popular. Schmidt & Bender and IOR/Valdada ones have been popular in Europe as have Leupold and NightForce in the USA. Scopes such as Leupold's 6.5-20x50mm LR/T or NightForce's NXS 5.5-22x56 mm—both with illuminated reticles for night usage—allow a .338 Lapua or .50 sniping rifle to be used over a wide range of distances quite effectively. One scope that has proven useful with the self-loading M21 rifle from Springfield Armory is one from BW Optics that incorporates a reticle designed to allow the marksman to quickly score hits at varying distances.

Many skilled snipers still prefer a fixed power scope of 10x and continue to use one of the high high-quality traditional models. To score precise hits at long range requires a good rifle, good ammunition, and a good scope, but most of all a skilled marksman. Whether fixed or variable, current scopes for precision rifles offer the sniper great light gathering capability, clearness, range-finding capability, and, if desired, illuminated reticle. Although many sniping scopes do incorporate range-finding capability, most snipers will also use a laser range finder today so that they can dial in elevation precisely. Speaking of dialing in elevation and also windage, modern scopes for precision sniping rifles allow very precise adjustment to $^1/_4$ MOA or even to $^1/_8$ MOA.

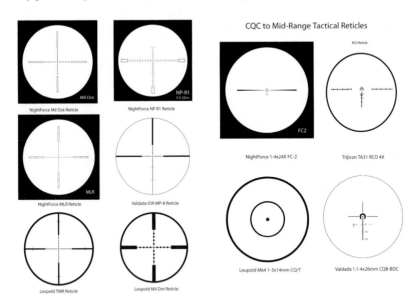

Left Tactical Reticles for Long Range Sniping Scopes
Right CQC to Mid-Range Tactical Reticles

There is also a category of scopes that falls between the CQC red dot type and the sniper rifle scope. Many scopes are designed for use on a self-loading carbine that may be used at close or long range. The advantages of the ACOG or the ELCAN have already been discussed for this usage, but there are other scopes that are designed for a specific scenario that may arise in antiterrorist operations. Operators have found that when they clear a building they need an optic with a wide field of view and a quick acquisition reticle such as a red dot, normally with 1x magnification. However, they may come out of that building and find themselves under fire from a sniper at 100 or 200 yards away. To most effectively engage that sniper, they need a scope with more magnification. Two optical sights designed to meet this need are the Trijicon ECOS, which has a standard ACOG for longer range with a small Doctor red dot sight piggybacked atop it. The ELCAN's Specter DR offers another solution since it can be quickly switched from a 1x red dot to a 4x by just flicking a lever on the scope's body. Schmidt & Bender, NightForce, and IOR/Valdada all offer scopes that can serve in this situation as well.

Antiterrorist units will also have specialized night vision optics. Since many antiterrorist operations take place in darkness, often shortly before dawn, night vision scopes are an important adjunct to their weapons. Various types of night telescopic sights are available, including those that rely on available light or those that are used in conjunction with infrared illuminators. There are also passive infrared telescopic sights that pick up the heat signatures of individuals or objects even in rain, fog, or other adverse conditions. Compact night optics, which may be mounted in front of standard day optics and used in conjunction with the optical sight that is already zeroed, are very useful, especially with some of the compact battle rifle optical sights. A discussion of how night vision devices and scopes work is given below under NVDs (Night Vision Devices).

Some companies offer a dual day/night scope system that is very versatile and fits the needs of antiterrorist snipers who may enter a hide at night yet still be waiting for a shot when day arrives. A couple of scopes from ATN offer good examples of this type of optic. A 2-6x68DNS or 4-12x80DNS is available. In either case, the scope functions as a standard day scope but by removing the day eyepiece and replacing it with a night eyepiece, the sniper is ready for a shot in darkness. Changing the eyepiece does not affect zero of the scope so the sniper is ready to go from day to night or night to day while remaining ready to take a shot if given the "green light." These scopes are also supplied with infrared illuminators that may be used in conjunction with the scope in total darkness. For use by combat swimmers, some night vision optics are available that may be used to depths of 50 meters.

Among U.S. manufacturers of high-tech night vision optics are Insight Technology Raytheon, Litton, Varo, and ATN. The Russians make a wide array of night optical sights that have a reputation for durability. Since these sights are quite reasonably priced compared with some produced in the West, they are especially popular with antiterrorist units in some developing countries as well as those formerly in the Soviet sphere of influence. In the UK, Pilkington night optics have seen substantial use as well as having been exported to friendly nations. Various other nations with a sophisticated electronics manufacturing base have produced night vision optics as well.

ILLUMINATORS

The term "illuminators" is often used to cover an array of lights and lasers that may be mounted on weapons. The simplest type of illuminator is the white light illuminator (i.e. flashlight). Early examples were commercial flashlights mounted on some type of mount affixed to the weapon. Early SAS lights mounted on the HK MP5 were of this type. Later, weapons incorporating rails designed specifically to take a light and/or laser were offered. Various companies now offer white light illuminators that slide onto a Picatinny or other type of rail and lock in place. In the USA, Insight Technology, BlackHawk, Streamlight, and SureFire offer an array of very high- quality ones. Most antiterrorist units now choose a handgun with rails for mounting a light and operators often carry the weapon with the light mounted. Lights are also affixed to SMGs, carbines, or shotguns. Some units use IR (infrared) illuminators, which allows them to see targets without signaling their position with a visible light. NVGs (Night Vision Goggles) are necessary when using an IR illuminator.

BlackHawk's Xiphos weapons light is interesting as it adds an additional feature that may be useful in antiterrorist operations. In addition to the constant or intermittent On features incorporated into other weapons lights, the Xiphos also offers a strobe feature. Antiterrorist units have experimented with strobes for disorienting terrorists during an operation; hence, the Xiphos offers the option of strobing during an entry, which may disorient the terrorist while also illuminating him for a shot.

Visible and IR lasers are also widely used. Operators zero the laser so it matches the point of aim of the weapon at a certain distance. Once the laser is zeroed, the weapon will shoot where the red dot points. As part of the U.S. SOPMOD (Special Operators Peculiar) Kit, Insight Technology developed various illuminators and laser pointers to fit on the M4 carbine. These included the CVL (Carbine Visible Laser), AN-PAQ-4C IR Aiming Laser, AN/PEQ-2A combo IR Aiming Laser and Illuminator. More recently Insight has offered the ATPIAL (Advanced Target Pointer/Illuminator/Aiming Light), which is very compact and combines visible and IR lasers and IR illuminator. The ATPIAL is primarily designed for the M4 carbine. Some years ago when the HK Mark 23 SOCOM Offensive Pistol was developed, Insight Technology had pioneered such multifunctional illuminators with the LAM (which combined visible and IR illuminator, visible laser, and IR laser in one module).

A similar device, the MOLAD (Multi-Operational Laser Aiming Device) is offered by Laser Devices, Inc. The MOLAD combines visible and IR illuminators and lasers in one module only about 4 inches long, 1.85 inches high, and 7.3 ounces in weight. The MOLAD fits any pistol with a Picatinny (MIL SPEC-1913) rail.

Above Most antiterrorist units today use handguns that allow the mounting of a light or laser. This Rock River Tactical 1911 has an Insight Technology M6X Tactical Laser Illuminator mounted that combines a white light and a laser in one compact package.

To keep the weight of the M4 carbine or other weapon down while still offering wide capabilities in illuminators, the latest trend is toward devices combining a red dot sight with

Above Units such as the Insight Technology LAM (Laser Aiming Module) were developed to give operators multiple types of illuminators in a compact package.

multifunction illuminators/pointers. Insight Technology's ISM-IR combines a red dot sight with a visible and IR laser that is co-aligned with the red dot. Lasers Devices Inc. offers the EOLAD, which combines the popular EOTech red sight with a visible and IR laser. The value of these combo sight/ laser pointers is that as the operator adjusts the red dot sight to zero it he is adjusting the sight/laser to be zeroed as well. Hence, the operator may engage by placing the red dot of the sight or the red dot of the laser on the target, depending upon the tactical situation.

Although most pointers use a red laser, LaserMax, among others, offers a green laser. Generally, the green is considered more powerful. It also offers the advantage that if two operators enter a room, one with a weapon mounting a red laser and one a weapon mounting green, it is quickly apparent where each weapon is pointing if two potential targets are near each other or a target is near a hostage.

NVDs (NIGHT VISION DEVICES)

NVDs are electro-optical devices that are designed to amplify existing light. Using an image-intensifier tube, image intensifiers amplify ambient light thousands of times and display images using a phosphor display. The phosphor screen used on most NVGs (night vision goggles) is green as the human eye can differentiate more shades of green than other colors viewable on a phosphor screen. The distance at which NVGs are viable varies, based on the magnifying power of the objective lens and the strength of the image intensifier. With very high-quality NVGs, a person can be detected at 200 yards on a moonless night. Current generation NVGs available to antiterrorist units amplify available light 30,000–50,000 times. There are very versatile multi-use NVGs. The Belgian-made OIP Lightweight Night-Observation System, for example, may be used as helmet/mask mounted NVGs for driving or, by changing to a 6x lens with reticle, may be mounted on a bipod and used for surveillance/intelligence gathering. Because this system is modular it gives operators who must travel relatively lightly a lot of options.

One of the big disadvantages of NVGs is that they severely affect peripheral vision, lowering it from 180 degrees or more to about 40 degrees. As a result, operators must be trained to constantly turn their heads from side to side to scan for threats. They must also train with their NVGs constantly to counter the tendency to overestimate the distance of objects viewed through them. Training will also prepare operators for navigating through darkened buildings or carrying out surveillance of a darkened building prior to an assault.

Some Night Vision Devices are worn as a monocular, but to gain depth perception pairs worn as aligned binoculars are more effective and are true Night Vision "Goggles." Binocular goggles may have a single lens or stereo lens. Monocular devices in some cases may be mounted ahead of telescopic sights or red dot sights to give night vision capability. Some red dot sights are specifically designed for use with night vision devices.

Also used sometimes are FLIR (Forward Looking Infrared) detectors, which sense the difference between an object and its environment. FLIR has the advantage of allowing the operator to see through fog, smoke, etc.—an advantage when clearing buildings after deploying stun or gas grenades which that create smoke and haze.

Night vision devices that are termed passive rely on available light that is magnified by the device. Active infrared devices work in conjunction with infrared illuminators that operate in a spectral range just beyond the visible spectrum of the human eye. Although antiterrorist units may use active infrared devices, since active infrared light may be detected by NVGs, they are not normally used on the battlefield.

BODY ARMOR

Members of antiterrorist units operate against dangerous criminals or terrorists as a matter of course and hence have a high likelihood of facing gunfire. As a result, ballistic protection is very important. However, operators must also be able to move quickly and climb or carry out other movements that require agility. As a result, their ballistic protection must offer a tradeoff between protection and mobility.

The ballistic vest, which protects vital organs, has normally used a combination of Kevlar inserts backed with ceramic or titanium plates to cover the most vital organs. Operators will normally have ballistic protection which reaches Level III (designed to stop fully jacketed 7.62 bullets) or Level IV (designed to stop 7.62 caliber armor piercing rounds). There is a Level V body armor, but it is designed for bomb disposal personnel and severely inhibits mobility. Kevlar and other ballistic protection materials degrade in effectiveness when wet; hence, they may have to be kept in sealed water-resistant enclosures. In an attempt to address the problem of weight versus ballistic strength, the next generation of body armor may incorporate nano technology. Some of the nano materials currently being tested can withstand shocks of up to 250 tons per square centimeter or more. Today, an array of sturdy vests which are designed to both take ballistic panels and to carry weapons and equipment are available for operators.

Those antiterrorist units, such as GIGN or RAID, that use dogs as an integral part of the unit will have ballistic vests for the dogs.

Coupled with the ballistic vest, operators will also wear a ballistic helmet and face shield. The ballistic helmet must also be designed for protection and mobility since the operator must be able to turn his head and use his peripheral vision. Currently, the best ballistic helmets being used by operators reach Threat Level IIIA (capable of stopping a .44 Magnum revolver round). The ballistic helmets used by most operators offer compatibility with communications and night vision equipment and some helmets offer compatibility with nuclear, biological, and chemical equipment. Manufacturers try to reduce the profile of the helmet enough to degrade peripheral vision as little as possible. Helmets are also designed to be compatible with the ballistic vest so that the operator can retain a full range of motion, even when prone. Although it doesn't affect the ballistic protection of the helmet the internal pad system and an adjustable head band are very important for comfort since an operator may have to wear the helmet for an extended period while awaiting the "Go!" order. Helmets should also allow the use of a ballistic collar to protect the gap between the ballistic vest and helmet.

Along with the helmet, operators will need a compatible communications system. "Active-Ear" type ear plugs screen out the sharp sounds of a stun grenade or gunfire while still allowing an operator to hear communications from his team or command post. The ballistic face shield is designed to offer some ballistic protection—multiple hits from up to a 9x19 mm or .357 Magnum handgun—while allowing the operator to still be able to see well enough to use his weapons and move surely. Constructed from polymer bond , the ballistic face shield is designed to be compatible with standard ballistic helmets. Normally, face shield visors are designed to be locked in one of three positions: full-elevated, midlevel, and deployed to cover the face. It is important, too, that the operator be able to quickly move the shield between these positions in case the tactical situation requires him to lift the shield to check something or quickly move it to cover his face. Some units choose ballistic goggles rather than a full face shield.

Above A good view of the FNH P90 SMG and ballistic helmets and visors used by Portugal's GOE (Portuguese Police)

The first operator through the door will often have a ballistic shield. Generally, the shields are designed to protect the point man but also to offer some protection to the rest of the "stack," who may be partially exposed behind him. Shields will generally have a small porthole made from ballistic material such as that used in the ballistic face masks. Some shields will also have a built-in illumination system for use when moving into a darkened room. The operator with the shield will normally carry it with his support hand and have a handgun in his strong hand. Because a shield must be light enough for an operator to carry it with one hand, ballistic shields normally only give Threat Level IIIA protection against powerful handguns. Shields that will stop rifle ammunition are available, but they are so heavy that they are on wheels, which severely limits the mobility of the operators. Some of these shields are transparent with hydraulic controls. They may have firing ports.

Though not offering ballistic protection, knee and elbow pads are an important part of the operator's body "armor" as well since rapid movements through doorways, into and out of vehicles, in ship's passageways, and so on, can result in hard knocks to the joints, which could incapacitate the operator. Additionally, a Nomex fire retardant coverall and protective gloves are worn by operators for non-ballistic protection. Boots are also important and will be specially designed to protect the feet while allowing the operator to retain agility and rapid movement. Some types of boot incorporate a steel insert in the sole as some drug labs or other possible raid sites will have sharp objects strewn on approaches as booby traps. Gas masks may be worn if operating amidst an environment where gas, smoke, or chemicals are present.

ENTRY TOOLS

When an antiterrorist team is given the order to go in, it normally has to gain entry as fast as possible. Although operators may in certain circumstances carry out an explosive entry by blowing an opening through a wall or blowing a door off of its hinges, more often, they will need an array of tools especially designed to deal with doors or windows. Many operators will have been trained to pick locks and may carry a lock pick set with them. As obvious as it seems, operators must also be trained to check if doors are unlocked as they sometimes are.

The basic tools will normally include a ram, which must be heavy enough to pop a door's lock yet compact and light enough for an operator to carry and handle it. You can generally spot the "ram man" of an entry team by looking for the largest and strongest. An alternative to the ram is a heavy-duty sledge hammer, usually with an aggressive-sounding name such as "Thor's Hammer" or "Thundermaul." Perhaps the most useful tool is the "Hallagan Tool," sometimes referred to as the "Hooligan Tool," which may be used to pry doors or carry out other operations. Hallagan Tools are generally nonconductive of electricity and flame retardant in case they are used following up a frame charge or otherwise to pry through burning materials. The other basic tool is a heavy-duty bolt cutter

These are the basic man-portable entry tools, which will usually be carried in a special backpack by one of the operators. He can quickly release the pack, or other operators can release individual tools from the pack for quick deployment.

Above Members of Portugal's GOE offer a good view of equipment as the assault up a dual ladder. Note the ballistic helmet and visor, flame-retardant balaclava, dual magazines for the HK MP5 SMGs, gun-mounted lights, and elbow pads. Note also the cover men at left and right of the ladder. (Portuguese Police)

A typical entry kit carried on the back of an antiterrorist operator—the SAS has used a kit of this type—might consist of a heavy-duty bolt cutter, a ram, and a Hallagan Tool. That combo with its pack weighs 45 lb. Some alternate kits will contain a maul/heavy sledgehammer instead of the ram. Rams or mauls are generally designed to be nonconductive as well.

Though not designed as an entry tool, one US Firm, TOPS—Tactical Ops USA— offers a very compact kit that is carried in a sheath on the operator's belt. Designated the Pry Knife and PPP (Pry, Probe, Punch), it incorporates two versatile tools that an operator can use to pry some internal doors or windows, or to cut, or punch out safety glass.

Other tools that may be available include the Breaching Saw, which is on a long handle—one model is 64 inches overall—that allows an operator to safely stand back while cutting inspection holes in ceilings, sheet rock walls or other lightweight building materials. The head of the saw is fabricated of high carbon

Above Operators from Spain's GEO use a pneumatic spreader and other heavy-duty entry tools to get past a barred doorway. (Policia Nacional)

steel, and the saw is designed to be nonconductive of electricity. Another tool—sometimes called a "break and rake"—is designed for use when a team will enter through a window. This tool is designed to punch through the glass, then be raked around the window frame to remove glass shards that could injure the operator coming through the window. Many of these tools will also have a hook designed to pull blinds or curtains free and out of the window.

When carrying out combat boardings of ships during MAT operations or in other situations where steel doors may be encountered, operators may have cutting torches/thermal lances or power saws. Doors may be opened, too, with a spreader-cutter, a device with blades that may be wedged into a seam or gap between a door and its facing. A hydraulic pump then pushes the blades apart with great force. Once this seam has been widened, the cutter portion of the tool may be used to cut a wider opening. The spreader-cutter and many other breaching tools were originally developed for fire or rescue personnel but work well for assault teams as well. Other powerful tools are available, but they are not portable and require more time to deploy.

To effectively use these tools during a rescue, operators must have had a chance to practice with them so that they learn the proper place to hit a door or how to quickly pry a door open. As a result, antiterrorist teams often find a construction company that tears down structures, and will arrange to go in just before a building is demolished to practice removing doors or windows.

Another aid to gaining entry is a fence climber designed to allow an operator fully loaded with equipment to quickly scale a fence. The assault ladder, which is a light weight telescoping ladder that weighs only 20–25 lb yet may be telescoped from 2.5 ft to 12.5 ft allows operators to quickly approach a building window, a train or bus window, or aircraft doors.

Above One of the specialized entry tools developed for antiterrorist teams; this one is a "break and rake" type designed to break out windows, rake them clear of glass, and pull out blinds or window frames.

For combat boarding of ships, teams have what is usually termed a "hook-and-pull" ladder, which incorporates a long pole with a hook to affix to a ship's rail. Once it is attached, a boarding ladder may be deployed. Other highly sophisticated ladders may be attached to vehicles and will be discussed later in the section on team vehicles. Some units have tested a climbing system based on suction pads that affix to the hands and feet. Another aid to scaling walls is the grapnel, which in some cases may be launched by a grapnel launcher.

Antiterrorist teams will be trained in explosive entry and will have available prefabricated frame charges and LINEX, a flexible tubular explosive that may be molded to fit the point of placement. They will also use stun or distraction grenades during entries, some of which separate into multiple submunitions that will help to confuse terrorists even more.

SEARCH AND SURVEILLANCE EQUIPMENT

The most basic item of search and surveillance equipment for the antiterrorist

Above Operators from Italy's COMSUBIN naval antiterrorist unit carry out an approach to a building prior to an assault with their HK MP5 MSGs at the ready—note the lights mounted and the holographic sights. (Marina Militare)

operator is normally a small folding mirror that can be used to check around corners or doors or over windowsills. A more sophisticated version employs a pole mounted camera and sometimes a microphone, which may be thrust through doorways or over windowsills. When used by an entry team, some pole mounted cameras send their images to a small monitor mounted on the back of the point man who wields the pole. This enables other members of the team to see what's ahead and allows the point man to be ready to engage a threat should it emerge. Some pole mounted cameras employ fiber optics, which even allows them to be thrust under doors. An interesting recent development is the Tactical Mirror Sight,which employs a small folding mirror mounted in conjunction with an EOTech sight to allow an operator to thrust his carbine around a corner to check for the enemy and to effectively engage the enemy without ever having to expose himself.

Various other types of search and surveillance equipment may be employed based upon the tactical situation. Some units will place cameras and microphones around an incident site so that they may constantly monitor

Above An interesting innovation that allows operators to check around corners and engage without exposing themselves is the Tactical Mirror Sight, which is mated with an EOTech.

activity and so that the unit commander can see what is going on from all angles. Surveillance teams may also train parabolic microphones toward the incident site to gather intelligence. Laser microphones may be aimed at windows to pick up sound vibrations that may be understood. (Note that weather and other conditions can adversely affect laser microphones.) Frequently, operators will infiltrate near to or even into a building where hostages are being held to place surveillance microphones. Operators at the Nord Ost Theater incident in Moscow and at Prince's Gate among others placed clandestine microphones.

Infrared surveillance cameras may be installed as well. Using thermal imaging, terrorists and hostages may be observed at night. Skilled operators may even be able to sort out terrorists from hostages by the "cold" silhouette of the weapon against the "hot" silhouette of the terrorist. Some current systems using microwave radar may be used through walls, ceilings, or floors. These systems can also determine on which side of a wall a subject may be located as well as the composition of interior walls (i.e. where studs are located). Some of these systems, such as the Camero Xaver 400, weigh only 6.5 lb and may be easily carried and held against a wall—using two handles that are incorporated—by an operator.

GPS satellite tracking equipment may be used on suspected terrorist vehicles to track them and, perhaps, stop them before they perform an act of terrorism. GPS tracking may also be used on vehicles supplied to terrorists as part of negotiations during an incident. Many vehicles now have tracking systems built in that may be used should terrorists hijack a bus or truck with internal tracking.

Today, many antiterrorist units will have access to an array of drones carrying cameras and other surveillance devices and capable of infiltrating near a terrorist target quite unobtrusively where they can gather real time intelligence. Some such as the Sikorsky Dragon Warrior are mini VTOLs with a daylight camera, FLIR (Forward Looking Infrared), and a laser designator. Many countries offer some design of small UAV. The USA produces more than a dozen different types. Versions using pusher engines are available as are mini-helicopters. Some are even armed and may be used to take out a high-value terrorist target if acquired!

One reason that major antiterrorist units have technical specialists assigned is that computer and surveillance technology advance at such a rapid rate that it's difficult for operators who must train in so many other skills to stay current. The technical specialist can attend all of the high tech trade shows and carry out tests to determine which devices will provide the operators with the ability to locate the terrorists, divine their intent, then counter them.

VEHICLES

Antiterrorist units normally have an extensive fleet of specialized vehicles to fit different missions. Among these will normally be a group of fast sedans, normally of local manufacture if the country has an auto industry. Hence, German units are likely to have Mercedes, the British Rovers, the French Peugeots, etc. These vehicles will likely have police performance packages and sophisticated communications equipment and are designed to get operators to an incident scene as rapidly as possible. Units such as GIGN that use dogs will have vehicles suitable for transporting the animals as well. Teams that sometimes perform the VIP protection function will likely have one or more armored limos and possibly a CAT (Counter Assault Team) vehicle that will have a rear facing seat for a tail gunner, possibly a mount for a light machinegun, and other special features.

Teams will also have all-terrain SUV-type vehicles capable of hauling half a dozen or more operators plus basic equipment. In some cases, these vehicles will have high-performance packages and communications equipment and can replace the high-performance sedan.

Many teams will have a specialized SWAT (Special Weapons and Tactics) van that is configured to fit the team's needs. Although some SWAT vans may be used to transport operators, they are best suited for carrying the wide array of equipment likely to be needed to deal with an incident—breaching tools, including those needed for explosive breaching, communication equipment, surveillance equipment, extra weapons and ammunition, less lethal munitions, medical kits, winches, and so on. Some SWAT vans are equipped to operate as a mobile command center for the team leader. Others may be equipped to serve the negotiators.

Some teams also have one or more light armored vehicles to insert teams near to an active shooter or evacuate wounded citizens or operators under fire. Normally, these are wheeled rather than tracked vehicles and are of the armored car/APC (Armored Personnel Carrier) type. They may be armed with machineguns and often will have a ram that may be used to take down doors. Some are also equipped to insert CS gas.

In addition, major antiterrorist teams will also have one or more SUVs or vans fitted out with a ladder or ramp system that is designed to insert personnel directly into second- or third-story windows, buses, trains, or aircraft. The ladder/ramp kit will generally be installed on a heavy-duty SUV or van fitted with high-performance options. One of the most widely used systems can carry nine fully equipped operators ready for insertion.

Although many of these vehicles will be built within the unit's home country, two U.S. packages that are widely exported offer good examples of this type of system.

The MARS (Mobile Adjustable Ramp System) incorporates:

1) Perimeter Breach Ramp, comprising a 15-ft mechanically operated ramp
2) Evacuation Stairway consisting of a folding stairway that may be deployed in 30 seconds for use on aircraft or multistory buildings
3) Observer/Sniper Bench, which can carry a sniper and/or observer and may be adjusted to offer the best surveillance or shooting position.
4) Ladder Turret, which may be rotated to properly align a ladder for an assault
5) Tactical Ladder of either 8 ft or 12 ft, which may be quickly deployed to insert operators.

Above GIGN operators along with their ramped vehicle used for various types of assault. A helicopter of the type used by GIGN for insertions is overhead. (Gendarmerie Nationale)

The MARS system may incorporate armored panels to protect operators during an approach and may be fitted to an armored SUV or van to protect the driver against fire. The advantage of a vehicle system such as MARS is that it allows operators to be inserted for an assault very quickly above ground level. Another widely used system is RAID (Rescue, Access, Interdiction, Deployment), which incorporates the following features:

1) 3 Configurations—flat for an 8 or 12 ft elevation, Gooseneck for a level platform, or 18 ft fully elevated

2) RTS (Rear Tactical Step), which can be used for entry or exit from the ramp system but can also carry operators ready to jump off at some point during the approach.

3) Side Deployment Rail, which may be used for access to alleys or other confined areas.

4) SAS (Side Assault System), which can be configured to either side of the vehicle depending upon the tactical situation. Armor may be added to protect the operators.

The vehicle carrying either of these systems will likely be a 4x4, armored, with heavy-duty suspension. It will often have retractable running boards to allow operators to ride ready for a quick drop off.

HELICOPTERS

All antiterrorist units have helicopter support, though few have the helicopter assets as an integral part of the unit. Normally, there is a portion of the Army, Air Force, Naval, or Police air service that trains with the antiterrorist unit and is designated as their air support.

The most obvious mission for helicopters in antiterrorist ops is to move the unit from its base to the site of the incident. If operators are practicing an assault on a site and the situation turns bad, the helicopters can quickly return them to support those unit members left as an alert "Go Team." Most units, in fact, have helicopters on standby at the nearest air base for such movement. Some major units also have fixed wing transport aircraft available as well. However, helicopters serve myriad other purposes. After rescuing hostages, for example, helicopters can quickly move them to safety or to a medical facility. In many cases, special operations helicopters will not be used but instead medical evacuation choppers will be called in. However, if operating in a hostile environment, then the helicopters assigned to the antiterrorist unit may carry out an evacuation as well as extracting the operators.

Helicopters may also be used as part of the actual assault on a site. They can insert operators onto a roof or on nearby rooftops. Operators can fast rope directly onto the roof or balcony or other possible entry point. In MAT operations, helicopters can come in low behind the vessel to avoid detection, then flare up to allow operators to fast rope onto the deck to seize the ship. Since many of these assaults will take place at night, pilots must be skilled at flying using night vision goggles. In some cases, helicopters may be used to create a distraction by flying overhead or landing nearby.

Helicopters may also be used as a sniper platform. When carrying out the combat boarding of a ship, a support helicopter on each side with trained snipers can prevent crew members from engaging the operators who are fast roping onto deck. Helicopter-borne snipers may also be used against vehicles transporting terrorists or dangerous materials. In some situations, such as an incident in a high-rise building, snipers in helicopters may offer the best chance of taking out a terrorist without assault. Whether carrying snipers or not, helicopters offer an excellent source of intelligence. In MAT operations, for example, the helicopters carrying the snipers can also guide members of the assault team and warn them of possible dangers.

Above The Osprey aircraft has great potential for use by special operations and antiterrorist forces. (USAF)

In a hostile environment where operators must evacuate the area under fire, helicopters can provide fire support using an array of guns and rockets. Prior to an assault on a compound containing hostages, gun ships may also be used to eliminate guard towers, armored cars, and such like, or attack nearby barracks to keep troops from reinforcing guards during the actual rescue mission.

To perform these myriad missions and others, helicopters will have to be specially configured. Secure attachment points for fast roping must be rigged inside the helicopter and reinforced skids on which the operators stand just prior to fast roping must be incorporated. (Note: To keep the helicopter balanced, operators will fast rope from both sides of smaller helicopters simultaneously.) Specialized shooting seats or harnesses will be incorporated for helicopters that may carry snipers. Some special ops helicopters will also incorporate bench seats so that operators can ride along the side of the chopper ready to quickly deploy onto a rooftop or elsewhere. On the U.S. 160th SOAR (Special Operations Aviation Regiment) MJH-6 Little Birds, fold down bench seats are incorporated on each side for such usage.

Helicopters assigned for antiterrorist missions and other special ops, must be designed for flying at night and in adverse weather conditions. Their electronics will include FLIR (Forward Looking Infrared) and in some cases, warning radar to alert the crew if targeted my by enemy surface-to air-weapons. An Air Launched Expendable Countermeasures Dispenser may be incorporated to launch chaff or flares if a SAM launch is determined. Some larger special ops helicopters will be capable of being airily refueled for long- range missions.

The U.S. 160th SOAR uses three main types of helicopters. The two types of "Little BIrds," the MJH-6, for insertions of a small group of operators directly onto an objective and the AH-6 as a gunship armed with 7.62 mm Mini-Guns and, normally, 2.75-inch rockets. The AH-6 may also be armed with AGM-Hellfire missiles, .50 machineguns, or MK19 automatic grenade launchers. 160th SOAR Blackhawk helicopters include the MH-60K, which is a special ops utility chopper; the MH-60L, also known as a DAP (Direct Action Penetrator),which is designed to carry out fire missions or act as aerial gun support to other 160th SOAR helicopters using a 30mm chain gun and M134D Gatling Guns; and the MH47D or MH47E Chinook, which can carry a substantial number of operators. The MH47D is designated as an "Adverse Weather Cockpit" version and is designed to operate in severe weather conditions. The MH47D has various other features configured for anti-terrorism/special ops. For the CSAR (Combat Search and Rescue) mission it is fitted with the PLS (Personnel Locator System) for finding downed aircrews. It also employs the FRIES (Fast Rope, Insertion Extraction System) for inserting or extracting operators quickly. The MH47D incorporates an internal rescue hoist with 600-lb capacity to allow extraction of injured operators or others.

A U.S. aircraft that offers many options for the antiterrorist unit is the V-22 Osprey which can combine the functions of a transport helicopter and transport fixed wing aircraft using VTOL (Vertical Takeoff and Landing) technology. It can hover to insert or extract operators but can also fly at speeds much faster than a Blackhawk helicopter while carrying 24 operators plus crew. The Osprey also incorporates some armament for suppressing ground fire.

Many allied countries use some of the same basic helicopters as the 160th SOAR, though normally without the most sophisticated equipment. Others use their own choppers. The French use the Puma to insert operators and as a gunship. They also use the Cougar HUS (Hélicoptère d'Unité Spéciale) and the Gazelle. The Russians use the Mi-8 HIP as their heavy helicopter as well as other Russian models such as the Kamov Ka-52 gunship or versions of the Hind, which can function as a combined troop carrier and gunship

Just as the USA has the 160th SOAR other countries have specially trained helicopter units for antiterrorist and special ops mission. The French unit is the EHS (Escadrille Des Hélicoptères Spéciaux). This unit is assigned to COS, which is the French equivalent of the U.S. SOCOM (Special Operations Command). Italian special ops helicopters are within the 26th Helicopter Squadron. The RAF Special Forces Flight provides helicopter support for British antiterrorist units. Others include the Jordanian Special Operations Helicopter Squadron, Philippine 740th Combat Group, and Republic of Korea 259th Special Ops Squadron.

BOATS AND OTHER CRAFT

Practically every antiterrorist unit has some waterborne capability even if it does not have the MAT mission. Of course, units such as the SBS, DevGru, Delphin, and Commando Hubert will have a wider array of small special operations craft from which to choose. The smallest craft will be intended to insert a couple of operators soundlessly along a shore or river bank while the largest craft normally used by an antiterrorist unit will be able to carry a full team plus give fire support if needed.

The most basic boat used for special operations is probably the kayak. Those used for special operations are foldable with a skin that's over a wood, aluminum, or fiberglass frame. Hulls are usually of a coated synthetic fiber and decks of similar material or a cotton/hemp blend as with Kleppers. Although one usually thinks of operators paddling kayaks to their objective some are equipped with small motors. Among the manufacturers that have supplied boats for antiterrorist/special ops units are Klepper, Folbot, Long Haul, and Nautiraid. Kayaks may normally be transported in a couple of bags and are known for their extreme durability even in rough seas.

What can generically be called the CRRC (Combat Rubber Raiding Craft) may be the most widely used special ops craft among non-specialized combat swimmer units. Often known as "Zodiacs" from their best-known manufacturer, CRRCs are designed to be inflated in a couple of minutes from a foot pump, compressor, or $CO2$ tank. They may be launched from various types of vehicles, including specially equipped submarines or from the shore, or they may be dropped from helicopters or aircraft. U.S. Navy SEALs have experimented with driving them directly from or onto helicopters hovering with their tail gates just below water, though this techniques requires a great deal of training. CRRCs can cover quite a bit of sea quickly, often using a 40–55 horsepower two-stroke engine and carrying up to ten operators. For clandestine approach, oars may be used once close to the objective. Operationally, CRRCs normally carry six operators plus two coxswains, who may also be operators, plus equipment. Empty weight on a typical CRRC is around 320 lb, which allows a team to easily carry it ashore and camouflage it.

Slightly larger RHIBs (Rigid Hull Inflatable Boat) or RIBs (Rigid Inflatable Boat) may operate in heavier seas and attain a speed of up to 45 knots. The latest RHIB used by U.S. Naval Special Warfare personnel is powered by a 470 horsepower engine and has a 200 nautical mile range with the standard fuel load. The RHIB's shallow draft—just under 3 ft—allows it to be used close to the shore and for riverine operations in very shallow rivers. The RHIB can carry more

Above The U.S. Navy's Special Boat Teams have craft that can operate on rivers or close to the shore to insert SEALs on raiding or antiterrorist missions and support them with firepower. (USN)

personnel and can also have light weapons mounted for support. When modified for such insertions, it may be airdropped into the sea. The most widely used RHIB has an overall length of 36 ft as opposed to about 15.5 ft for a CRRC.

Even more sophisticated boats are just coming into service. The new Zodiac Hurricane MACH 2, for example, is capable of speeds of up to 60 knots and can carry 12 operators plus 2 pilots. Because of its high speed, it incorporates shock absorbing seats and other technology to make the ride smoother. Despite its 900 horsepower, provided by 3,300 horsepower outboard engines, the MACH 2 is surprisingly quiet.

The PBL (Patrol Boat Light), sometimes designated the Boston Whaler, is a 25-foot craft with a speed of 30 knots. It can mount .50 caliber or 7.62 mm machineguns. The foam core and fiberglass construction lends itself particularly well to special ops usage since it is so durable and survivable.

Among larger craft used for antiterrorist ops are those that fall into the type of the MkV SOC (Special Operations Craft). Designed to transport 5 crew members plus 16 operators, the MkV can travel at up to 50 nautical miles per hour and has a range of 500–600 miles. The MkV may be used to get operators close to their objective, then launch them in CRRCs, of which it can carry four. The MkV has a ramp that allows the craft to ride directly onto the boat during a quick extraction. A MkV SOC may be transported by a large aircraft such as a C-5 or aboard the deck of a larger ship. The MkV may be fitted with an array of sophisticated electronics and communication equipment and has five mounting points for weapons. These mounting points may be used for a combo of M-2 .50

caliber heavy MGs, M240 7.62 mm MGs, M60 7.62 mm MGs, or Mk19 40 mm automatic grenade launchers. The MkV SOC is very fast and also harder to track than many fast boats, which makes it effective for operations close to the coast.

Specialist combat swimmer units with MAT missions may also use a swimmer delivery system such as the U.S. Navy's SDV (SEAL/Swimmer Delivery System) or ASDS (Advanced Seal Delivery System). Designed to silently let combat swimmers approach an objective underwater after launch from a submerged submarine, the MkVIII SDV (SEAL/Swimmer Delivery System), forerunner to the ASDS, has an onboard breathing system with masks containing communication equipment so that operators can talk with each other while aboard the vehicle. The Mk VIII also has a sophisticated Doppler navigation system that allows operators to steer to their objective quite precisely while submerged. The MkVIII will carry six operators at a depth of up to 500 ft at twice the speed of a skilled combat swimmer. The MkVIII is what is termed a "wet system," meaning that the operators are still exposed to the water while riding the SDV. The current generation ASDS, on the other hand, is actually a mini-submarine that allows the combat swimmers to stay dry during transport. The

Above A combat swimmer from Italy's COM-SUBIN prepares to engage a target with his Colt carbine as he comes ashore. (Marina Militare)

Above A GIGN operator in full combat swimmer gear. (Gendarmerie Nationale)

Russians have their own swimmer delivery systems as do a few other countries. Some U.S. allies have purchased systems from the U.S. including some of the predecessor SDVs to the MkVIII. The term SDV designating "Swimmer Delivery Vehicle" has become somewhat generic and many countries make variations. Among those producing some type of underwater transport for combat swimmers are: Croatia (the Velebit midget sub), Germany (the Orca), Italy (Chariot, used by COMSUBIN but also combat divers in India, Argentina, and Egypt among others), and Russia (the Protei-5 single swimmer vehicle). Various countries also make mini-submarines for use by combat special ops personnel.

It should be mentioned that combat swimmers or antiterrorist unit divers will use a SCUBA system for approaches involving a relatively long swim underwater, though they are also trained to use snorkels, which limit their depth to just below the surface. Most antiterrorist/special ops swimmers will use closed circuit SCUBA gear that does not give off bubbles that may identify the position of the swimmer. Widely used around the world is the Austrian Draeger closed-circuit system. Using mixed gases, this system recycles the "air" after the diver breathes out to scrub the CO_2 from it so it may be reused. Using a closed circuit system a trained diver may remain submerged without detection for up to four hours. Note that there are rebreather systems designed for shallow water and those for deeper waters. Units operating primarily in lakes or rivers will likely choose the shallower water systems.

Above U.S. Navy combat swimmers leave a submarine aboard an SDV (SEAL delivery vehicle). (USN)

Weapons and Equipment

Other rebreathers for deep operations are very sophisticated and may include an electronic controlled mixed gas system as well as a buoyancy control system. The Stealth Divex used by the SBS is a good example of deep rebreather systems usable to a depth of 100 meters.

Special submersible headsets are available for combat swimmers, which may be used while approaching the shore or once the operation begins.

Units may well have other forms of transport for insertion of operators over the water. The Subskimmer, which can operate as a fast surface craft or operate submerged, offers versatility for some units. Other units have used the Jet Ski as a method to quickly insert operators onto a shore. Virtually any type of transport that can be used to insert an operator onto a shoreline or target vessel has probably been tested by one or more units.

Chapter VI

Missions and Tactics

Although antiterrorist units train constantly for a wide range of hostage rescue or terrorist scenarios, months or even years may go by between incidents where their skills are called upon. Units used to carry out arrests of dangerous felons or military units that are deployed on terrorist hunts in Afghanistan or Iraq see more action and hence hone their skills. Real world deployments as well as realistic training teach operators to remain flexible in tactics so they can quickly adjust to an unfolding incident. Although each incident will differ, there are some basic precepts that will normally apply. Knowledge of these basic precepts and tactics is important to understand how antiterrorist units operate.

Hostage Rescue

The primary mission for the antiterrorist unit is hostage rescue. Some units only have the mission of rescuing hostages within their national territory while others will be tasked to rescue their citizens anywhere in the world. In some cases, too, the responsibility for specific types of hostage rescue may be divided among multiple units. In many countries, for example, the rescue of hostages at sea falls to naval or marine special forces. A few countries also grant responsibility for rescues aboard hijacked airliners to special forces drawn from the Air Force. In any case, though, there are basic precepts that apply to most hostage rescue operations. These will be discussed below, along with tactics for specific situations.

In the earliest stages of a hostage incident, the antiterrorist unit wants to establish a secure perimeter to keep the terrorists contained and to prevent them from being reinforced by additional terrorists. As was shown at Beslan, it can be highly critical to keep family members or others from getting too near the incident site as well. Generally, operators will not be used to establish the perimeter. That mission will rest with police or military personnel.

Above GROM Operators practice entering windows using other operators for assistance or by free climbing. (GROM.mil.pl)

The antiterrorist unit will begin to gather information about the site, the terrorists, and the hostages as early as possible to enable them to begin planning a rescue. Normally, too, a portion of the unit will be designated as a "Go Team," which will be responsible for developing a plan to carry out a rapid entry should the terrorists begin executing hostages. The "Go Plan" will not be particularly sophisticated but will offer some chance of saving a portion of the hostages. As more intelligence is gained, the Go Plan will evolve until eventually it becomes a final entry plan.

Intelligence may be gained from a wide variety of sources. Freed hostages, for example, offer invaluable insight into the terrorists' mood, weapons, location, and state of mind. Family members of hostages, co-workers, friends, and others can offer useful information about the hostages such as medical problems that may affect their ability to survive an assault. For example, the presence of small babies, or hostages with severe heart problems can weigh against using stun grenades. Blueprints of a building or aircraft, train, bus, or ship diagrams can aid the hostage rescue team in planning an assault. Members of the unit's intelligence unit will also begin searching for a site where an assault can be rehearsed. If the incident is taking place in an apartment building, factory, office, or theater, one that is relatively close and was designed to the same plan will be chosen. The availability of buses, aircraft, trains, or subway cars of the same type can also normally be arranged.

Above A Lithuanian ARAS sniper/observer team in position on a rooftop. The rifles appear to be the PGM UR. (Lithuanian Ministry of the Interior)

Snipers/observers will have been positioned early in the incident and will feed information to the command center. If the number of terrorists is low, snipers may also be on alert for a "green light": to take them out should all terrorists be in the crosshairs simultaneously. Unit surveillance experts will have attempted to place listening devices and other types of surveillance systems to gather intelligence about terrorist locations and intent. Obviously, having operators or intelligence experts who speak the language of the terrorists and hostages is important for gleaning information. In the case of some Islamic terrorist groups such as the Chechens at Nord Ost and Beslan, analysts will be very alert to signs that the terrorists may be preparing to die or execute the hostages. The chanting of certain prayers may be an indicator. Other acts such as separating certain hostages and hooding them may indicate that they are about to be executed. Intelligence analysts from the unit will also evaluate previous incidents in which members of the terrorist group have been involved to determine whether they are dealing with a group likely to kill hostages and then fight to the death or with a group known to negotiate for a compromise.

Speaking of negotiations, hostage negotiators will attempt to establish contact with the terrorists as early as possible. The primary objective of a negotiator is to end a hostage incident without loss of life by convincing the terrorists to lay down their weapons and release the hostages. However, if this is not possible, the negotiator will attempt to buy time for the assault teams to practice and prepare to "go in." Skilled negotiators may also be able to convince terrorists to release some of the hostages (i.e. children, those who are sick, pregnant women, and such like). In some cases, they will make minor concessions such as turning on the air conditioning in exchange for the release of some hostages. Often, though, the negotiator will attempt to convince the terrorists that it will be easier for them to control fewer hostages or it will show their good faith if they release some hostages. Hostages who are released can then provide intelligence experts with very useful information. They also reduce the number of hostages for whom the rescuers must account during an entry.

Above Operators from Czech URNA prepare to clear a room by entering from both sides of the door. (Czech Republic Ministry of the Interior)

Above A four-man team of Italy's NOCS simultaneously rappels down the side of a building while operators already on the ground give them cover. (Polizia di Stato)

One style of negotiating is to wear terrorists down over trivia. If they ask for fast food to be sent in, for example, the negotiator will ask which type, which condiments, which side dishes, and so on, and discuss them. This establishes a certain amount of empathy, but may also calm the terrorists as they are required to make decisions about mundane things.

As the negotiator talks with the terrorists, he or she must be skilled in gaining intelligence from the conversations and in gauging the mood of the terrorists. Note the words "he or she" in the previous sentence. There may be circumstances where a female negotiator will be an advantage while in others only a male negotiator will be able to establish the correct relationship.

A good negotiator will normally not give direct answers to demands as he will have to "refer that to my superiors." One of the most important jobs of the skilled negotiator is to alert the assault teams if he believes the incident will not be negotiated out and that the terrorists are preparing to kill hostages. (Note: even when negotiators are trained members of the antiterrorist unit, SOP (Standard

Operating Procedure) is normally not to let them actually see the entry teams preparing to go in, in case some slight change in their voice or manner might give the terrorists a warning. On the other hand, skilled negotiators can keep a terrorist leader occupied on the phone as the assault team goes in, lengthening his reaction time to give orders and giving the operators a few more seconds. This was the case with the negotiator at Prince's Gate.

Specific tactics for dealing with different types of hostage situation will be discussed below, but units normally employ certain basic tactics for most incidents. Operators will be organized into teams usually of between four and seven, with the five-operator team being quite common. These teams will have trained intensively to carry out an entry of a building or onto a form of public transport. Their moves will be choreographed and they will have practiced their movements so they do not cross each other's lines of fire.

For building entries, the "point man" will often be armed with a handgun so that he can hold a mirror, a pole camera, or a ballistic shield in his support hand. The second operator in a "stack" will be the primary shooter and will normally be armed with a submachinegun or carbine so that he can fire over the shoulder of the point man if a threat emerges. Once the initial members of the team have effected entry, the remainder of the stack, with the exception of the rear security man (the "tailgunner"), will follow them into the room to secure it and prepare to move on. On many teams, the rear security man is also the breacher who will use a shotgun to blow off hinges or locks or will swing a sledge. Once the door is breached he will stand aside and cover the rear of the rest of the team. If the operators are clearing rooms along a hallway, he will stay in the hallway to cover them as they emerge to move onto other rooms. As soon as a room is secured by the entry team, well-trained teams will move through it to carry out an entry on the next room.

Many units will also incorporate a follow-up team, which will take charge of any captured terrorists and help secure and evacuate any hostages encountered by the entry teams.

Operators may initially approach the site where they will carry out an entry using stealth and will only "go dynamic" at the moment when everyone is ready to carry out the entry or when they are compromised. Often, an explosive entry will be carried out after the team has gotten into position using a stealth approach. Diversions may also be incorporated such as the arrival of an ambulance with sirens blaring or something else transpiring on the side away from the intended point of entry.

When carrying out rescue missions that are complex, due to the number of hostages, the size of the building, or the complexity of the entry, operators will almost always effect entries from multiple points. Communication must be good and care must taken, however, that operators are aware of each other and do not engage each other during the chaos that can ensue. One reason that many units wear black "ninja suits" or other distinctive attire is so that other operators can instantly identify them. The "men in black" with helmets and masks also offer a certain intimidation factor to their targets.

Prior to entering a room, operators may deploy stun grenades or tear gas. In

Above Members of GSG9 ready to carry out a simultaneous entry on two stories of a building. (BGS)

the fast-paced milieu of a hostage rescue operation anything that can gain a few seconds may well save lives. Just prior to an entry the power may be cut to a building to give the operators the advantage of using NVGs.

Snipers will have been deployed to provide intelligence or to take out threats that present themselves. In some cases, the actual entry will be "sniper initiated" as the sniper or snipers eliminate terrorist lookouts. Snipers will continue to watch for terrorists who present themselves or who may attempt to escape. In some cases when the sniping distances are relatively close, shooters may be equipped with suppressed submachineguns or certain types of suppressed rifles for the quiet elimination of lights or terrorist sentries. Operators may also be equipped with suppressed weapons to make it more difficult for terrorists within a structure to hear their initial shots.

Once the shooting starts, terrorists holding hostages in other parts of a building may well be alerted that an assault is underway and may start killing hostages. If another entry team can be ready to go in through a window, wall, or ceiling at this point to take out the terrorists the chances of saving the hostages are much higher. Obviously, though, intelligence about where the hostages are being held is very important. Although the rescue

Above An LAPD SWAT sniper prepared to give sniper cover from a helicopter. (LAPD)

team must beware of booby traps or hidden terrorists, they must still move as quickly toward the points where hostages are being held.

In an active shooter scenario such as gunmen at a school, the rule followed by most antiterrorist teams is to move toward the sound of the gunfire. If they encounter wounded or injured civilians they leave them for follow-up teams with medical personnel attached. The team must get to the shooters as quickly as possible and neutralize them. That is the highest priority.

Above Operators from Spain's GEO hone their rappeling skills. (Policia Nacional)

In the sections below, specialized tactics used by antiterrorist units for assaulting different types of building and modes of transport will be discussed.

BUILDINGS

When dealing with a hostage incident in a building, one of the first considerations is the number of stories in the building. As soon as possible rescue personnel will also want to determine to the best of their ability the number of hostages and terrorists and their location or locations within the building.

As soon as the incident is known, the first law enforcement or military personnel on the scene should set up a perimeter to keep the public and press as far from the incident site as possible. One of the initial mistakes made by German officials during the Munich Olympic massacre was not securing the area around the dormitory where the Israeli athletes were held. As a result, crowds in their thousands were allowed to congregate quite close or to observe from nearby dormitories. Not only did this expose a large number of people to possible gunfire, but it also allowed possible sympathizers to observe the area and relay intelligence about actions of the police or military to the terrorists. Camera crews were allowed to get close enough to film the police infiltrating over the roof for a potential rescue. Of course, the terrorists were watching the entire rescue unfold on television and took action to counter the rescue.

At the Beslan School siege, there were so many local residents, many of them family members of hostages, surrounding the school that Russian security personnel never did get complete control of the scene. As a result, drunken bystanders taunted and fired weapons at the terrorists. Even as the operators from Alpha and Vympel went in for the rescue, firing from the crowd meant that they had to fear being shot in the back.

On the other hand, during the siege of the Japanese Ambassador's residence in Lima, Peru, a secure perimeter was established. As a result, Peruvian security personnel were able to dig a series of tunnels into the compound and under the residence to allow the operators to get into position prior to the rescue. Had a very secure perimeter not been established this extensive digging operation might have been compromised.

To prevent terrorists from receiving communications from accomplices on the outside, these days an electronic perimeter is normally established as well as a physical one. Within the perimeter, cell phones are blocked, as are television reception and computers.

Once the perimeter has been established and operators arrive on the scene, one of the first steps is to establish a "Go Plan"—what the SAS calls an IA (Immediate Action) Plan. Designed for use should the terrorists start killing hostages, the Go Plan is usually simple—along the lines of "Run Fast, Break Doors, Shoot Bad Guys!" Go Plans are not likely to save all of the hostages because they are not as refined as final rescue plans. They may, however, keep all of the hostages from being executed. Normally, as an incident progresses, the Go Plan will evolve, often eventually becoming the actual rescue plan. Sometimes, too, circumstances will dictate that the Go Plan will have to replace the more detailed rescue plan. At Beslan, for example, most of the Alpha operators who were to be tasked with the entry were at another location practicing their entry tactics when explosive devices planted by the terrorists reportedly exploded causing them to begin killing hostages. As a result, the members of Alpha and Vympel who were manning the close perimeter and who were tasked with carrying out a Go Plan had to quickly enter and attempt to save as many hostages as possible. Alpha members practicing the more sophisticated entry plan, meanwhile, were quickly helicoptered back and followed the initial operators in.

Very early on, too, sniper/observer teams will be placed to support future actions and gather intelligence. When the U.S. Delta Force carried out the rescue of Kurt Muse from a prison in Panama, Delta snipers infiltrated to shooting positions the day before in civilian clothes. Others infiltrated to the hills above the prison. They continued to rely on intelligence about the activities of guards and when the actual rescue started they eliminated guards and took out the prison's electrical system with rounds from a .50 sniper rifle.

To aid in communication between the snipers and other personnel, a system of identifying points on the building will be used. A standard one widely used by antiterrorist units is to identify each of the four sides of the building with a color. Each floor will then be identified with a number. For example, "1" for the first floor, "2" for the second floor, and so. If there is a basement with visible windows it might be "0." Windows and doors are also identified with numbers usually from left to right. As a result, the sniper might whisper into his radio, "Tango, white, 3, 3" indicating a terrorist is visible at the front of the building on the third floor in the third window from the left."

Normally, an attempt to establish contact and begin negotiations will begin as soon as possible. Negotiators try to establish a rapport with the terrorists and if possible negotiate a peaceful solution to the incident. They will also attempt to gauge the mood of the terrorists and gather intelligence from things said and things heard in the background. By stretching out the negotiations, it is hoped that some degree of affinity will develop between terrorists and hostages—the "Stockholm Syndrome"—which will make it less likely that the terrorists will execute the hostages. By stretching out negotiations, the negotiator also buys the operators time to prepare a rescue. An absolutely critical skill for any negotiator is to be able to judge whether it appears that negotiations will not work and to be willing to pass the word that an assault is going to be necessary. In some recent incidents, particularly the Beslan School siege, it became apparent that the terrorists really did not have serious demands. They just wanted to create a massive incident and kill a large number of hostages. This has been a signature of incidents carried out by Chechen terrorists. Occasionally, "negotiations" can proceed in a more "indirect" manner. When Kurt Muse was being held in Panama, a soldier was stationed outside his cell with orders to kill him if a rescue attempt was made. As a result, shortly before Delta launched their rescue, a U.S. military officer visited Muse and in a loud voice likely to be heard by guards and picked up by microphones informed Muse (and anyone listening) that should Muse be killed no Panamanian would leave the prison alive! Ultimatum or negotiation with guards?

Unit intelligence specialists will begin to gather information about the site, terrorists, and hostages as soon as possible. Freed hostages may be a good source of information about the terrorists, their weapons, their mood, their positions in the building, the presence of explosives, and the identity and state of other hostages. Normally, intelligence specialists try to interview freed hostages immediately upon release to capitalize on fresh information they may bring. If the incident drags on, they may re-interview released hostages to see if they remember other details once they have calmed down. Hostages who have been held for awhile will usually have more information than those released almost immediately. During the siege at the Japanese Ambassador's residence in Lima, Peru, for example, a large number of hostages were released after 17 days and gave intelligence personnel a great deal of useful information.

Electronic intelligence gathering methods may be used to gain real time intelligence about the terrorists. At Prince's Gate listening devices had been placed and proved useful. During the Nord Ost Theater siege in Moscow, FSB operators infiltrated into the basement and placed listening devices. (Note that at the Beslan School siege the terrorists had learned from Nord Ost and blew holes in the school's floors to make movement to place devices difficult.) One of the best sources of intelligence at Nord Ost was an FSB agent who was attending the performance and was allowed to keep his cell phone. He gave the FSB constant updates about the locations of the terrorists and the explosives. The listening devices at Nord Ost alerted FSB intelligence specialists when some of the female suicide bombers and other terrorists started chanting prayers, which seemed to be a forerunner to killing the hostages. This galvanized the Alpha rescue team to prepare for its entry.

During the siege at the Japanese Ambassador's residence in Lima, communication devices were actually smuggled in to some of the military officers held hostage. These were used to communicate with the rescue planners throughout the siege and also to warn hostages when the assault was coming in.

Myriad other sources of intelligence will be tapped prior to a rescue. Those who work in the building will be questioned about entrances, air conditioning ducts, sewers, stairways, and various other aspects of the building that may be useful. Just knowing what type of glass is used in windows, the composition of exterior and interior walls, which way doors open, and locations of surveillance cameras can prove invaluable. Often, the local fire department will have building plans and possibly video tapes of the building that may be used in planning a rescue. Antiterrorist units also frequently carry out threat assessments at embassies, public buildings, national monuments, and other high risk locations and have videotape and diagrams on file. Units may well have practiced at the site for a rescue.

Ever since the massacre at the 1972 Munich Olympics, antiterrorist teams have planned how to deal with incidents at Olympic Games very carefully. The Chinese Snow Wolf Commando Unit (AKA Snow Leopard Commando Unit), for example, trained extensively on every venue being built for the Beijing Olympics. This has been the case at every Olympics over the last 30 or more years. Some units have gone so far as to pre-mark with coded symbols the positions for placing explosives to allow an explosive entry on some venues.

Psychologists trained in analyzing terrorist behavior may provide useful intelligence about what to expect from the terrorists. Prior to the Munich Olympics, one psychologist virtually predicted the likelihood of Israeli athletes being taken hostage, but Munich Olympic officials did not want to consider such a negative scenario!

As intelligence comes in from all of these possible sources including negotiators and sniper/observer teams, the Go Plan will evolve into a rescue plan. Operators will have found a building as similar as possible to the one where the siege is taking place. At the Nord Ost Theater siege, for example, Alpha practiced on another Moscow Theater built to the same plan. Highly trained Vympel operators acted as the terrorists during the practice assault.

Using the intelligence gathered, the team will begin creating an approach and entry plan. If a stealth approach is possible that is normally the best option as it delays the instant when the terrorists will realize an entry is under way. Darkness is the friend of operators carrying out a stealth approach, one reason that so many units wear black utilities and gear. Terrain around the building will be analyzed to determine if ditches, wooded areas, even rivers offer a route of clandestine approach. In some cases, gaining entry to buildings next door to the target one will allow operators to get close and prepare for a rescue.

Some special operations helicopters are designed to operate very quietly due to carefully balanced rotors and mufflers on the engines. It may be possible for these helicopters to deposit operators directly on the roof of the target building. Louder helicopters landing nearby may be used to cover the helicopter hovering to allow operators to fast rope onto the roof. U.S. operators train to be inserted directly from benches on the sides of 160th SOAR Little Bird helicopters that hover just above a roof. This method was used in Panama to insert operators onto the prison roof during the rescue of Kurt Muse.

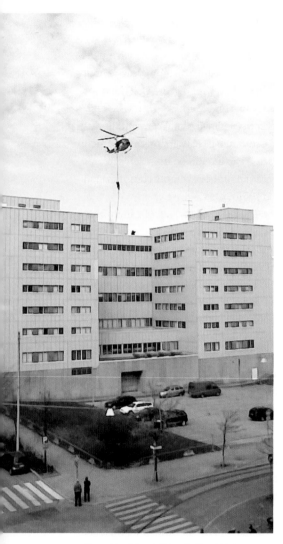

Above Members of Finland's Bear Unit fast rope to the top of a building prior to an assault. (Helsinki Police)

Often, to cover an approach, the ambient sound level around the area will be raised. When the Italian NOCS unit rescued Brigadier General James Dozier from the Red Brigades in 1982 they had road construction crews operating loudly in the area. During the Prince's Gate siege, aircraft on approach to Heathrow were brought in over the area of the Iranian Embassy at a lower level than usual to cover the sound of any movements. Around the Japanese Ambassador's residence in Lima, loud martial music was played to cover the sounds of digging.

As part of a stealth approach, it may be necessary to eliminate guard dogs or sentries with suppressed weapons. Lights may also need to be shot out with a suppressed weapon. In some cases, the power to the building may be cut to plunge it into darkness. The downside of this ploy is that it alerts the terrorists that something is happening. If the power is to be cut, it is better if it is done just as the entry begins to give the operators the advantages of their NVGs. Once a dynamic entry does begin, operators will throw in stun grenades, blow holes in walls, detonate frame charges on doors or windows, quickly accelerate towards the building on vehicles carrying ramps or ladders—whatever it takes to get shooters into position to neutralize terrorists and protect hostages.

Part of the preplanning is making sure the correct equipment is available and working. Proper frame charges or charges for breaching walls, roofs, or floors must be prepared. Unit explosive experts may also carry LINEX, which may be fashioned into a breaching charge on the scene. Proper rappel ropes must be prepared for building descents. Fence climbers or other special climbing gear should be prepared, and any necessary breaching gear should be allotted to breachers going in as part of the entry teams.

Operators must also determine which weapons are the best choice for the operation. For example, if the terrorists are known to be wearing body armor then rifle caliber carbines or other weapons that can punch through body armor must be used. During the Lima rescue, it was known that some of the terrorists were wearing body armor; hence, some operators carried FN P90 SMGs loaded with 5.7x28 mm AP (Armor Piercing) ammunition to deal with this problem. M4 carbines loaded with AP ammo may be chosen in some circumstances as well. In other scenarios, the possibility of hostages being held in multiple rooms nearby where overpenetration of bullets could be an issue might dictate the use of pistol caliber SMGs or handguns loaded with expanding ammunition. Operations where there may be large amounts of steel, as in a factory containing machines, might also indicate the need for frangible ammunition to limit ricochet. A rescue carried out around chemicals or flammable gases would indicate the need for suppressed weapons to limit muzzle flash, which might cause an explosion or fire. Approaches through sewers normally dictate suppressed weapons for the same reason.

An important consideration is the number of operators that will be required to carry out a successful rescue. Planners must allow for operators running into unforeseen problems, being injured, becoming engaged in a fire fight that ties them down, and so on. As a result, a reserve will usually be built into the assault force. For the assault on the Japanese Ambassador's residence in Lima, Peruvian special ops deployed 140 operators. Given the size of the residence, the fact that terrorists were holding 72 hostages in various locations, and the presence of 14 terrorists plus the complexity of the plan—which involved operators approaching through tunnels and carrying out explosive entries through the building's floors as well as other operators coming in through the gate—140 is not an excessive number. Despite the complexity of the operation, only one hostage was killed along with three operators. All of the terrorists were killed and the rest of the hostages were rescued, though some were wounded.

By practicing on a building as similar as possible to the one being assaulted, operators can anticipate many of the problems they will encounter, but not all. At Prince's Gate, the SAS encountered a wall its intelligence had not indicated was there. Well-trained operators, however, are used to scenario training in which the "intelligence" is faulty, thus requiring them to quickly improvise. No matter what obstacles are encountered, the primary mission of antiterrorist operators is to move toward the sound of the guns and the location of the hostages. Sometimes, too, during the practice for an assault, operators will determine a major flaw in the rescue plan and it will have to be adjusted.

As was shown during the Beslan School siege, finding a building that most closely duplicates the incident site but is at some distance may be a disadvantage. At the point when an entry was required at Beslan. most of the Alpha operators tasked with the rescue were practicing some distance away, which delayed their arrival on the scene. In some cases, to keep the rescue team close by, it may be preferable to find a large parking lot or park area that is close by but out of sight of the terrorists. The building may then be recreated by chalking lines on the parking lot or setting up tape. This is not an optimum solution, but it does keep the rescue team close by. It can also be an advantage for smaller countries, the entire antiterrorist force of which may have fewer than 50 operators, with not enough to constitute a "Go Team" as well as a rescue team to be practicing far from the scene.

Once the rescue has been planned and rehearsed and operators have checked their equipment and their routes, the time for the assault must be determined. Generally, very early in the morning when terrorists will be least alert is considered a good option. However, intelligence may indicate that at a certain time, many of the terrorists gather at one point in the building ,as was the case during the Lima rescue. Therefore, the chance to neutralize a good portion of the terrorists at once makes that a desirable time to strike. In some cases, the rescue has to go in because there are indications that the terrorists are about to kill hostages. Snipers sometimes determine when the assault will go in as well. If they have multiple terrorists in their crosshairs and can cut the odds against the entry team by taking them out that may convince the team leader to give the "Execute, Execute, Execute!" order.

Generally, antiterrorist teams plan entries from multiple locations. When terrorists have separated hostages and hold them at multiple locations within the building, multiple entry points are a virtual necessity. Multiple entry points also allow operators to get to hostages quickly using an alternate route should one group run into problems at their entry point. Since terrorists will often occupy upper floors or hold the hostages on upper floors, units practice entries on upper stories extensively.

Various techniques may be used to reach upper stories. Entries may also take place on upper stories even if terrorists and hostages are on lower stories because of the advantages gained by helicopter insertion onto the roof. When Delta carried out the rescue of Kurt Muse in Panama, they landed

Building Entry – Multiple Points
In this illustration of a building entry from multiple points, it is assumed that the hostages are held in the upstairs room; hence, two operators rappel down to neutralize the terrorists with the hostages by shooting through the window. On the ground floor the breacher is ready to hit the door with a ram, while the rest of the entry team is stacked ready to storm in as soon as the door is breached.

Above Members of Austria's MPs engage targets as they rappel through windows. (Osterreichs Bundesheer)

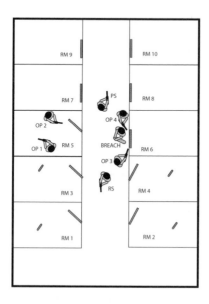

Rapid Hall Clearing Technique Illustrated is one technique used by operators to rapidly clear a hallway when checking for terrorists and hostages. A point security man (PS) moves ahead of the team to make sure a threat does not materialize ahead of them. A rear security man (RS) observes the area to the rear of the clearing teams to make sure a threat does not arise from that direction. Two teams of two operators (OP 1- OP 4) carry out the actual clearing while the breacher (BREACH) pops open the doors. Each team leapfrogs down the hall. As illustrated, the breacher has popped open the door of Room 5 and it is being cleared by Operators 1 and 2 (OP 1 and OP 2). As soon as they carried out their entry, he moved to pop the door of Room 6 (RM 6) where the team composed of Operators 3 and 4 (OP 3 and OP 4) have moved into entry position after clearing Room 4 (RM 4). Note that a green lightstick has been thrown into each room after clearing to show it has been secured.

on the roof, then did an explosive entry through a door and cleared down to the cell block eliminating any guards they encountered. During the Ma'alot School siege in Israel, Sayaret Matkal operators originally planned to enter the school via ladders as the children were being held on the second floor. However, terrorists threw grenades, which caused the operators to leap from the ladders to take cover. As a result, an alternate first floor assault through the doorway was quickly launched. Unfortunately, in clearing upward, operators missed the second floor where the terrorists held the children and went directly to the third floor. As a result, 18 children were killed (three more later died of wounds) and at least 50 more were wounded before the terrorists could be killed.

To reach the upper stories of a building various methods may be used. Most antiterrorist units practice free climbing on urban buildings, which may allow them to reach lower stories relatively quickly. Vehicles mounting ladders or ramps may also be used to quickly insert operators onto lower stories. More basically, operators carrying ladders may be used to gain entry. When coming down from the roof or a higher story, operators may clear down stairways as Delta did in Panama, but more often they will attempt entry from a window or balcony. Operators practice rappeling down the side of a building, then shooting through a window or crashing through to take the shot. They also practice shooting with their feet braced against the side of the building, braced against the windowsill as they enter, or after landing just inside a window. Some operators practice a variation on the Australian rappel, in which they come down the building head first, which allows them to peek into a room from above a window and, if feasible, take a shot from that position. Some European teams practice a technique based on the wide windows with shutters or large windows that open inward. Operators swing out as they rappel and crash through the windows or shutters feet first. As soon as they are in the room, they can then neutralize any terrorists. Normally, as they crash into the room they gain a few seconds from the surprise generated. During any of these entries from windows or balconies, stun grenades may be pitched in first to disorient the terrorists.

When the time comes to carry out the actual entry through doors, operators will normally form a "stack" of between four and six operators. For most external doors, they will line up along one wall as the breacher either blows the door with explosives or forces it with a ram or other entry tool. As soon as the door is breached, the breacher will move aside and the first two operators will quickly clear the doorway to avoid silhouetting themselves. Normally one will move to each side of the doorway and will engage any terrorists within their fields of fire. An imaginary line bisecting the room into two triangles is often used to delineate who looks where in the room. The imaginary line will also determine, to some extent, who shoots which terrorists to make sure all are engaged. By positioning themselves along the walls and with delineated fields of fire the chances of a "Blue on Blue" shooting are lessened as well.

If a room is large and contains a substantial number of hostages and terrorists, more operators may carry out the entry with at least two additional shooters following the first two into the room and along the walls. Too many shooters, however, can endanger the hostages and the operators. If the design of the building is such that one room leads into another, as soon as the first two operators secure the room, two more may move to the door to the next room to carry out another entry. Techniques will vary somewhat depending on the units, the floor plan of the building, and the location of the hostages.

When a building contains a hallway or hallways that must be cleared, one method is to approach a door, kick it in, pitch in a stun grenade, and shoot any terrorists encountered. This method is designed to be quick and dirty when many rooms must be cleared quickly. If the exact locations of the hostages are not known, the need to move quickly becomes even more imperative. However, when clearing a building it must also be borne in mind that the terrorists may have booby-trapped doors, floors, stairways, and so on. Operators must remain alert, therefore, while also moving quickly.

Because hostage rescue operations do require speed of movement and coordination among operators who may be carrying out entries from multiple points, communication is extremely important as operators must let each other know where they have encountered terrorists, whether booby traps have been discovered, whether hostages have been located and rescued, whether hostages are being evacuated and by what route, and where teams are in the building. Not only does good communication help operators carry out a difficult multifaceted plan but it also helps prevent them from shooting each other because they were taken by surprise. To help avoid Blue on Blue shootings, many teams wear some distinctive elements. Since when engaging a threat the eye is usually drawn to an opponent's weapon, some units put some distinctive element of color on the forearms of their carbines or SMGs. The black "Darth Vader" outfits worn by many antiterrorist units normally help make them recognizable to each other as well.

When stairways are encountered, operators will move up them as quickly as possible while covering upward as they move and secure landings. The larger the building, the more operators and the more entry points will be needed. It should be obvious, though, why intelligence about the location of the hostages is so critical. Once the hostages are rescued, then any terrorists hiding elsewhere in the building may be mopped up more deliberately. At Beslan, for example, operators spent hours clearing remaining terrorists barricaded in the basement.

Some members of the rescue team will be detailed to evacuate the hostages as soon as the direct threat of the terrorists has been removed. They will normally be rushed from the building as quickly as possible with operators watching to eliminate any terrorists who might attempt to take a shot at the fleeing hostages. At Beslan, terrorists were hanging out of windows shooting fleeing children; hence, Spetsnaz snipers found themselves having to give constant covering fire to fleeing hostages. Some Alpha and Vympel operators died while acting as human shields for the fleeing children.

In case terrorists may have hidden themselves among the hostages as happened at Prince's Gate and some other incidents, hostages will be secured and guarded until their identity can be sorted out. Of course, severely injured hostages will receive medical treatment.

Speedy medical treatment was especially necessary after Alpha used Fentanyl gas during the Nord Ost Theater siege. Although the gas did knock out most of the terrorists and prevent them detonating the massive explosive charges designed to bring down the theater, the lack of immediate medical treatment for hostages who had been gassed resulted in somewhere around 125 deaths. Given the large number of hostages and terrorists and the massive explosive charges, the decision to use Fentanyl was most likely a good one since, given that hostage incidents involving Chechen terrorists normally end badly, all of the hostages could have died. However, preplanning should have anticipated the need for ambulances and trained medical personnel to be readily available and to have the information about how to treat those exposed to the gas.

Building clearance is incredibly complex and it requires extensive training to choreograph the movements of multiple operators through a large building amidst smoke from stun grenades and the sound of gunfire. An overview has been given here of techniques, which will normally follow a basic pattern but will be adjusted to fit the specific situation and individual unit preferences.

AIRCRAFT

Although antiterror units must train in advance for all types of hostage incidents, this is even more of a necessity when dealing with a hijacked airliner. Units must take every opportunity to familiarize themselves with the types of aircraft used in their civilian and military fleets to transport passengers and freight as well as those types of airliners that fly into and out of their country under other national flags. They must also be familiar with private passenger jets that are widely used. Major units have mockups and in some cases actual fuselages of major aircraft types at their training facility. Normally, too, national units arrange with the airlines to train on actual jets when they are undergoing maintenance. Heads of security for major airlines are frequently veterans of national police units or military special ops units and hence will cooperate. Having access to the actual aircraft allows operators to learn where the various doors are located and how they open. It lets them practice approaches to learn where blind spots are beneath the aircraft, on wings, and so on. Airlines will often also allow them to do force-on-force training with Simunitions dye-marking cartridges aboard the aircraft.

Pre-planning and training for possible aircraft hijackings will also entail studying aircraft heights and obtaining ladders of the correct height to enter through aircraft doors. Today, major units have specialized assault vehicles with built-in ladders and ramps. They should have practiced so that they know in advance at what heights the ramps or ladders will need to be positioned to access different types of airliners. Some units, including the SAS, will send operators through simulator training on airliners so that they can fake being pilots to access the cockpit. If they actually have flight training that is even better. Other operators will learn how catering services work for aircraft or how ground crew operates—once again to gain knowledge that will allow them to get close to or board the aircraft. Units with female members may send some of them through

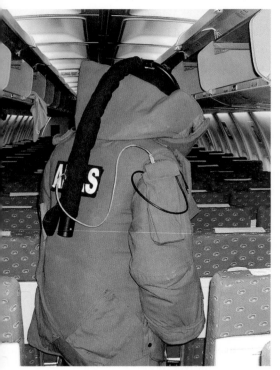

Above A member of Lithuania's ARAS antiterrorist unit checks an aircraft for explosive devices wearing full bomb search gear. (Lithuanian Ministry of the Interior)

training as cabin crew as terrorists will be less likely to suspect a woman in a stewardess outfit.

When a hijacking actually takes place it is most likely to happen while the aircraft is in the air. If there are air marshals aboard, whether from the antiterrorist unit or not, they may take action. If, however, the aircraft is taken over, the two major threats are that the hijackers will attempt to turn it into a flying bomb, as on 9/11, or that they will begin to kill hostages. If the plan is to turn the aircraft into a flying bomb and attempt to kill hundreds or even thousands and if the terrorists do not land for fuel, then shooting down the aircraft may become the final option, although some aircraft today do have special security features that can be implemented to prevent this scenario. Cockpits are much harder to access today and some pilots fly armed.

If, however, the plane lands, then an antiterrorist team has a chance to seize the aircraft to prevent its use as a flying bomb or to save the hostages. The primary problem faced by the antiterrorist unit is being in position to carry out an assault when the aircraft lands. If they are not in their own country, normally extensive negotiations will have to take place prior to permission being given to carry out an assault. Sometimes this will entail including members of the local police or military in the operation. This is an instance where friendly relations established during joint training will prove invaluable. Even so, permission may not be granted. In some cases, the aircraft may take off and land at another airport where negotiations to allow a rescue must again take place. If the aircraft does land where operators can carry out the assault, they will try to influence the location to where air traffic controllers taxi the aircraft. They will want it positioned in an optimum location for rescue, perhaps one where snipers and operators have already been secreted nearby.

Once an aircraft is on the ground, the antiterrorist team has to plan and carry out a three-step operation to successfully take down the hijacked aircraft: (1) the approach, (2) the entry, and (3) the assault.

If the aircraft has been taxied to a point where there is low ground beside the runway, buildings nearby, or brush or high grass growing along the side of the runway, operators may be able to get close to the plane before beginning their actual approach. Positions near the plane will offer the chance to gain intelligence as well. At Mogadishu, for example, GSG-9 operators observed the aircraft with NVGs from 30 meters away during the night and determined the location of two of the terrorists. The approach should make use of blind spots to the rear and beneath the aircraft. If a request has been made to service the aircraft or refuel it, operators can hide aboard service vehicles or pose as ground crew to get close. In some cases, operators may even gain access to the aircraft. The Israelis carried out the first successful rescue aboard a hijacked airliner in May 1972, against a Sabena aircraft using operators dressed as service crew. During the December 1994, hijacking of an Air France plane to Marseilles, GIGN operators posing as members of the service crew got aboard the aircraft and placed mini-cameras and listening devices, thus giving them excellent intelligence prior to the assault.

Often a distraction will be used to cover an approach, but it is more likely the distraction will occur just before the entry. If the hijackers are in contact with the tower and/or a negotiator, an attempt to keep them on the radio will help

Above GSG9 practicing the combat boarding of an aircraft; note that some operators crouch on the wing below the emergency exit while others are beneath the aircraft where they will not be seen. (BGS)

cover an approach. In some hijackings, terrorists have actually placed lookouts in the open door or on the ground to watch for an approach by rescuers. This makes a stealth approach very difficult and may dictate that visible terrorists be eliminated by snipers, possibly with suppressed weapons, to be followed by a ramped vehicle driving directly to the doorway to begin the assault. Note, too, that a contingency Go Plan will have been developed in case the hijackers start killing hostages. Normally a careful, stealthy approach will no longer be feasible at that point, and operators will try to board the aircraft and eliminate terrorists as quickly as possible.

If the team do manage to approach the aircraft through stealth and get into position, they will normally position themselves beneath the aircraft. GSG-9 first discovered that on many types of airliner there is a blind spot just below the emergency exit over the wing that allows two operators per side to crouch by that window/exit. If operators can infiltrate to that point they are ready to enter through the emergency exits. Care must be taken not to set up vibrations in the wing that may be noticed.

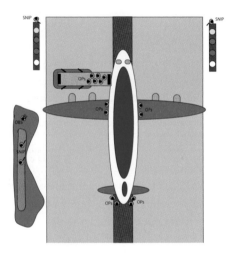

Once the actual entry begins speed becomes paramount. A classic example of the advantage of speed of entry and assault took place during the March 1991, hijacking of SIngapore Airlines Flight 117. Singapore's SAF stormed the aircraft killing all four hijackers and rescuing all crew and passengers within 30 seconds!

Aircraft takedowns require a substantial number of operators, too.

Aircraft Assault Illustrated is one possible scenario for taking down a hijacked aircraft. Snipers (SNIP) and observers (OBS) have been placed wherever cover is available near the aircraft. Operators (OPs) have infiltrated to positions at the rear of the aircraft to access rear doors and on the wings to access the emergency exit doors. Other operators are on the ramp of an assault vehicle ready to enter through the passenger door. The operators on the wings will normally do the initial entry and attempt to take out as many terrorists as possible while the team on the ramp gains entry. The operators at the rear doors will normally protect and remove the hostages as quickly as possible.

Above Members of Czech SOG prepare to do a practice aircraft boarding using two ladders, one for the assault team and one for the operator who will open the door. (Amada Ceske Republiky)

For example, when GIGN assaulted the hijacked Air France aircraft at Marseilles in December 1994, in addition to snipers and support personnel, GIGN deployed 25 operators beneath the aircraft and 15 on one of the airport's mobile stairways to carry out the initial assault.

Familiarity with an array of aircraft types becomes very important during the entry phase. Operators need to know the locations of all possible entry points as well as how to open them quickly. Knowledge of the height of wings from the ground will aid in climbing onto them and knowing the height of passenger doors and other doors will help in the selection of ladders and vehicle-mounted ramps or ladders. Just to give an example of the type of information needed in the team's database, possible entry points for popular airliners break down as follows: DC-10: 8; 727-200: 9;747-400: 11; 737-400: 8; and Airbus 380: up to 16.

When possible, a distraction to cover the entry is desirable. At Mogadishu, GSG-9 used a fire on the runway in front of the aircraft to draw the terrorists to the cockpit just prior to the entry. When GIGN responded to the hijacking of

Flight 8969 to Marseilles in December 1994, snipers were positioned with .50 sniper rifles to shoot into the cockpit if necessary. When the aircraft moved toward the control tower without permission and terrorists fired at the control tower, the snipers were given the green light to fire high into the cockpit to keep everyone's head down since they did not know the location of the flight crew. In addition to stopping the hostile actions on the part of the hijackers, these shots acted as a distraction and launched the entry.

Generally, entry will take place from multiple points. A possible scenario would be to place two operators on each wing to go in through the emergency exits, other operators on a vehicle ramp (which may be armored to protect them during approach) to enter through the passenger door, and still other operators to go in through a rear door, most likely to evacuate the hostages. If ladders are used for entry to passenger doors, most teams practice using two ladders—one for the operator opening the door and one for those who are actually entering.

Above Operators from Italy's GIS with their ramped vehicle, which can be used for aircraft assaults. (Carabinieri)

Once operators are successfully aboard the aircraft they will carry out their assault to clear the aircraft of threats as quickly as possible. When they go in over the wing through the emergency exits, they will normally be the first "shooters" on board and will attempt to neutralize as many of the terrorists as possible. Aircraft configured with one aisle are easier to clear than those with two aisles but teams practice for dealing with both. On a one-aisle aircraft, the 2 two-man teams coming in over the wing will normally split with one team clearing forward and one team clearing backward. With an aircraft with two aisles it is more important to get additional operators on quickly, though there are ways for four men to begin clearing with two aisles. One on each side can clear forward and one rearward or 1 two-man team can still clear forward and one rearward. They may have to engage terrorists across the heads of frightened passengers in this scenario, however. In either case, operators must yell at passengers to stay down. Even when passengers seem panicked, however, operators must listen to them as they may be attempting to identify a terrorist hidden among them.

Above GIGN operators pour onto an aircraft from the ramp of their assault vehicle. Note the operator in the foreground covering the assault team. (Gendarmerie Nationale)

GIGN and RAID practice using dogs for tubular assaults as on aircraft. GIGN teams have inserted the dogs through the emergency exit on the wing. Since the dogs are trained to attack anyone with a weapon they encounter they can be very effective once in the cabin. They move quickly along the floor or over seats, making very difficult targets, and give the operators following them in a few more seconds to get into action.

Follow-up operators will normally come in through the passenger door via their ramped assault vehicle and will engage any remaining terrorists as soon as they enter. Care must be taken, however, that they communicate with other operators already on the plane to prevent a Blue-on-Blue shooting. These follow-up operators may be the ones assigned to secure the cockpit since the passenger door may be right behind the cockpit door. GIGN and some other units practice using dogs with entry teams coming in through the passenger door as well.

Still other operators will normally enter through the rear and help control and remove passengers and also watch for additional hidden terrorists. Other operators on the ground will secure the hostages until they can be sorted out. Team medical personnel will usually be available to deal with wounded hostages or operators immediately.

Once the plane has been cleared and all crew, passengers, surviving terrorists, and operators are off, it will be checked for explosives. Hijackers will often either have placed explosives or claim to have explosives rigged on the aircraft. As a result, operators assaulting an aircraft must be aware of this. Generally, if there

Above While two members of Slovenia's Specalna Enota cover the aircraft cabin, other operators move down the aisles checking the passengers. (Slovenian National Police)

is any fear that the terrorists do have explosives, any terrorists encountered, even if no gun is visible, will be shot in the eye-nose triangle (some teams prefer the mouth or the area between nose and mouth) to prevent them detonating a device. The hijackers of the Lufthansa aircraft at Mogadishu had grenades and threw some of them, but they rolled under the aircraft seats, which cushioned much of the blast. The design of passenger aircraft is such that seats are likely to dissipate the effect of grenades, though they remain very dangerous.

The seats on an aircraft can also dissipate the effect of stun grenades. Or, should the grenade land among passengers and be confined to the space between seats, its effects will be magnified. Generally, too, the use of smoke or gas grenades aboard aircraft is not advised since terrorists and hostages will be so close to each other that operators will have enough trouble acquiring targets without the problems of a smoke-filled cabin. There is also a chance of fire in the confined space of an aircraft cabin with passengers dying from smoke inhalation before they can be removed. The Egyptian Unit 777 assault on a hijacked airliner in Malta in November 1985 is a perfect example of how not to carry out a rescue. Various factors contributed to the botched operation, including lack of familiarity with the 737 and the use of smoke grenades. During this "rescue" 57 hostages died.

Of course, the best rescue would be one in which an entry did not prove necessary. Although information has been scant about the incident, reportedly, an attempt to hijack an Aeroflot passenger plane was thwarted due to the fact that each passenger's seat was bugged with listening devices during the era of KGB omnipresence. Allegedly, by using these devices, operators were able to determine the locations of the terrorists and shoot them with full-jacketed rifle ammo through the fuselage of the aircraft!

TRAINS (UNDERGROUND AND CROSS COUNTRY)

There are so many miles of track crossing the continents of the world that terrorist sabotage is a constant threat to rail systems. Attacks on the London, Moscow, and Tokyo undergrounds by terrorists and planned attacks on the New York and other underground systems have shown the vulnerability of these systems to bombs, sabotage, and biological agents. Cross country trains have suffered terrorist attacks in India, Russia, and Spain among other countries, once again illustrating vulnerabilities. The derailing of a passenger train or an explosion aboard a packed train can create devastating loss of life. These are threats that security personnel must attempt to counter, normally with access control, surveillance systems, and vigilant security personnel and passengers.

For the antiterrorist unit, however, the primary concern is with the possibility of passengers aboard a train being taken hostage. In Japan alone, there are 22.2 billion journeys by trains every year. Japan's SAT must, therefore, put great stress on training to take down trains. The busiest underground system is Hong Kong's with 7 million passengers per day; hence, the SDU must be ready to take down a subway train if necessary. In virtually every country, operators train to assault a variety of types of train: cross-country passenger trains, cross-country freight trains carrying hazardous materials, underground commuter trains, urban trolley systems, elevated trains, and airport people mover trains.

Above Operators from Slovenia's Specialna Enota swarm aboard a train during assault training. (Slovenian National Police)

Antiterrorist operators plan for and rehearse rescues on all of these types of transport, using "war game" scenarios that simulate a worst case scenario on the assumption that if they can develop tactics for the worst case, they should be prepared for lesser incidents. For example, what would a unit do if the Eurostar Train were hijacked and stopped beneath the North Sea? The SAS and GIGN have planned for such a scenario.

In many scenarios, terrorists who seize a train will stop it in a location that they feel offers them the best security against an assault by antiterrorist operators. By stopping a train on a railway bridge above a river or in an underground tunnel, for example, terrorists can make a rescue far more difficult. Perhaps the best-known hostage incident aboard a train took place in 1977 at De Punt in Holland, where South Moluccan terrorists held hostages aboard a train for weeks. If the terrorists do not choose to stop the train but instead try to keep it moving, then it will be necessary to stop it, preferably at a point that lends itself to a rescue operation. In the past the SAS and other units have been trained to board moving trains by leaping to car tops from overpasses or using other methods. Reportedly, operators have been killed or injured practicing these techniques.

Since train routes are predetermined by the track system, if it is necessary to stop a hijacked train plans can be made to divert it onto a siding, which offers a relatively high chance of success for a rescue. For a train powered by electricity, once the train has been diverted power can be cut. For a diesel train, it may be necessary to move another train in behind it once it has been diverted to keep it from moving. Once a train is immobilized, then negotiations and rescue plans may begin. Immobilizing a freight train that has been hijacked because it is carrying explosives, chemicals, nuclear materials, or other dangerous substances before it can reach an urban area is obviously critical as well.

Two key considerations when developing a rescue plan are the linear nature of trains and the likelihood that a large number of hostages will have been taken since terrorists will be most likely to strike during a time when the train is packed. Not only will they gain the maximum number of hostages, but on a busy train they will have been more likely to escape notice from security personnel.

If a hijacked train is stopped above ground, then antiterrorist snipers will attempt to deploy into concealed shooting positions offering the best shooting angles. Trains have many windows that may offer shots at a substantial number of the terrorists. Because of the possible deflection of a shot through windows, however, it would be preferable to assign multiple snipers to each terrorist. The use of a heavier caliber sniper rifle that can punch through the car's body is preferable as well. A weapon in .300 Winchester Magnum or .338 Lapua should give the sniper a better chance for a kill. The shooting angle may well be slightly downward or upward depending upon the situation of the train and the snipers, but skilled snipers will have trained to factor in angles when planning a shot. Although snipers in the traditional sense will not be appropriate for use in the confined spaces of dark underground tunnels, it may be possible to place marksmen with carbines or SMGs mounting night vision optics to take out some terrorists from yards away.

The snipers will also provide intelligence from observing the train. Additionally, the nature of train cars and rail beds makes it possible to place listening devices and possibly fiber optic cameras by crawling close to the cars at night. Plans of the trains should be obtained from the rail company. Normally, too, cars are standardized so operators should be able to find duplicates upon which to practice. In fact, most major teams frequently practice on passenger cars in use on

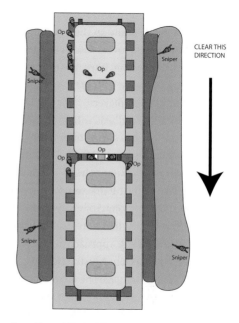

CLEAR THIS DIRECTION

Assaulting a Hijacked Train To carry out a rescue on a hijacked train requires a substantial number of operators (Op) and snipers. In the illustration, snipers are positioned in cover overlooking the rail bed. Their mission is to track the terrorists and eliminate as many as possible when the assault goes in. Operators are set to enter two cars containing terrorists and hostages simultaneously. Note also that two operators are ready to enter through a sky light in one car. When multiple cars must be cleared, operators will move in the same direction—either forward or backward—to avoid a blue on blue situation which could arise if they entered the same car from opposite directions.

their country's railways and underground systems. They must be familiar with how to move through the doorways connecting cars quickly and how to breach doors or windows if necessary.

The large number of hostages likely to be involved makes gathering intelligence about passengers, crew, and terrorists important. Photographs of as many of the terrorists, crew, and passengers as possible should be obtained for operators to study so they can quickly sort friend from foe during an assault. Terrorists may well switch clothing with crew members or take other steps to make themselves hard to spot and shoot/no shoot decisions must be made instantaneously. Observers with the snipers may be able to shoot digital photos of many of the players.

Because roadbeds will often position a train a few feet above the ground and because windows tend to be somewhat high as well, a stealth approach along the side of a train will be possible in many cases. Once operators are in position, snipers can take out as many of the terrorists as they can. The "Go" order may not be given until the maximum number of terrorists are in snipers' crosshairs. If there is high ground or an overpass, operators may also fast rope onto the top of the train. A helicopter insertion atop the train may well attract too much attention to the approaching helicopters, though the helicopters might also offer a distraction. A distraction to give the operators time to get aboard the train and ready to engage the terrorists would certainly be desirable. At De Punt, the assault on the train by Dutch Marines was preceded by Dutch Air Force jets flying low over the train and kicking in their afterburners, which forced everyone—both terrorists and hostages—to duck.

Stun grenades may be used, but the compartmentalized nature of trains can dissipate their effect, or, on the other hand, magnify it so that small children or those with medical problems might be seriously injured by the blast. There are special smaller stun grenades that are often used for assaults on linear targets such as trains. Some units also practice throwing the stun grenades to one side of the train to draw the attention of the terrorist away from the side where the assault will take place.

French units such as GIGN and RAID use dogs when assaulting linear targets. The dogs are trained to move quickly down an aisle and attack anyone with a gun.

Above Ukrainian Alpha operators use ramps thrust through a train's windows to allow operators to quickly board and engage terrorists. (Ukrainian Ministry of the Interior)

The growling dogs make excellent distraction devices against the terrorists as well as effective counters!

Some units—among them Russia's Alpha and Vympel—practice using ramps that they ram through the train windows. Operators then run up the ramps and engage anyone with a gun. Still other units break windows and go through on the backs of other operators to engage terrorists. All of these entry methods are valid if well practiced and a team may well want to have all of them in its repertoire. The primary objective is to neutralize as many of the terrorists as possible immediately through sniper fire or operators entering the cars. Well-trained dogs work, too.

Because trains are linear and may contain hostages and terrorists spread over many cars, the rescue plan must get operators into position all along the train.

If there are enough operators available, a team may be assigned to each car, which they will clear, then secure. If not, great care must be taken that operators moving through cars do not encounter and engage members of their own unit moving from the opposite direction. If there are not enough operators to cover each car, then teams assigned multiple cars may be ordered to clear the train front to rear or rear to front so that they are not moving toward each other. The tactical situation will dictate the plan that is used.

Other types of trains can present different challenges. Elevated trains that run above urban areas, for example, can present real problems if seized and then stopped in the middle of a city. On the positive side, there are likely to be buildings where snipers may be deployed. If the terrorists can be located within the cars, shots from above or below might possibly be used to take them out through ceilings or floors of the cars. If an assault is necessary, however, the options become fast roping onto the train from above or using ladders to reach it from below. A stealth approach along the tracks or rail at night remains a possibility as well, though power would have to have been cut so the rail was not hot. Some units have special vehicles with ladders and ramps attached and, depending on the height of the elevated train, these might be used. Fire trucks or trucks for repairing overhead stop lights or street lights might be used as well.

If a hijacked subway train is stopped in a tunnel, operators will have to approach in darkness using their night vision equipment. Power may have been cut to the train, but if it hasn't terrorists may actually be easily spotted by operators from the darkness. If power has not been cut, operators will have to be extremely aware of the third rail, which will have enough current to kill them if they encounter it. Most underground systems today have cameras in the cars, tunnels, and platforms that should provide intelligence. On the other hand, terrorists may well disable the cameras as soon as possible. Still, images of the terrorists may have been captured that will make identifying them during an assault easier. If the car has remained illuminated, it would be advisable to cut power just before the assault to give the operators using NVGs and possible IR illuminators an advantage and also to make it more difficult for terrorists to identify targets. Because of the possibility of flammable gases being in some tunnels, suppressed weapons would be advisable for tunnel operations. Should the terrorists have hand grenades, the presence of rows of seats in trains will be an advantage as they will help stop fragments from spreading too far. It is quite possible, too, that some grenades will roll under seats and have most of their blast absorbed.

There are training facilities specifically designed to train operators to deal with underground train incidents. In the USA, the Washington Metro Area Emergency Response Training Facility has a 260-ft long section of subway tunnel that contains two 75-ft long underground railway cars. As a result, all types of training scenarios may be staged for operators. Many units will also have one or more railroad and/or underground cars available at their live fire training facility and can use them for live fire training or "force on force" training using Simunitions.

BUSES

The number and array of buses used around the world makes them an attractive terrorist target. Urban transit buses, cross country buses, airport buses, school buses, even buses transporting military or police personnel have been terrorist targets. As a result, the antiterrorist unit must prepare to carry out a rescue on any buses likely to be used in their country.

Like trains, buses are a linear target, though a more contained one. Normally,

Above Members of Poland's GROM antiterrorist unit demonstrate techniques for assaulting a suspect vehicle in an urban area. (Grom.mil.pl)

terrorists and hostages will be spread out to some extent on a bus. During the Munich Olympic hostage incident, while moving the hostages to waiting helicopters via bus the terrorists placed the hostages in the back of the bus and they remained in the front. This was a situation designed for the use of snipers. If the terrorists can be identified, the large number of windows on a bus makes it relatively easy for a sniper to identify and neutralize them. When terrorists seized a school bus transporting French children in Djibouti, GIGN chose to use snipers to end the incident. They sent drugged food to the bus, which put the children to sleep causing them to lie down on the seats. This left the terrorists as very visible targets. Snipers eliminated all but one of the terrorists with precise shots, but an assault team had to rush the bus to eliminate the final one. One consideration today, however, is that many urban and cross-transit buses have tinted windows, which make the passengers more comfortable but can make a sniper's job more difficult.

Terrorists may also mingle with the passengers making the use of snipers problematic. In that case an assault will be necessary. First, however, the bus will

Above Vympel operators have used ramps to quickly gain entrance to a bus with large windows. Note that one operator provides rear security while other operators cover the bus or remove terrorists or hostages. (FSB)

have to be immobilized. Having a large truck stop in front of the bus and behind the bus can stop it. If this technique is used it should be made to appear a normal traffic jam. Road construction may also be used to stop the bus. Some units have practiced using a large vehicle to ram a bus to immobilize it; however, this method may well result in injuries to many hostages, and is normally only used as a last resort. A bus may also be immobilized if a trained operator can reach the back or undercarriage of the bus while it is stopped. Many buses have an ignition switch in the rear so mechanics can work on the engine. Using it, the bus may be switched off. Cutting certain brake lines may also cause the brakes of the bus to lock up. Puncturing the gas tank will eventually result in the bus stopping, but operators have no control over where it will stop and the risk of fire is increased.

In some incidents, terrorists will request a bus to take them to an airport or elsewhere with hostages. Should a unit commander on the scene decide that there is a better chance of carrying out a rescue if the terrorists remove the hostages from a building they could be granted a bus. Operators can supply a bus with a remote cut-off or with a gas tank that is almost empty—the gas gauge

Above Members of FSB Vympel are hoisted into shooting position and braced by other operators during bus assault training. Operators are armed with Makarov pistols. (FSB)

Left A member of Holland's BBE deployed off the Somali coast on anti-piracy duties practices engagement from the deck with his C8 carbine with Aimpoint sight. (Royal Netherlands Marine Corps)

may be altered to show full. It is highly preferable that the bus be stopped at a point determined best for a rescue; hence the remote cutoff has advantages as does using a fake road crew or a stopped truck. An alternative, however, is to have operators hidden in a commercial truck that can pull alongside the bus as it stops, at which point the operators rush the bus.

When buses are supplied, they may also be prepped to make a stealth approach prior to an assault easier. Side mirrors may be adjusted to allow for dead spots along the side of the bus, for example, or doors may be rigged to allow easier entry. Prior to assaulting a bus, if there is time, practice assaults should take place on a bus of the same type. Most units will also have already practiced on a variety of buses and are quite likely to have one or more at their training facility.

Whichever method is used to immobilize the bus, operators must act fast to prevent the terrorists from killing hostages. The SOP is to get operators to the windows on one side of the bus quickly to eliminate as many terrorists as possible. Various techniques are used to get the shooters into position. Some teams use ladders that are thrust against the bus to allow shooters to run up and take their shots. Often another team member will help support them. Learning to balance and take the shots requires some practice. Other teams have some operators crouch while shooters run onto their back to take their shots. Russian units such as Alpha and Vympel have practiced running a canvas-topped truck up next to the bus, then jamming ramps through the windows. Operators then run across and take their shots as they enter the bus. The Russians and other units have also used ladders, which they ram through the windows of a bus so operators can run up and engage. At least some teams have practiced taking out terrorists through the roof of the bus with a short burst of fire if their location is known and hostages are not too close. Normally, submachineguns or handguns that can be swung quickly to engage are the preferred weapons. As with train assaults, stun grenades may be effectively thrown to the side of the bus away from the assault to draw attention.

Although snipers and assault teams along the side of a bus may take out all of the terrorists, it will still normally be necessary to board the bus. If a terrorist has been driving the bus, an operator on the driver's side may eliminate him, then reach in to open the door. If the driver is a hostage, an operator can come along his side and order him to open the bus, or if the driver freezes reach in and release the door himself. Doors may also be pried or rammed open. If the entry is through windows via ramps or ladders, then those operators carrying out the entry can gain control of the bus.

Many buses have multiple doors—either at the rear as on school buses or the rear side as on commercial transport buses. Although there can be advantages to entering from the rear, entry from the front is normally best as it allows operators to watch faces to identify terrorists and to watch hands for weapons or explosives. As soon as the first two operators are in position to control the bus—usually from the front with one on each side of the aisle—they should order everyone to raise their hands and show they are empty. Normally, then, a pair of operators will board the bus and move down the aisle checking each row for terrorists, weapons, explosives, and so on. Due to the narrowness of the aisle operators will normally move, one right behind the other, each facing the seats on his side of the aisle. As soon as they check an aisle, those in the aisle may be ordered to move toward the door with hands raised. A team will take control of them and restrain them until their identity has been determined. While clearing a bus, some hostages may have panicked and will attempt to leap up or rush for the doors. Operators must be willing to elbow them back into a seat or take other firm action to retain control until the tactical situation becomes completely clear.

At this point, there still may be terrorists hidden among the hostages. Some teams prefer to keep everyone seated until all rows are cleared; then a team will begin to remove them. By keeping everyone seated with their hands raised, operators limit terrorists' speed of movement should they still be among the hostages. If there is reason to believe the bus is wired with explosives, getting hostages off quickly will be a priority. The two cover men will remain in position to cover seated passengers, though great care must be taken not to point their weapons at the team moving down the aisle to clear. If the operators who took positions to fire through windows remain in position they can help cover, but they will have to point their muzzles in a safe direction as the clearing team reaches their position.

Once the bus has been evacuated, medical personnel can deal with any injured hostages and EOD personnel can give the bus a thorough check for explosives. Once hostages have been checked and cleared, they will be debriefed and released.

Maritime Antiterrorism

Antiterrorist units charged with the MAT mission might be called into action for a variety of reasons. A hijacked cruise ship, for example, would create a massive hostage situation and would call for a carefully planned assault. Pirates might also seize a tanker, or freighter. The crew could be considered hostages but, depending upon the cargo, should the terrorists kill the crew—as they often do—and abandon

Above Members of Croatia's ATJ Lucko unit carry out a surface approach during a combat boarding operation. (Croatian Police)

the ship, a tanker might create an ecological nightmare as could some container ships. Ships such as natural gas tankers might well be hijacked and turned into massive bombs to be exploded in a harbor or near a defense installation. An antiterrorist unit might be charged with retaking the ship or, in some cases, sinking it. Still another scenario might involve a ship being used by terrorists to transport WMDs. Once again the ship might be seized, but it might also be destroyed. Other ships might be targeted because they are transporting high-value terrorist suspects to be snatched by the antiterrorist operators.

The first critical element that will affect how an antiterrorist unit deals with a ship is whether it is at sea or anchored, either in a harbor or off shore. If the decision is made that the best option is destruction of the ship, then combat swimmers will approach an anchored ship and place explosive charges or teams in fast boats will approach a moving ship and place charges. Of course, if a ship carrying dangerous materials is anchored in a harbor, destruction is not an option since it would create the same dangers as if the terrorists detonated the ship.

For ships at sea that are to be assaulted, the options are a surface assault from small boats and a helicopter assault by fast roping operators onto the ship. A

Top Members of the Icelandic Viking Squad prepare to do a combat boarding. Note the special hooked ladders they will use to reach the deck. (Icelandic National Police)

Above Members of Pakistan's Naval SSG practice combat boarding operations in conjunction with U.S. Naval personnel. (USN) combination of these two may prove an even better option. When a ship is at sea and small boats are to be used, the boats and the operators may be inserted into the sea from helicopters or aircraft over the horizon prior to the approach. For ships that are anchored, surface or helicopter assaults are viable, but an underwater assault by combat swimmers might be even more effective. Many of these techniques are being used by units countering Somali pirates.

When inserting operators from helicopters, normally at least two transport choppers will be needed. These will have been rigged for fast roping and the pilots will have trained for MAT operations. That means they will be skilled at flying at night and will be capable of skimming the waves and approaching from behind then flaring up to insert the operators while trying to match the helicopters' movements to the bobbing deck. Helicopter insertion onto the deck of a ship takes a great deal of practice. Generally, operators will be inserted as close to the bridge as possible so that it can be seized quickly. The first members of the assault team

Above U.S. Navy SEALs fast rope to the deck of a ship while team members already on deck provide cover for them. (USAF)

to hit the deck will set up a security perimeter for those following them. Once the operators are on deck they will begin to move toward their objectives, leapfrogging to give each other cover. Different teams will train to move through the ship with slightly different techniques. The SBS, for example, avoids stairs or ladders that might be booby trapped while other teams move up stairways with one or more team members stopping at each level to provide cover.

The type of helicopter in use will determine how many operators may be inserted by each bird. For example, U.S. CH-46 helicopters can each carry 16 SEALs or Marine operators, while Blackhawk MH-60s of the 160th SOAR can only carry 8. In addition to being rigged for fast rope insertion, the transport helicopters should also be rigged for extraction via a trooper ladder or SPIE rig since the helicopters will not normally be able to land to remove operators after an operation or if some are injured.

Two additional helicopters will probably escort the transport choppers and act as sniper platforms. These are usually smaller, more lively choppers of the Lynx

Above Members of Spain's UOE provide cover with a .338 Lapua and a .50 BMG rifle during a combat boarding of a North Korean ship. (USN)

type used by the SBS or 160th SOAR LIttle BIrds. One sniper chopper will flare off to each side of the ship and provide cover for the fast-roping operators. Generally, an approach angle of between 45 and 60 degrees to the deck is considered best to lessen the chances of a sniper round hitting one of the operators. Any crew members who appear with a weapon will be taken out. Normally, each helicopter will carry only one sniper. The sniper will generally be armed with a self-loading rifle with a relatively low power scope that offers a wide field of view. In the past, the SBS has used the G3 rifle with a 4x scope. The sniper helicopters can also offer an intelligence source as they hover above and to the sides of the ship. They can warn operators of obstacles or crewmen as they move across the decks.

As mentioned above, surface assaulters may have initially been delivered into the water with their boats by aircraft or helicopter, but they then speed toward the ship, once again approaching from the rear. Operators with small boats can also be inserted via submarine. Since the small surface craft used by MAT teams

Above Members of Lithuania's ARAS antiterrorist unit move to secure the bridge during an antiterrorist exercise. (Lithuanian Ministry of the Interior)

can exceed 50 knots, they can normally run down any target ship from the stern. Teams normally have some type of hook and pull ladder system, which may be extended for hooking the deck. A ladder is then dropped, which the operators climb to board the ship. The first couple of operators up the ladder will often have suppressed pistols to silently eliminate any sentries encountered. Even if the surface assault is simultaneous with a helicopter insertion, the first operators to reach the deck from the boats will normally provide cover for the others coming over the rail. Although the specific type of ship and tactical situation will determine movement, generally on a combined helicopter/surface assault, the operators who fast rope from the helicopter will move to secure the bridge and other areas above decks while those inserted by boat will move to secure the areas below deck.

A subsurface assault allows a more clandestine approach to a ship that is stopped at sea, docked, or anchored off shore. When ships are close to shore,

Above Members of Lithuania's ARAS practice a sub surface approach then boarding during an antiterrorist exercise. (Lithuanian Ministry of the Interior)

operators may swim from points along the beach to the ship. At sea, the swimmers would likely be inserted from a submarine. They might then use an SDV (SEAL Delivery Vehicle) to approach the ship underwater. Once swimmers reach the ship they might climb anchor chains or ropes to reach the deck or deploy hook and pull ladders of the type already mentioned. As with a boat insertion, the first operators over the rail will normally have suppressed pistols to deal with sentries. Subsurface assaults can be used in conjunction with helicopter or surface assaults as well.

In some cases, distraction may be used to gain time for operators preparing to carry out a combat boarding operation. A "yacht" with attractive girls sunbathing on deck offers a distraction in daylight while a "yacht" with a party—once again with attractive girls—can offer a distraction at night. Very bright lights on the "yacht" or a spotlight from a passing ship can degrade the night vision of sentries aboard the target ship. Numerous other options might be used (i.e. a fire boat with sirens and horns blaring or a fishing boat with a large catch hanging in plain view). A device known as an LRAD (Long Range Acoustic Device) emits a very high-pitched and disabling sound in a 15–30 degree arc that can be very painful at 100 meters and remains effective to 500 meters. If a nearby ship is equipped with an LRAD and it is pointed at the target ship just before the boarding operation, it can help disorient the crew. Obviously, operators will need to wear ear protection. Passing yachts or ships can also carry hidden snipers who will help cover the assault. Most of these distractions will only work in harbors or near to shore, however.

An important determinate for choosing the type of assault or

Above Divers from Russia's Omoh. (MVD)

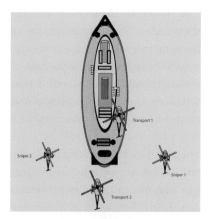

Ship Assault At Sea I This diagram shows the initial stage of an assault on a ship at sea. All four helicopters have approached from the rear, hugging the waves to escape detection until the last minute. The two smaller helicopters, each carrying a sniper, flare off to the sides to allow the snipers to give fire support to the operators fast roping onto the deck. The two transport helicopters carry operators. Note that Transport 1 is inserting its team as close to the bridge as possible so that it can take control of the ship quickly.

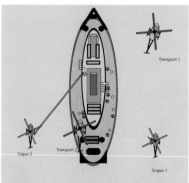

Ship Assault At Sea II Once operators from Transport 1 have fast roped to the deck that helicopter moves off to allow Transport 2 to deposit its operators. Note that the operators (O) on deck have moved to secure the bridge and set up perimeter security for the landing of the next flight of operators. The helicopters carrying snipers continue to give overwatch and provide covering fire as needed. Note that the sniper in Sniper 2 is engaging an armed terrorist (T).

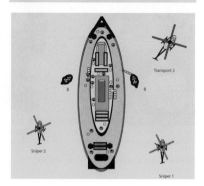

Ship Assault At Sea III Once operators (O) from both transport helicopters have reached the deck, they move out to secure the upper deck areas and check any cabins. The transport helicopters move off and may circle in case they are needed for extraction of casualties or personnel. The helicopters bearing snipers continue to give overwatch. In some cases, additional operators are inserted via boats (B) and will climb the sides of the ship to help secure the lower decks and guard any prisoners.

combination of assaults will be the nature of the mission. If there are hostages, possibly in multiple points around the ship, then getting a large number of operators aboard and beginning to clear above and below decks quickly is a high priority. If, however, the ship is carrying WMDs or has been turned into a potential floating bomb, then gaining control of the bridge and engine room so the ship may be stopped is most critical. Whenever possible, operators will have studied diagrams of the ship from their unit's database of world ship types.

Once operators are aboard using any of the techniques described, they will begin clearing the ship using fairly standard tactics. Normally, weapons loaded with frangible ammunition and often with suppressors will be used during combat boarding operations. As has already been mentioned, securing the bridge is a priority. A four-man team is fairly standard to secure personnel on the bridge.

Above Australian Clearance Divers armed with C8 carbines mounting ELCAN sights are assigned to MAT (Maritime Anti-Terrorism) duties with the Tactical Assault Group East. (Royal Australian Navy)

If desirable, the ship may be stopped from the bridge or its course changed if moving. The ship's master and other bridge crew can be secured and possibly used for intelligence about the remainder of the crew or others on board.

Because passageways below decks are tight on most ships, two-man entry teams are used to clear compartments. Usually one or more breachers combine with these entry teams. If a compartment door needs to be breached, a breacher does so, then moves to the next compartment. In that way two-man teams leap frog down a passageway. Normally, for follow-up personnel some method of marking cleared compartments is used (i.e. throwing in a light stick). Larger compartments such as the engine room will normally merit a four-man clearing team. A few operators will have set up a holding area where captured crew or others aboard may be detained after having been searched and secured with flex cuffs.

Upon reaching cross passageways, point men will check the passageway, then

Above During a MAT exercise members of Greece's DYK move to secure the bridge. (Hellenic Navy)

the clearing teams will move into them with rear security covering the passageways. Internal stairways will also normally be cleared by a point man moving ahead of his team. External stairways—because they are exposed from multiple directions—will normally require a four-man team to clear. Once the stairway is secure another team will move through the team securing to take the next level. The teams will carry out this maneuver until reaching their objective. It should be apparent by now that clearing below decks of a large ship will require a substantial number of personnel. In some cases, additional teams will be inserted via boat or helicopter once the upper decks are secure.

When the location of hostages or crew taken by pirates is known, then getting operators to that area quickly is a priority, though they still must maintain security while moving and be alert to booby traps.

If the ship is carrying suspected WMDs or explosives wired to detonate a dangerous cargo, then operators will normally shoot any nearby terrorist to prevent him detonating the devices. Once the area is secured, if feasible, specialists in nuclear, biological, chemical, or EOD, will be inserted onto the ship. Members of the antiterrorist team with EOD or WMD training will normally be assigned to the team going for the devices so they can make an initial assessment of the threat and what will be needed to neutralize it. A ship containing possible WMDs or explosive devices will normally be stopped at sea or, in some cases when taken over in harbor, moved out to sea.

As with other types of hostage situation, hostages will be initially secured as well until operators have a chance to sort out who is who. Those hostages or, in the case of pirates, freed crew members, will be medevaced as soon as possible. Once the ship is secured and terrorists detained, hostages will be removed as will the terrorists. Operators will then normally leave the ship in the hands of other security personnel such as Marines and specialists to deal with any dangerous materials.

A variant type of MAT operation is assaulting an offshore oil platform. The combination of possible destruction of a high value economic target, creation of an ecological disaster, and the taking of hostages makes oil platforms a potential terrorist target. Nations that have offshore oil platforms, therefore, normally also have a unit tasked with carrying out antiterrorist operations against them.

Generally, oil platforms are relatively isolated but remain a static target. The same basic options exist for assaulting an oil platform as a ship. Operators can come in via helicopter, small boat, or subsurface via SDV and scuba. Most maritime antiterrorist units have determined that the subsurface assault may be the best initial option. Operators train to swim to the rig under water, then climb the legs to eliminate any terrorist guards on the platform. Because of the waves in areas such as the North Sea, operators train to time the rise and fall until they can grab a guy wire or strut to begin their climb. Units normally have their best free climbers do the original climb, then lower ropes for the rest of the team.

Once on the platform, operators move to eliminate any terrorists who are visible, normally with suppressed weapons. At this point, some units practice having additional operators inserted from a helicopter via fast rope or from small boats. However, some units have the entire operation carried out by swimmers. In either case, the next step is to clear the interior spaces of the platform as quickly as possible to free hostages and to check that there are no explosives wired to the platform.

Terrorist activity in Nigeria, where foreign workers have been taken hostage on oil rigs, has caused some units to specifically practice for an operation to rescue their citizens who are working in the Nigerian oil industry. U.S., British, Australian, and other Western oil workers are employed on rigs all over the world so the possibility of mounting a rescue of their citizens or assisting local operators with a rescue remains a constant for units such as the SBS, OAT, DevGru, Commando Hubert, and COMSUBIN.

Dignitary Protection

For virtually all antiterrorist units, dignitary protection is a secondary mission to hostage rescue. In a few cases a country's Presidential or Royal Protection Team actually goes through the same training as the antiterrorist team. Although France's GSPR has recently been re-organized, it was originally formed from personnel who had been trained as part of the GIGN antiterrorist unit. Indonesia's PASPAMPRES draws its members from those trained as part of the country's special forces or antiterrorist units. Normally, however, antiterrorist units are assigned dignitary protection roles to supplement regular protection teams.

Members of the SAS, for example, have augmented Royalty Protection teams if the Queen or other members of the Royal Family are traveling in areas of heightened threat level. Operators from the U.S. Delta Force or DevGru have augmented protection teams for U.S. officials in war zones. Many antiterrorist teams rotate operators through their embassies in more dangerous areas so that they can assist in hardening embassy security and augment the diplomatic protection teams. Such assignments also allow them to become familiar with the embassy in case a rescue is ever required there.

In some cases, members of the antiterrorist unit provide specialized members for a close protection effort. For example, the U.S. Secret Service has its own CAT (Counter Assault Team), which provides heavier firepower should a motorcade be attacked. In other countries, however, members of the antiterrorist unit provide this function. The SAS has carried out this mission for the British Prime Minister and the Queen. In Italy, NOCS often functions as a counterassault team for Italian officials, the Pope, or visiting dignitaries. Because of the skill of their snipers, many antiterrorist teams will also provide highly trained countersnipers during VIP visits.

Units drawn from a country's national police will often provide actual close protection for important visiting dignitaries. Among those carrying out such duties are Austria's EKO COBRA, the Slovak Republic's UOU, and Italy's NOCS. Some units have specialized hardened vehicles—NOCS has both hardened limos and SUVs for counterassault teams.

Members of antiterrorist units can also be useful in preparing threat assessments. Operators drawn from military special ops units that may have a wartime mission of taking out enemy leaders can offer chilling insights into the weaknesses of a standard protection effort based on their analysis of what they would do in the terrorists' boots. Many operators have served in Iraq and Afghanistan and have become quite knowledgeable of the current state of IEDs (Improvised Explosive Devices) and can apply that expertise to helping protective teams guard against them.

Training Exchanges and Training Assistance

At any given time a few members of most antiterrorist units will be carrying out exchange training with other friendly units around the world. Teams will also take part in tactical competitions against other teams to hone skills and to learn techniques. Training exchanges are useful for many reasons. The most obvious is that operators learn different techniques and see new equipment they may not have encountered before. However, by working together units also develop relationships that will be very important should they ever have to mount a joint rescue operation or work with a unit to rescue their own citizens in another country. Some units work so closely together on training exercises that operators become almost interchangeable. Operators from the Combat Applications Group (Delta), British SAS, Australian SASR, and Polish GROM have worked together so often that this is the case with them.

Another advantage of exchange training is that certain units have a special expertise in certain areas or their country offers special facilities or geographical features that lend themselves to a specific type of training. The United States has a substantial number of excellent combat shooting schools, for example, and many foreign operators who are on exchange with DevGru or Combat Applications Group take advantage of the expertise at these schools. The USA also has a facility in Washington, DC, with two subway cars and a subway tunnel that's excellent for training to carry out assaults on underground systems. Because the Israelis deal with suicide bombers and other terrorist acts constantly, many units send operators to Israel to learn from this experience. Although there are areas of the USA and possessions that can be used for jungle training, American operators will often go through jungle warfare training with the Malaysians, the British SAS in Belize, or the Australian SAS.

Such exchange training often results in lifelong friendships. Since operators in antiterrorist units can rarely share their lives with those outside of the antiterrorist community, having friends around the world who understand the life offers them a chance to take a holiday away from home yet still with trustworthy colleagues.

Training assistance is slightly different from training exchanges in that members of a unit sent on an assistance mission are normally helping a friendly state form an antiterrorist unit or improve the skills of the one already in existence. Operators sent on such exchanges must not only have a sound knowledge of tactics and weapons, but also the ability to teach these techniques. Foreign language skills can be very helpful in such exchanges. Training a unit in another country, especially in the developing world, may come with a few pitfalls. For example, in one country a well-trained antiterrorist unit was developed with assistance from a major power. The commander of the unit then used his highly trained operators to stage a coup and install himself in power.

Normally, though, the benefits far outweigh any potential disadvantages. Some have speculated that training foreign antiterrorist units, especially in parts of the world with endemic terrorism, could be giving potential terrorists knowledge that they could use against an antiterrorist unit should alliances change. There is some truth in this, but tactics are constantly changing and major units upgrade tactics and equipment. Also, the same message applies that I used to impart when training VIP protection units around the word. Occasionally, a student would ask, "What if I should become an assassin and turn what you've taught me against a principle you are protecting?" My standard answer was, "Just because I taught you everything you know doesn't mean I've taught you everything I know!" No unit teaches everything during training assistance missions!

As with exchange training, one of the most important benefits of training assistance is that contacts may be invaluable should an incident occur involving citizens of the country that has supplied the training assistance. Should British citizens, for example, be taken hostage in a country the antiterrorist unit of which was trained by the SAS, the odds are quite good that an offer of SAS assistance would be accepted. Although most major units offer training assistance, the French have been especially willing to send teams from GIGN or RAID to former colonies in Africa to develop teams. Pakistan's SSG has carried out a great deal of training assistance to some other Muslim states, their religion being considered as important as their expertise.

Countering Weapons of Mass Destruction

Since dealing with potential weapons of mass destruction falls under the umbrella of antiterrorism in some countries the antiterrorist unit has members trained to carry out operations in a hazmat environment. Normally, the actual handling of WMDs (Weapons of Mass Destruction) requires people with substantial scientific training in nuclear, chemical, or biological sciences. As a result, scientific units will be on call to assist antiterrorist operators.

The larger the country, the more likely it is to have multiple agencies that will be involved in a terrorist scenario involving WMDs. A good example occurred shortly after the 9/11 attacks on the USA. There were grounds to believe that as a follow-up there would be an attempt to use a nuclear device in the USA. As a result, joint teams comprised of members of NEST (Nuclear Emergency Search Teams), who have sophisticated equipment and the training to locate nuclear devices, and members of the FBI HRT were formed. The plan was that HRT members would take out the terrorists who had the device after NEST had located them.

Because of attempts to smuggle nuclear materials in the former Soviet Union, Russia, Ukraine, and other countries have units trained to counter nuclear smugglers. The Slovak Republic's UOU had an instance in April 2007, in which they helped seize 37.4 lb of radioactive material being smuggled through their territory. In the USA, the Atomic Energy Commission offers overseas training for SWAT teams specializing in countering an incident at a nuclear power plant. In many countries, however, the national antiterrorist unit will have this mission.

Training in full hazmat gear is very difficult as it limits physical movements, field of vision, and use of certain types of weapons. Nevertheless, operators have to practice donning the suits and actually learn to be inserted, move through an installation, and engage possible terrorists while wearing their hazmat gear. Units that also have the mission of seizing drug labs often get a chance to carry out real operations wearing at least some of their hazmat gear.

Functioning as Air Marshals

In at least a few antiterrorist units, operators sometimes fly as air marshals on their country's airliners. This may only occur in times of increased threat or operators may rotate through the air marshal assignment on 30–90 day assignments before returning to the unit. The problem that arises is whether the air marshal job is a proper use of highly trained operators. Air marshals do need to be well trained in close combat with and without firearms and proper techniques for engaging terrorists aboard an aircraft as well as first aid, recognition of IEDs, and terrorist psychology; however, they do not need all of the sophisticated hostage rescue or special ops training normally given to operators. Since many national antiterrorist units may number 60 operators or less and there are quite likely more flights than that per day, it becomes a numbers game.

When members of an antiterrorist unit are tasked to function as air marshals, it will often be on flights that have been determined to carry an especially high risk due to their point of origin or destination. In other cases, intelligence may indicate that a flight has a higher risk of terrorist attack, in which case members of the antiterrorist unit could be assigned to function as air marshals on that flight. Many countries do not have air marshals, but US requirements that flights to the USA must have an air marshal aboard might dictate that members of an antiterrorist unit are assigned that mission just for those flights.

In addition to putting highly skilled "shooters" aboard aircraft, there are other advantages to having members of the antiterrorist unit who have undergone air marshal training and have flown as security on flights. Operators who have undergone air marshal training and flown to provide security often gain more insight into how commercial aircraft and airports work. As a result, should they have to take down a hijacked airliner, they will have additional knowledge of aircraft entry points and vulnerabilities. They will also have gained practice shooting within the confines of an airliner. Putting members of an antiterrorist unit through air marshal training gives them additional useful training and makes them available should they be needed for that mission.

There are a few antiterrorist units that have the air marshal mission full time. In some cases, these units are within the special operations forces of their country's Air Force. They have the antiterrorism mission for any situation involving aircraft whether assaulting a hijacked aircraft on the ground or acting as air marshals while flying.

Glossary

ARW Irish Army Ranger Wing
ATJ Croatian Antiteroristicka
Jedinica
BBE (now UIM) Dutch Bijzondere
Bijstandseenheid
BEOH Argentinian Brigada Especial
Operativa Halcón
BLUE ON BLUE A shooting that
arises when an operator fails to
recognize another operator or
another friendly in the heat
of battle
BOPE Brazilian Batalhão de
Operações de Policia Especiais
CAG U.S. Combat Application Group
CCC Belgian Communist Fighting Cells
COBT Bulgarian Spetsializiran
Otriad za Borba s Terorizma
COES Peruvian Compañía de
Operaciones Especiales
COMMANDO HUBERT French
Maritime Antiterrorism unit.

COMSUBIN Italian Comando
Raggrupamento Subacquei ed
Incursori Teseo Tesei (Maritime
Antiterrorism unit)
CQB Close Quarter Battle
CQC Close Quarter Combat
DEVGRU U.S. Naval Special Warfare
Development Group (Formerly SEAL
Team SIx)
DFLP Democratic Front for the
Liberation of Palestine
D4 Israeli MAT unit, Shayetet 13
DINOES Peruvian División Nacional
de Operaciones Especiales
DYK Greek Dioikisi Ypovrychion
Katastrofon (Naval Special
Warfare Unit)
EKAM Greek Eidiki Katalstaiki
Antitromokratiki Monada
ELN Ejercito de Liberación Nacional
(Colombian National Liberatiion Army)
EKO Austrian Einsatzkommando

Kobra (Formerly GEK–Gendarmerieeinsatzkommando)
EOD Explosive Ordnance Disposal
ESI (=SIE) Belgian Escadron Spécial d'Intervention
ETA Basque Euskadi Ta Askatasuna (Freedom for the Basque Homeland)
FALN Venezuelan and Puerto Rican Fuerzas Armadas de Liberación Nacional (Armed Forces of National Liberation)
FARC Colombian Fuerzas Armadas Revolucionarias de Colombia (Revolutionary Armed Forces)
FBI U.S. Federal Bureau of Investigation
FLB Front de la Liberation de Bretagne (Breton Liberation Front—active against France)
FLCS Front de la Liberation de la Cote des Somalis (Front for the Liberation of Somalia
FLIR Forward Looking Infra-Red
FLNC Fronte di Liberazione Naziunale Corsu (National Front for the Liberation of Corsica)
FNSH Albanian Qendrore e Forcave Speciale e të Ndërhyrjes së Shpejtë
FOPE Paraguayan Fuerza de Operaciones Especiales
FRAME CHARGE An explosive charge to fit on a door or window for explosive breaching

FSB Russian Federalnaja Sluzba Bezopastnost (formerly KGB)
FSK Norwegian Forsvarets Spesialkommando
GEO Spanish Grupo Especial de Operaciones
GEOF Argentinian Grupo Especial de Operaciones Federales
GIGN French Groupe d'Intervention Gendarmerie Nationale
GIPA Andorran Grup d'Intervencio Policia d'Andorra
GIPN French Groupe d'Intervention Police Nationale
GIS Italian Gruppo di Intervento Speciale
GOE Brazilian Grupo de Operações Especiais
GOE Portuguese Grupo de Operações Especiais
GOPE Chilean Grupo de Operaciones de Policia Especiales
GOPES Mexican Grupo de Operaciones Especiales
GROM Polish Grupa Reagowania Operacyjno Mobilneyo
GSG-9 German Grenzschutzgruppe 9
GSIGN French Groupement de Sécurité et d'Intervention de la Gendarmerie Nationale
GSPI Romanian Grupul Special de Protectie si Interventie
GSU Kenyan General Service Unit(s)

HAHO High Altitude High Opening

HALO High Altitude Low Opening

HAMAS Harakat al-Muqawwama al-Islamiyya (Islamic Resistance Movement, very active against Israel)

HQSF British Headquarters Special Forces

HRT U.S. FBI Hostage Rescue Team

IRA Irish Republican Army

ISA U.S. Intelligence Support Activity

ISI Pakistani Inter-Services Intelligence

JRA Japanese Red Army

JSOC U.S. Joint Special Operations Command

JTF-2 (=FOI 2) Canadian Joint Task Force 2

KSK German Kommando Spezialkräfte

KOPASSANDA Indonesian Komando Pasukan Sandi Yudha

KOPASSUS Indonesian Komando Pasukan Khusus

LINEX A flexible, tubular explosive that may be molded

LTTE Sri Lankan Liberation Tigers of Tamil Eelam

MAT Maritime Anti-Terrorism

M-4 Carbine Standard weapon of U.S. special ops troops and many other antiterrorist units around the world

MLN Movimiento de Liberación Nacional (Uruguayan National Liberation Movement)

MP5 The HK MP5 Submachinegun, the most widely used SMG among anti-terrorist units

MRTA Movimiento Revolucionario Túpac Amaru (Peruvian Tupac Amaru Revolutionary Movement)

NEST Nuclear Emergency Search Teams

NOCS Italian Nucleo Operativo Centrale di Sicurezza

NSG Indian National Security Guards

NZSAS New Zealand Special Air Service

OAG Australian Off-Shore Assault Group

OAT Australian Off-Shore Assault Team

OMON (cyrillic OMOH) Russia and former Soviet Republics Otryad Militsii Osobennogo Naznacheniya

160th SOAR U.S. 160th Special Operations Aviation Regiment

OUSO Macau Unidade Táctica de Intervenção da Polícia

PASKAL Malaysian Pasukan Khas Laut (Naval Special Forces)

PFLP Popular Front for the Liberation of Palestine

PIJ Palestinian Islamic Jihad

PIRA Provisonal Irish Republican Army

PKK Kurdistan Workers' Party (active in Turkey)

PLA Palestine Liberation Army

PLF Palestine Liberation Front

RAID French Recherche Assistance Intervention Dissuasion

RENEA Albanian Reparti i
Eleminimit dhe Neutralizimit
te Elementit te Armatosur
SAF Singapore Special Action Force
SAG Malta Special Assignments Group
SAS British Special Air Service
SASR Australian Special Air
Service Regiment
SAT Japanese Special Assault Team
Sayaret Matkal Israeli antiterrorist
unit
SBS British Special Boat Service
SDU Hong Kong Special Duties Unit
SEK German
Sondereinsatzkommando
SFF Indian Special Frontier Force
SIE (=ESI) Belgian Speciaal
Interventie Eskadron
SSF Qutar Special Security Force
SSG Pakistani Special Service Group
STAR Singapore Special Tactical
and Rescue
TAG Australian Tactical Assault Group
TANGO Widely used radio code in
English for a terrorist
TLF Sri Lankan Tamil Liberation Front
UDA Ulster Defense Association
UEI Spanish Unidad Especial
de Intervención
URA Japanse United Red Army
URNA Czech Utvar Rychleho NAsazeni

Suggested reading

Beckwith, Col. Charlie A., *Delta Force* (Harcourt Brace Jovanovich, San Diego, 1983)

Bennett, Richard M., *Elite Forces: An Encyclopedia of the World's Most Formidable Secret Armies* (Virgin Books, London, 2003)

Camsell, Don, *Black Water: A Life in the Special Boat Service* (Lewis International, 2000)

Cohen, Aaron, *Brotherhood of Warriors* (Harper Collins, New York, 2008)

Coulson, Danny O., No-Heroes: Inside the FBI's Secret Counter-Terror Force (Pocket Books, New York, 1999)

Courtois, Jean-Louis, *Le Raid: L'Unité D'Élite de la Police Française* (Pygmalion, Paris, 1999)
—— *Le RAID: L'Ultime Recours* (Editions Crepin-LeBlond, 2000)

Davies, Barry, *Fire Magic: Hijack at Mogadishu* (Bloomsbury, London, 1994)
—— *SAS, Shadow Warriors of the 21st Century* (Lewis International, Miami, FL, 2002)

Deflez, Gilbert, *La Brigade des Missions Impossibles* (Jacques Grancher, Paris, 1979)

Gagueche, Yvon. *GIGN, GSPR, EPIGN: Gendarmes de L'Extreme* (Editions Vanneau, Paris, 1990)
—— *GIGN, 10 Ans D'Action, Collection Action* (Editions des Acacias, Nancy, 1985)

Giampietri, Luis, *41 Seconds to Freedom: An Insider's Account of the Lima Hostage Crisis 1996–97* (Ballantine Books, New York, 2007)

Giduck, John, *Terror at Beslan* (Archangel Group, Inc., Golden, CO, 2005)

Haney, Eric L., *Inside Delta Force: The Story of America's Elite Counterterrorist Unit* (Delacorte Press, New York, 2002)

Harclerode, Peter, *Secret Soldiers: Special Forces in the War Against Terrorism* (Cassell & Company, London, 2000)

Hufnagl, Wolfdieter, *Cobra: Das Gendarmerie-Einsatzkommando GEK* (Motorbuch Verlag, Stuttgart, 2002)

—— *Jagdkommando: Sondereinheiten des Österreichischen Bundesheeres* (Motorbuch Verlag, Stuttgart, 2002)

Katz, Samuel M., *The Elite: The True Story of Israel's Secret Counterterrorist Unit* Pocket Books (New York, 1992)
—— *The Illustrated Guide to the World's Top Counter-Terrorist Forces* (Concord, Hong Kong 1995)
—— *The Illustrated Guide to the World's Top Naval Special Warfare Units* (Concord, Hong Kong, 2000)

Le RAID, Unite D'Élite de la Police Nationale (Crepin-Leblond, Paris, 2005)

Mannucci, Enrico, *In Pace e In Guera* (Longanesi & C., Milan, 2004)

Marcinko, Richard, *Rogue Warrior* (Pocket Star Books, New York, 1992)

Micheletti, Eric, *French Special Forces* (Histoire & Collections, Paris, 1999)
—— *GIGN*, Histoire & Collections (Paris, 2005)

Pugliese, David. *Canada's Secret Commandos: The Unauthorized Story of Joint Task* —— *Force Two* (Esprit de Corps Books, Ottawa, 2002)

Pushies, Fred J. et al., *U.S. Counter-Terrorist Forces* (MBI Publishing, St. Paul, MN, 2001)

Pushies, Fred J., *Weapons of Delta Force* (MBI Publishing, St. Paul, MN, 2002)

Ryan, Paul B., *The Iranian Rescue Mission: Why It Failed* (Naval Institute Press, Annapolis, 1985)

Scholzen, Reinhard. *KSK: Das Kommando Spezialkrafte der Bundeswehr* (Motorbuch Verlag, Stuttgart, 2004)

Southby-Tailyour, Ewen, *Janes Special Forces Recognition Guide* (Collins, London, 2005)

Thompson, Leroy, *Hostage Rescue Manual* (Greenhill, London, 2001)
—— *The Rescuers: The World's Top Anti-Terrorist Units* (Paladin Press, Boulder, CO, 1986)

Tophoven. *GSG 9: German Response to Terrorism* (Bernard & Graf Verlag, Koblenz, 1984)

Trofimov, Yaroslav. *The Siege of Mecca* (Doubleday, New York, 2007)

Whitcomb, Christopher. *Cold Zero: Inside the FBI Hostage Rescue Team* (Little, Brown, and Co., Boston, 2001)

Williamson, Tony, *Counterstrike Entebbe* (Collins, London, 1976)

Index